LEVINAS AND THE POLITICAL

Emmanuel Levinas is one of the most influential philosophers of the twentieth century and is best known for his work on ethics and theology. Even though he has been very influential in literature and cultural theory, the political implications of his work have so far been neglected. *Levinas & the Political* is the first book to explore systematically the relation of Levinas's thought to the political, and how the ethical resources he offers can enrich our understanding of the political arena.

Levinas & the Political explores the political from Levinas's early writings in the face of National Socialism through to his controversial political statements on Israel and French politics. It analyses themes such as the deconstruction of metaphysics as a reconfiguration of the political, embodiment, the face and alterity. Howard Caygill also explores Levinas's engagement with the heritage of Heidegger and Bergson, and the implications of his rethinking of the political for an understanding of the significance of the Holocaust.

Levinas & the Political is essential reading for all students of philosophy and politics and all those interested in Levinas.

Howard Caygill is Professor of Cultural History at Goldsmiths College, University of London.

THINKING THE POLITICAL
General editors:
Keith Ansell Pearson
University of Warwick
Simon Critchley
University of Essex

Recent decades have seen the emergence of a distinct and challenging body of work by a number of Continental thinkers that has fundamentally altered the way in which philosophical questions are conceived and discussed. This work poses a major challenge to anyone wishing to define the essentially contestable concept of 'the political' and to think anew the political import and application of philosophy. How does recent thinking on time, history, language, humanity, alterity, desire, sexuality, gender and culture open up the possibility of thinking the political anew? What are the implications of such thinking for our understanding of and relation to the leading ideologies of the modern world, such as liberation, socialism and Marxism? What are the political responsibilities of philosophy in the face of the new world (dis)order?

This new series is designed to present the work of the major Continental thinkers of our time, and the political debates their work has generated, to a wider audience in philosophy and in political, social and cultural theory. The aim is neither to dissolve the specificity of the 'philosophical' into the 'political' nor to evade the challenge that the 'political' poses the 'philosophical'; rather, each volume in the series will try to show it is only in the relation between the two that the new possibilities of thought and politics can be activated.

Volumes already published in this series are:

LEVINAS AND THE POLITICAL

Howard Caygill

London and New York

First published 2002
by Routledge
11 New Fetter Lane, London EC4P 4EE

Simultaneously published in the USA and Canada
by Routledge
29 West 35th Street, New York, NY 10001

Routledge is an imprint of the Taylor & Francis Group

© 2002 Howard Caygill

Typeset in Sabon by Taylor & Francis Books Ltd
Printed and bound in Great Britain by MPG Books Ltd, Bodmin

British Library Cataloguing in Publication Data
A catalogue record for this book is available from the British Library

Library of Congress Cataloging-in-Publication Data
A catalog record for this book has been requested

ISBN 0–415–11248–6 (hbk)
ISBN 0–415–11249–4 (pbk)

It is dominated by the presentiment and the memory of the Nazi horror.

Levinas, *Difficult Freedom*

CONTENTS

LIST OF ABBREVIATIONS

AT	*Alterity and Transcendence*
BV	*Beyond the Verse: Talmudic Readings and Lectures*
BW	*Basic Philosophical Writings*
CP	*Collected Philosophical Papers*
DE	*De l'évasion*
DF	*Difficult Freedom: Essays on Judaism*
DH	*Discovering Existence with Husserl*
EE	*Existence and Existents*
EI	*Éthique et infini*
EN	*Entre nous: On Thinking-of-the-Other*
EP	*Épreuves d'une pensée*
GDT	*God, Death and Time*
GM	*Of God Who Comes to Mind*
IH	*Les Imprévus de l'histoire*
LR	*The Levinas Reader*
OB	*Otherwise than Being, or Beyond Essence*
OS	*Outside the Subject*
RB	*Is it Righteous to Be?*
RH	*Reflections on Hitlerism*
THP	*The Theory of Intuition in Husserl's Phenomenology*
TI	*Totality and Infinity: An Essay on Exteriority*
TN	*In the Time of the Nations*
TO	*Time and the Other*
TR	*Nine Talmudic Readings*

ACKNOWLEDGEMENTS

This book would not have been finished without the patience and generosity of many friends and colleagues. My thanks first of all go to Edi Pucci for the lessons in phenomenology and other more important things, and to Jay Bernstein and Greg Bright for blowing on the embers. My thanks also to the editors of the 'Thinking the Political' series - Keith Ansell Pearson and Simon Critchley - both for their invitation and their patience. I learnt a lot from conversations at various times and places with Gary Banham, Richard Beardsworth, Sara Beardsworth, Alexia Defert, Francesco Di Donato, Mick Dillon, Joanna Hodge, Peter Osborne, Gabriella Pucci and Michael Shams, but especially with my colleagues in the Philosophy and Human Values group at Goldsmiths College – Josh Cohen, Vic Seidler and Nigel Tubbs. I thank also my students on the Goldsmiths College course in Contemporary Thought, especially the group of 1998–99 with whom I read *Totality and Infinity* in the shadow of the war in Kosovo. Finally, the greatest thanks go to Piero, who forced me to defy the gravity that attends much of the matter in this book.

Howard Caygill
Molin Nuovo
December 2001

INTRODUCTION

This reading of Levinas began as a response to a radio broadcast in which Levinas participated shortly after the massacres in the Chatila and Sabra camps in Israeli-occupied Lebanon in 1982. In that broadcast, Levinas revealed a coolness of political judgement that verged on the chilling, an unsentimental understanding of violence and power almost worthy of Machiavelli. The ruthless political clarity that could claim 'in alterity we can find an enemy' was not what I expected from the philosopher I had been taught to regard as the thinker of ethical alterity and the subject of a growing body of sentimental commentary. The perplexity was compounded by an interview in 1992 in *Le Monde* in which, going against the grain of that historical moment, Levinas developed a cogent defence of the USSR. Rather than ignore these political judgements, or regret them as relaxations of an otherwise irreproachable ethical rigour, I decided to reread the texts of Emmanuel Levinas from the standpoint of his political judgement.

What quickly emerged was a thinker who engaged with the question of the political horror of the twentieth century with an intensity and a bleakness unrivalled in philosophical writing. Levinas repeatedly described his life and work in terms of the presentiment and mourning of the Nazi horror under which he and his immediate family had suffered; he entitled a late meditation on his teacher Martin Heidegger 'As if Consenting to Horror', and, in the 1992 reflection on the USSR, he could claim that 'in spite of the horror of this regime' it remained the bearer of a promise of liberation. Levinas thus arrived at the horrors of Chatila and Sabra after a lifetime of reflection on political horror and the refusal of any alleviation of its memory and persistance. What one of Levinas's interlocutors in the 1982 broadcast, Alain Finkielkraut, observed of Sartre – that engagement consisted in continuing the war in the time of peace – holds perhaps even more for Levinas. There is a sense in which his writings are warnings against being duped by the post-war truce, admonitions to remember the political horror that continued to cast its shadow over the peace.

1

The extent to which Levinas had been 'touched'[1] by the events of the twentieth century has recently begun to be more fully appreciated. The degree of his personal proximity to the fault lines of twentieth-century political history is unparalleled. More than any other thinker of the epoch, Levinas was scarred by some of the most critical events of European and World history. He was born in Kovno in 1906 and passed his childhood in Lithuania and the Ukraine, where he witnessed the Russian Revolution and the violence of the Civil War fought between the black, white and red fronts. He left Lithuania to study at Strasbourg in 1923, five years after that city and its region had passed from German to French administration and at a point in which its university was dedicating itself to the re-statement of the principles of French republican culture. In 1928–29 Levinas crossed the Rhine to study at Freiburg, and attended the Davos seminar – founded to promote Franco–German understanding – with Heidegger and Cassirer. He left for Paris in 1930 where he attended the seminars of Brunschvicg and Kojéve and produced his first published writings under the growing shadow of fascism.

After mobilisation in the French army in 1939, Levinas was taken prisoner of war, and although he himself survived under the 'protection' of the Geneva Conventions, many close members of his family were murdered by the German National Socialist government.[2] After the war, as director of l'École normale israélite orientale (ENIO) responsible for training teachers from the Magreb and the Near East, he was in close contact with events in that region, including the foundation of the State of Israel and the decolonisation struggles. After being admitted to the French university system in 1961 at the University of Poitiers, he moved in 1967 to the University of Nanterre on the eve of the events of 1968.

While the details of Levinas's political life await a full biographical study,[3] even a glance at his life shows that reflection on politics and the political was for him a predicament rather than a choice. This is confirmed by Levinas's published writings and interviews which return continually to the issue of politics and the political, and venture into political judgements on issues such as the meaning of French Republicanism, German National Socialism, the Cold War, the State of Israel, the USSR and colonialism/anti-colonialism. It would be difficult for a philosopher to sustain such a level of political engagement without directly or indirectly developing a notion of the political.

Reading Levinas's texts within the horizon of political horror requires the reversal of many of the interpretative protocols that are associated with his work. Instead of extending what might be imagined to be a secured understanding of the ethical into the political, the ethical emerges as a fragile response to political horror. Instead of separating Levinas's 'philosophical' and his 'Jewish' writings, whether deliberately or by default, the importance of the relationship between 'Israel' and the State of

Israel in Levinas's thought makes it essential to insist on them being read together. And finally, given the inseparability of reflection on the political from political events, it is vital to pursue as far as possible a disciplined chronological exposition of the development of Levinas's thought and to avoid the luxury of the anachronistic pursuit of thematic parallels that is enjoyed by many commentators.

The concept of the political that emerges from Levinas's writing brings together his critique of ontology and his meditation on the meaning of the prophetic. In keeping with his critique of political ontology, his understanding of the political escapes any notion of the political present. When speaking of German National Socialism he refers to it in terms of intimation or memory, but never as a present experience; when speaking of Israel he does not necessarily always refer to the 'actually existing State of Israel' but often to a state of the future, as the prophetic promise of Israel. Levinas's political is haunted by an unassimilable past of political horror and an unforseeable future of political promise. The political present is largely absent in Levinas's texts, leaving marks as the memory of horror or the prophetic intimation of peace, as the politics of impossible mourning and prophesy, or even as the 'passion' of Auschwitz and the 'adventure' of the State of Israel. The political for Levinas is the unassimilable or the unforgettable that returns disruptively to insist on the *question* of the political.

The interweaving of political horror and promise emerges throughout Levinas's work, receiving its extreme figuration in the themes of war and fraternity. For Levinas it is irresponsible to speak of peace without war, or to imagine a peace that is but the cessation of war: war is inextricable from peace, violence is inextricable from ethics.[4] The omnipresence of war is central to understanding Levinas's view of the post-war political – the epoch of global 'Cold War' and the perpetual war footing of the State of Israel. War and the political assume a proximity in Levinas's thought that were it recognised would prove extremely uncomfortable for liberal readers accustomed to keeping war – as the alleged pathology of civility – separate from peace. The proximity of war and politics is a thought that brings Levinas closer to the thought of Clausewitz and Carl Schmitt than to the liberal ethical theory that issued from Kant.

Levinas's emphasis on fraternity also diverges from the norms of liberal political theory. The dominant, liberal tradition of political thought since Kant and Hegel gives overwhelming primacy to the concept of freedom and then, to a lesser degree and under certain historical conditions, of the concept of equality. Yet, as Levinas constantly reminds us, the modern political has been trinitarian since the French Revolution, comprising not only freedom and equality but also fraternity. It is upon the third member of the trinity that Levinas focuses his attention. He seeks the promise of peace in an ethics of alterity that

3

points toward the rethinking of fraternity.[5] Yet to privilege fraternity over freedom and equality is to engage with the very element of the revolutionary trinity that was most vulnerable to becoming a warrant for violence.

By defining 'the brother' in national, confessional, racial or class terms it becomes possible to overcome in the name of fraternity the very universal claims of freedom and equality according to which all are brothers. The American Constitution and the French 'Declaration of the Rights of Man and Citizen' are classic examples of the ambiguity of frater-nity: according to these texts it can be understood universally according to the freedom and equality of all, or it can be understood as warranting the exclusive claim to freedom and equality of a p articular national, class, religious or racial fraternity. Levinas does not assume the universality of fraternity nor does he limit it to a particular group; instead he tries to rethink fraternity on the basis of alterity and thus to derive the concepts of freedom and equality from fraternity rather than leaving it as their supple-ment. In this movement the concept of justice assumes increasing importance. The shift of focus from freedom to fraternity characteristic of Levinas once again makes his concept of the political extremely question-able, even though few readers have been tempted to engage in the sustained exploration of its implications.[6]

The reading of Levinas and the political undertaken in this book proposes to show how the question of the political consistently troubles Levinas's thought. The first chapter describes the troubling of Levinas's reception of phenomenology by the reflection on the trinitarian politics of the French republican tradition and the rise of German National Socialism, accompanied by what Levinas described in an essay of 1934 as the 'Philosophy of Hitlerism'. The chapter closes with an examination of the implications of National Socialism for the question of Jewish iden-tity. The bringing together of Levinas's 'philosophical' and 'Jewish' writings of the 1930s is extended in Chapter 2 into the 1950s and Levinas's reflections on the post-war political of the Cold War and the State of Israel. In the third and fourth chapters the political questions expressed in his books *Totality and Infinity* and *Otherwise than Being* are shown to emerge from a matrix of philosophical, political and reli-gious reflections, each of which determined the shape of the others and opened an original space for thinking the political.

The reading of Levinas's two great works in terms of the politics of 'messianic eschatology' and the elaboration of a 'prophetic politics' is followed in Chapter 5 by a reflection on Israel and the State of Israel that considers Levinas's critical relationship to Zionism, the place of Israel in universal and holy history and the fate of the Palestinians. The book ends by renouncing philosophical commentary and turning to the biblical theme of 'strange fire', here called upon to figure the ambivalent horror and promise that consumes and sustains Levinas's concept of the political.

1

PRESENTIMENTS OF NATIONAL SOCIALISM

> What remains for me is the general application of the
> phenomenological analysis discovered by Husserl, and also,
> the horror of 1933. (EI)

Political horror

In 'Signature' – the autobiographical sketch that closes *Difficult Freedom* –
Levinas described his life as a 'disparate inventory...dominated by the
presentiment and memory of the Nazi horror' (DF, 291). He expressed this
even more forcefully in a 1986 interview with François Poirié by asking 'Will
my life have been spent between the incessant presentiment of Hitlerism and
the Hitlerism that refuses itself to any forgetting?' (RB, 39) By locating the
consistency of his life and signature between the presentiment and the
memory of political horror, Levinas unambiguously aligned his philosophical
work with the thinking of the political, or, more precisely, with the thinking
of political horror. The event of National Socialism, feared and mourned,
marks all of Levinas's writing, from the early phenomenological texts of the
1930s to the late essays on prophetic politics and human rights.

Levinas's two major philosophical works – *Totality and Infinity:
Essay on Exteriority* (1961) and *Otherwise than Being, or Beyond
Essence* (1974) – are both works of mourning for the victims of
National Socialism. Levinas described the critique of totality worked
through in all its ramifications in *Totality and Infinity* as following 'a
political experience that we have still not forgotten'.[1] This political and
personal experience is explicitly recalled in the dedication of *Otherwise
than Being* to 'the memory of those who were closest among the six
million assassinated by the National Socialists, and of the millions on
millions of all confessions and all nations, victims of the same hatred of
the other man, the same anti-semitism', followed by the names in
Hebrew of Levinas's murdered family.[2] Yet, while the working through
of a life and an authorship suspended between the presentiment and
ineluctable memory of political horror marks everything written under

5

Levinas's signature, it does not exhaust its possibilities, for the work of mourning the political horror of Nazism and its consequences is also dedicated to exploring the possible openings for a non-fascist modern politics.

An important dimension of the attempt to mourn the event of National Socialism was the understanding of what it implied for philosophy. This required not only the analysis of the ways in which philosophy was implicated in National Socialism, an inquiry opened as early as the 1934 essay 'Some Reflections on the Philosophy of Hitlerism', but also the implications of continuing to philosophise after its defeat. The complicity of philosophy with political horror was unforgettably figured in the work and National Socialist political allegiances of Martin Heidegger. In almost every post-war reference to his former teacher, Levinas describes both National Socialism and Heidegger's involvement with it as 'unforgettable' events, after which neither politics nor philosophy could remain the same.[3] The question of the relationship between Heidegger's thought and his National Socialist politics remained open for Levinas until the end. In a late reflection (1988) on this question, 'As if Consenting to Horror',[4] Levinas confronted Heidegger's *Sein und Zeit* with Hitler's *Mein Kampf*. His erstwhile 'firm confidence that an unbridgeable distance' separated the 'extreme analytical virtuosity of the one' from 'the delirious and criminal hatred voiced by evil' in the other was already shaken in the early 1930s and hardly restored by Heidegger's posthumous self-justification in the 'Only a God can Save Us': the *Spiegel* Interview (1966). Just as it was impossible to forget National Socialism, so was it impossible to forget the complicity of Heidegger and, through him, of philosophy in its crimes.[5]

On a certain reading of Levinas's oft acknowledged debt to Heidegger, Levinas mourns the victims of National Socialism while remaining indebted to a philosophical language – Heideggerian phenomenology – deeply implicated in it.[6] Far from the later alignment of *Being and Time* and *Mein Kampf* ventured in 'As if Consenting to Horror', Levinas's thought can be taken as a development of the non- or anti-National Socialist elements that can be found in Heidegger's thought. Another reading would affirm Levinas's debt to Husserl over that to Heidegger, and see in his work a development and defence of Husserlian phenomenology against Heidegger's alleged misappropriation.[7] Each of these readings carry with them a particular politics and a particular way of working through the memory of National Socialism, but, by exclusively reading his work with respect to the phenomenological tradition, they underestimate the complexity of Levinas's development.

The price of locating Levinas too exclusively in the phenomenological tradition is a loss of political and philosophical focus. His debt to phenomenology was always qualified by other considerations, primarily by the Jewish prophetic and talmudic traditions but also by the historical climate of his French philosophical education at the University of Strasbourg during the 1920s. The latter institution was imbued with the philosophical and political 'principles of '89', namely the tradition of radical republicanism bequeathed by the French Revolution of 1789. The inquiry into the relationship between the republican principles of liberty, equality and fraternity was for the members of the Strasbourg school never far from even the most abstract of their philosophical analyses.[8] Levinas's immersion in these debates predated his turn to phenomenology, and in many subtle respects gave his reading of Husserl and Heidegger its peculiar direction and momentum. During the late 1920s and early 1930s it was the republican more than the Jewish or phenomenological traditions that shaped Levinas's presentiments of National Socialism, although from the mid-1930s these were articulated in the language of the phenomenological and Jewish traditions.

Liberty, Equality, Fraternity

...it is necessary to fight for the Republic (DF)

Levinas claimed that certain presentiments of National Socialism predated his arrival in France to study at the University of Strasbourg in 1923: he avoided studying in Germany not only because of the inflation and terror-istic disorders of the early Weimar Republic, but also 'a presentiment perhaps' (RB, 28). With the exception of certain incidents during visits across the border that exposed the ambient anti-Semitism of the German university, Levinas's years in Strasbourg were marked only indirectly by the emergence of the German National Socialist movement. Yet the question of the relationship between the Jewish experience and the founding principles of political modernity – liberty, equality and fraternity enshrined in the revolutionary declaration of the Rights of Man and Citizen – had taken on a new urgency in the wake of the 'Dreyfus Affair'. The debate on the meaning of these principles and their relationship to each other was as old as the Revolution, but it had been sharpened in the late nineteenth century by the anti-Semitic injustice of the fate of Alfred Dreyfus. The Affair provoked a debate on the character of the French Republic that continued directly and indirectly into the early decades of the twentieth century. Levinas arrived at Strasbourg carrying with him the Eastern European heroic folk memory of Dreyfus, and later often recalled how moved he was to discover that the ethical and political implications of the affair were still being worked through by French philosophers and sociolo-gists such as his teachers Charles Blondel, Maurice Pradines, Maurice Halbwachs and Henri Carteron.[9]

In his recollections of Strasbourg, Levinas recalled specifically the 'very strong impression' made by Maurice Pradines's course on the relation between ethics and politics. Pradines's use of the Dreyfus Affair as an example of ethics overcoming politics was obviously important for the development of Levinas's later thoughts on the relationship between ethics and politics.[10] Yet the direct and indirect significance of the Dreyfus affair for the development of Levinas's philosophy was far more profound. It formed a locus for the statement of his radical republican politics and its relationship to the issues of nation and race. The Affair highlighted the importance of the revolutionary principles of liberty, equality and fraternity but called also for their reformulation, especially with respect to the third principle of 'fraternity'. Instead of regarding the principle of fraternity in classical Jacobin terms of the male nation armed, or in those of the pre-political fraternal categories of class, gender, race or religious confession, Levinas was stimulated by his teachers at Strasbourg to seek an ethical concept of fraternity framed in terms of solidarity with the victim of injustice.

In her chapter on the Dreyfus Affair in *The Origins of Totalitarianism*, Hannah Arendt claimed that 'the Dreyfus affair in its entirety offers a foregleam of the twentieth century' and that its 'true sequel' took place not in France but in National Socialist Germany.[11] The controversy surrounding the Affair continued well into the twentieth century and even in 1924, the year of Levinas's arrival at Strasbourg, the rightist and anti-Dreyfusard *Action française* (1899–1944) republished the anti-Dreyfusard *Precis de l'affaire Dreyfus*, while in 1931 an anti-Dreyfusard play by Rehfish and Wilhelm Herzog, *L'affaire Dreyfus*, was staged in Paris.[12] The slogan 'Death to the Jews' that emerged at the time of the Affair was revived by the French fascists and widely used from the mid-1930s. For Arendt the Dreyfus Affair was a presentiment of National Socialism whose significance became increasingly ominous during the 1930s.

The facts of the Dreyfus case should now be uncontroversial, but at the time, and throughout the Third Republic and beyond, their significance was violently disputed. The discovery, by a French spy in the office of the German military attaché, of a piece of handwritten paper promising to deliver French military secrets initiated the chain of events that led to the rapid condemnation for treason of the Jewish officer Captain Alfred Dreyfus. In a wave of official secrecy and anti-Semitism, Dreyfus was convicted by court martial, stripped of his rank and sentenced to life imprisonment on Devil's Island. Two years later, new evidence emerged proving Dreyfus's innocence, but the army high command refused to admit their error and attempted a cover-up with forged documents and the transfer of the new and inquisitive Head of the Intelligence Division of the General Staff, Colonel Picquart (who had become convinced of Dreyfus's innocence) to Tunisia. In the face of mounting evidence for Dreyfus's inno-

8

cence, the army, supported by the Church and conservative public opinion, refused to reconsider its earlier verdict.

By 1898 a battle for public opinion opened with the publication of Zola's *J'accuse*, and the call for acquittal was supported by other liberal Dreyfusards such as Anatole France, Charles Peguy and Emile Durkheim, along with the foundation of the *League for the Rights of Man and Citizen*.[13] Zola was tried and convicted of calumny of the army, but with the emergence of new evidence and the confession of the real German spy Major Esterhazy, the high-level conspiracy to incriminate Dreyfus was revealed, and one of its architects, Colonel Henry, committed suicide. The case was re-examined by the Court of Appeal and, in 1899, the original sentence was annulled and the prison sentence reduced to ten years on the grounds of 'alleviating circumstances'. Dreyfus was pardoned by the President a week later but was not to be acquitted until 1906 by the Court of Appeal. The case was never fully closed and Dreyfus continued to be an object of hatred and assassination attempts by the French Right until his death in 1935.

Beyond the facts of the case itself, the Dreyfus Affair became a shibboleth: in Arendt's words, 'The Dreyfus Affair in its political implications could survive because two of its elements grew in importance during the twentieth century. The first is hatred of the Jews; the second, suspicion of the republic itself, of Parliament and the state machine'.[14] Behind both elements lay a broader, less articulated suspicion of the revolutionary principles declared in the Rights of Man and Citizen, and of their effect on the organisation of state and society. In the eyes of the *Action française* and Catholic France, the principle of fraternity – defined in terms of nation, religious confession or even race – was more important than the principles of liberty and equality. For liberals, however, the case called for a thorough rethinking of the place of fraternity within revolutionary principles, one that would make fraternity compatible with modern liberty and equality. An enlarged concept of fraternity would have to guard against excluding potential citizens from participation in the republic on the basis of their religious confession, gender or other distinguishing feature.

When Levinas arrived in Strasbourg in 1923, French philosophical culture continued to be marked by the reverberations of the Dreyfus Affair. More than an example in Pradines's lectures on ethics and politics, the Dreyfus Affair was the site of the battle for the soul of French Republicanism and, as such, determined the climate of French thought. It was never far from the surface of the three main currents of French philosophy with which Levinas quickly became familiar: the Cartesian rationalism associated with Leon Brunschvicg; the sociological approach to philosophy pioneered by Emil Durkheim and represented in Strasbourg by Maurice Halbwachs; and the brilliant, idiosyncratic and extremely influential philosophising of Henri Bergson.[15] In the highly politicised context of the Third Republic, each of these schools was situated within a particular political and cultural context inherited from the French Revolution and sharpened by the experience of the Dreyfus Affair. The first current regarded the founding declaration of the Rights of Man and Citizen along with its principles to be rational, and considered sociability to rest on the free use of reason. The second, Durkheimian, school accepted the rational kernel of the declaration but argued that a sociologically informed education would supply the deficit of fraternity (anomie) that had emerged in the liberal modernity of liberty and equality. Bergson's philosophy subordinated equality and fraternity to freedom, but freedom understood as radical spontaneity or 'creativity'.

While Levinas was later to pay elegant tribute to the person and work of Brunschvicg[16] by whom he was taught in the early 1930s, the main influence on his thought before the discovery of phenomenology came from the Durkheimian and Bergsonian schools represented by his teachers at Strasbourg. In the Nemo interviews, Levinas described his education at Strasbourg as an

> Initiation in the great philosophers Plato and Aristotle, Descartes and the Cartesians, Kant. Not yet Hegel, in the 1920s in the faculty of letters at Strasbourg! But it was Durkheim and Bergson who seemed to me particularly alive in the teaching and in the interest of the students. There were the ones to be cited and the ones to be opposed. They had incontestably been the teachers of our teachers. (EI, 16)

Levinas's teacher Maurice Halbwachs, later murdered in Buchenwald, worked in the Durkheimian tradition, applying Durkheim's concept of collective representations to social class and collective memory. His work was indebted to the framework of Durkheim's sociological analysis of modernity elaborated in the early 1890s and in its turn sharpened in response to the Dreyfus Affair.

The conceptual structure of collective representation and social solidarity adopted by Halbwachs from Durkheim was inseparable from the latter's radical republican critique of the Third Republic and his defence of the revolutionary principles. In a programmatic essay, 'Individualism and the Intellectuals', written in response to the Dreyfus Affair, Durkheim attempted to re-order the equation of liberty, equality and fraternity.[17] Insisting on liberty and equality, he argued that they were not only compatible with fraternity, but were in fact inseparable from it. Modern individual liberty and equality were the outcome of fraternity understood as 'organic solidarity' – one that emerged from the social division of labour. In his *Division of Labour in Society* (1893) Durkheim opposed mechanical or pre-modern with organic or modern solidarity: the former emphasised social uniformity, the latter social differentiation. For Durkheim, the anti-Drefusards represented social regression, a return to mechanical solidarity and an understanding of fraternity in terms of such categories of 'mechanical solidarity' as church and nation. Durkheim's work later led him to a closer analysis of the relationship of consciousness and social solidarity and the argument that a secular educational system would be the most appropriate institution for the teaching of the republican values of organic solidarity.

Levinas's later assessment of the significance of Durkheim's work and its often underestimated political and philosophical motivation is subtle, and explains why he did not abandon Durkheim's categories and why they persist even in *Totality and Infinity*. However hard Durkheim tried to present himself as the founder of scientific sociology, he was always for Levinas first and foremost 'a metaphysician'. Levinas perceptively understood Durkheim in terms of the derivation of 'the fundamental categories of the social, or as one would call it today, an "eidetic of society" starting from the *key tenet* that the social cannot be reduced to the sum of individual psychologies' (EI, 17). Unlike many critics of Durkheim, Levinas understood that the his critique of individualism was not undertaken in the name of totality or the renewal of mechanical solidarity, but in the name of differentiation or organic solidarity. It was intended to deepen and strengthen individual liberty and equality, rather than dissolve them into collective uniformity. Levinas's description of Durkheim's metaphysics of the social is framed in the language of his own later political philosophy:

> The idea that the social is the order of the spiritual constitutes a new intrigue in being beyond animal and human psychism. The plan of 'collective representations' defined rigorously inaugurates the dimension of the spirit in the individual life itself where the individual comes to be recognised and even emancipated. There is with Durkheim, in a sense, a theory of the 'levels of being' and the irreducibility of these levels to each other – an idea which receives its full meaning in the Husserlian and Heideggerian context. (EI, 17)

At its strongest, the Durkheimian 'social' points beyond being; more modestly it establishes levels of being – the social, the psychic, the animal, consciousness – which cannot be reduced to each other. Levinas's final comment may be read as a reference to his intellectual autobiography: what he learnt about the social from Durkheim was later given its 'full meaning' by Husserl and Heidegger. That is to say, the phenomenologists confirmed and deepened an insight into the nature of radical republican modernity that had already been prepared by the work of Durkheim. This insight was deepened through reflection upon the character of ontological difference, here pre-dating Heidegger and appearing within a very different political and intellectual context.

11

Levinas's reference to Husserl and Heidegger giving 'full meaning' to an existing intellectual engagement holds even more for Bergson than for Durkheim. In the interviews with Poirié and Nemo, Levinas is extremely candid in his assessment of the significance of Bergson for the development of his thought. He describes the neglect of Bergson after the Second World War in terms of scandal and 'immoral ingratitude', seeing him as condemned to wait a long time for his 'exit from purgatory'. At Strasbourg during the 1920s, however, the philosophy of Bergson was a powerful presence – it represented 'contemporary philosophy' itself. With respect to the teacher of his teachers, Levinas was and perhaps remained a Bergsonian; put provocatively, a Bergsonian with a phenomenological veneer. When asked in a 1988 interview published in *Autrement* of his debt to the phenomenological tradition, Levinas referred to his Strasbourg teachers and the 'importance (which was essential for me) of the relationship – always present: the background of those masters – to Bergson' (EN, 223). In this interview he went so far as publicly to give priority to Bergson over Heidegger, not only in his own development but in the development of twentieth-century thought:

> Bergson is hardly quoted now. We have forgotton the major philosophical event he was for the French university and which he remains for World philosophy, and the role he played in the constitution of the problematic of modernity. Isn't the ontological thematisation by Heidegger of *being* as distinguished from *beings*, the investigation of being in its verbal sense, already at work in the Bergsonian notion of durée, which is not reducible to the substantivity of beings? (EN, 223)

In the *Autrement* interview, Levinas elaborates the view already stated in the Poirié interview that 'everything new about the modern and postmodern philosophy of time, and in particular the venerable newness of Heidegger would not have been possible without Bergson' (RB, 30). He emphasised this in the *Autrement* interview, finding in the late work of Bergson an anticipation of 'the critique of technical rationalism so important in the work of Heidegger' while seeing *Creative Evolution* and *The Two Sources of Morality and Religion* as anticipating his own thought of a 'spirituality freeing itself from a mechanistic humanism' and an interpretation of *durée* 'as a relationship with the other and with God' (EN, 224).

Not only did Levinas regard Bergson as anticipating Heidegger, but he he also acknowledged him as providing the means to go beyond Heidegger. Levinas 'felt close to certain Bergsonian themes' especially to *durée* and with it the notion of a 'proximity that cannot be reduced to spatial categories or to modes of objectification and thematisation' (EN, 224). He went so far as to claim that 'Bergson is the source of an entire complex of interrelated contemporary philosophical ideas; it is to him, no doubt, that I owe my modest speculative initiatives. We owe a great deal to the mark left by Bergsonism in the teaching and readings of the 1920s'.[18] Referring to his own works, Levinas finds in Bergson a concept of being 'a little beyond being and otherwise than being, all the marvel of diachrony...' (RB, 31). The precise extent and nature of this debt will become clearer below; meanwhile it remains only to add Levinas's view that Bergson's *Time and Free Will* (1889) was one of the most important works in the history of philosophy, comparable with *Being and Time* and prized for its concern to justify the concept of freedom, to elevate freedom as a value above equality (which he considers inseparable from spatial equivalence).[19] Yet this freedom is considered in terms of a new humanism, a new vision of human fraternity based on 'the very event of infinity in us, the very excellence of the good' (RB, 31). This link between human fraternity and the infinite, adumbrated by Bergson as a possible future for modernity, is one that Levinas will take further in his ethics.[20]

Levinas's early admiration for the work of Durkheim and Bergson remained a significant feature of his thought and shaped his reception of phenomenology. Even so, he had no wish to become a disciple of either thinker, largely because of the constraints that working within a philosophical school would have placed upon him. He did not want to pursue 'sociology as an empirical science in the way Durkheim had recommended to his pupils and for which he had elaborated the *a prioris*' nor 'to reiterate the work Bergson accomplished, as perfect as a poem, or else offer variations on it' (EI, 19). It was in this context that Levinas discovered phenomenology through the work of Husserl, and with it the possibility of ' "working in philosophy" without finding myself closed in a system of dogmas but at the same time without running the risk of proceeding by means of chaotic intuitions' (EI, 19). With the discovery of phenomenology Levinas found a powerful and open philosophical language, but it was not one that he adopted uncritically. From his initial encounter with the works of Husserl while at Strasbourg until his final texts, Levinas was always testing the limits of phenomenology. His early phenomenological writings confront the new philosophical language and thematic with those of the French tradition and, in particular, that of Bergson and the question of freedom.

Before leaving the Dreyfus Affair for phenomenology it is important to note one final consequence of the Affair that would later prove of utmost importance for Levinas's philosophy and politics. The Paris correspondent of the Viennese *Neue Freie Presse* during the 1890s responsible for covering the Dreyfus Affair was Theodor Herzl. Herzl described the spectacle of the crowd taunting Dreyfus with the cry 'A la mort les juifs' as a turning point in the formulation of political Zionism. He drew from the Affair the conclusion that modern revolutionary principles of liberty and equality would never protect the Jews from the threat posed by Christian national fraternity. In his programmatic document of modern Zionism *The Jewish State* (1896), Herzl proposed a vision of a future Jewish state based on three factors: the political principle that the Jews are a nation without a homeland; the affirmation of technology as a means for realising a Jewish polity; and the 'driving force' of the 'Jewish tragedy' in Europe for which the Dreyfus Affair had provided a chilling presentiment.

Herzl's response to the Dreyfus Affair was a sombre rethinking of the modern revolutionary principles and the realisation that confessional fraternity would always threaten the principles of equality and fraternity. The Zionist movement will obviously be important when considering Levinas's subsequent judgements of the founding of the State of Israel and its acts. Yet at this point it is necessary to insist upon Levinas's closer familiarity with the French republican responses to the Dreyfus Affair. His rethinking of fraternity differed from Herzl's in that he did not see the future of the Jewish people fraternally bound in their own nation-state as the only response to the Jewish tragedy. He tried to conceive fraternity as universal, not as an identity, but as alterity and with Israel figured less as a nation state than as a messianic community. This introduced a tension into his judgement of the real existing state of Israel, but would also challenge the Western philosophical obsession with being and identity. It was through the 'open methodology' of phenomenology that he would try to redefine fraternity in terms of ethical alterity, and it would be through ethical alterity that he would question many of the premises of Zionism.

Phenomenology and freedom

Levinas was justly proud of his role in helping introduce the phenomenology of Husserl and Heidegger to a French-speaking public. Initially encountering their work 'by accident' as early as 1927 through the philosopher Gabrielle Peiffer and the theologian Jean Hering, Levinas immediately appreciated the revolutionary significance of the phenomenology of Husserl and its modulation into the key of fundamental ontology achieved by Heidegger in *Being and Time* (1927). Levinas was one of the first to appreciate the revolutionary significance of *Being and Time*, not only for phenomenology but for the entire tradition of Western philosophy.[21] His knowledge of German made it possible for him to move across the Rhine to Freiburg-in-Breisgau (1928–29) where he enrolled in classes with Husserl ('Phenomenological Psychology', 'The Constitution of Intersubjectivity') and subsequently with Heidegger. At the famous Davos seminar of 1929 that hosted the confrontation between Heidegger's and Cassirer's interpretations of Kant, Levinas acted as a bridge between French and German participants, and was remembered for his enthusiastic support of Heidegger and his willingness to explain the Master from

Germany's thought to French participants during mountain walks.[22] Levinas himself recalled with some embarrassment his parody of Cassirer during a student cabaret on the last night of the conference.[23]

From these initial links between Strasbourg and Freiburg emerged the series of exegetical and critical works on phenomenology that shaped the French reception of Heidegger and Husserl. Levinas's pivotal position in the transmission of phenomenological thought to France was hardly appreciated before the late 1950s, and perhaps is still not fully acknowledged. His early writings on Husserl, beginning with the long article 'On the *Ideas* of M. E. Husserl' (1929), and his thesis *The Theory of Intuition in Husserl's Phenomenology* (1930), are not the straightforward expositions of phenomenology for a French audience they are sometimes taken to be. His translation with Gabrielle Peiffer of the *Cartesian Meditations* (1931) reflects a deliberate choice of focus – intersubjectivity – with Levinas translating the crucial fifth and sixth meditations. The series of 'exegetical' articles he wrote during the 1930s registers the shock of Heidegger's public profession of allegiance to the National Socialist regime in Germany and his entry into the Nazi Party on 1 May 1933, but does not show any fundamental change in direction.[24] This direction was governed by Levinas's confrontation of phenomenology with the representatives and the thematics of the French philosophical tradition, particularly the work of Bergson and the theme of freedom.[25]

The role of Bergson and the problem of freedom in Levinas's reception of phenomenology is almost wholly unappreciated. Nevertheless it is the key, not only to Levinas's understanding and critique of Husserl and Heidegger and his concept of the political, but also to the centrality of the issue of freedom in the work of French phenomenologists such as Sartre and Merleau-Ponty. In reflecting on his debt to Husserl, Levinas was explicit about finding in Husserl's *Logical Investigations* a way of reconciling the demands of methodological rigour with the radical impetus of Bergson's concept of freedom. He found in phenomenology an access to 'a new possibility of thinking, to a new possibility of moving from one idea to another, different from deduction, induction and dialectic, a new way of unfolding "concepts" beyond the Bergsonian appeal to the inspiration in intuition' (RB, 31). The critique of Bergsonian intuition – similar to the critique of mystical intuition by the Lithuanian school of Talmudic exegesis – is carried through on the inspiration and according to the discipline of Husserl's doctrine of intentionality.

The essays on Husserl from the 1930s consistently – almost obsessively – address the theme of the relationship between intentionality and intuition in Husserl; the ubiquitous problem of 'self-evidence' or the Bergsonian 'immediate given of consciousness' by means of the search for an alternative to the opposition of rationalism and irrational intuition. Throughout the articles Levinas explicitly casts intentionality as an antidote to a Bergsonian intuition that was not immune to fascist appropriations such as those of Sorel and Hulme. Yet Levinas was reluctant to abandon the concept of freedom, and sought in Husserlian intersubjectivity a way of thinking freedom through the discipline of phenomenological method.

Throughout his pre- and post-war writings on Husserl, Levinas criticised the limits imposed upon the thought of freedom by the theoretical prejudices of Husserlian phenomenology. He paradoxically found Heidegger to offer a more convincing account of intentionality and intersubjectivity than Husserl; but then he had to confront the issue that the very philosopher who seemed most capable of protecting the concept of freedom from fascist appropriation became the most vulnerable to its attractions. For this reason it was important for Levinas to develop an account of intentionality and intersubjectivity that would protect freedom but without the risks attendant upon Bergson's prizing of intuition nor the certainty of the 'inner truth and greatness' of Heidegger's National Socialism.

Levinas was convinced that 'the path of Husserl was prolonged and transfigured by Heidegger' and that he himself 'went to see Husserl and found Heidegger' (RB, 32). However, the 'horror of 1933' put this continuous transition into question: the move beyond Bergson from Husserl to Heidegger was arrested, making necessary a return to Husserl. His understanding of the relation between the two phenomenologists was already problematic in the 1929 essay 'On the *Ideas* of M. E. Husserl' and the 1930 book *The Theory of Intuition in Husserl's Phenomenology*. Both texts are marked by the traces of an argument staged by Levinas between Husserl and Bergson on the problem of 'self-evidence' or the intuitive 'immediate given' of consciousness. In 'On the *Ideas* of M. E. Husserl' Bergson features in the three pivotal footnotes which determine the direction of Levinas's future reading of phenomenology.[26]

'On the *Ideas* of M. E. Husserl' appears at first glance to be an introductory commentary on Husserl's text, professing itself faithful to the commented work's 'general plan'. The commentary is thus organised according to the four parts of *Ideas: General Introduction to Pure Phenomenology*, beginning with the analysis of 'eidetics' and 'phenomenology as an eidetic science', moving to the object of phenomenology and then to its method, and ending, still with Husserl, on the problem of 'reason and reality' (DH, 4). Yet throughout the commentary Levinas seeks to justify a view of consciousness as an intentionality that is beyond the opposition of reason and intuition.

It is in the discussion of perception in the first section of the commentary that Levinas makes the first fundamental contrast between Husserl and Bergson on the issue of the relation to an object. Approaching this problem by means of the issue of the 'identical quality given in a changing stream of perceptions', Levinas glosses Husserl as proving a solution not only to sensationalist views of the objectivity of sensible qualities, but also to Bergson's contrary view that identical quality is a distortion introduced by consciousness. Husserl's distinction between the object and the act of consciousness allows him to derive quality from the 'animation' of sensation through intentionality. From this Levinas concludes, in the footnote, that

> This apparent antinomy between the multiplicity of sensuous moments which represent the object and the identical unity of the object itself does not, therefore, imply the Bergsonian thesis that the identical object is a distortion of consciousness: it allows for a resolution through the distinction between the act and the object of consciousness. (DH, 182).

Contrary to Bergson's view in *Time and Free Will*, Levinas claims that consciousness does not arrest or spatialise *durée* or the 'changing stream of perception' by distorting its temporal character and making it spatially present, but animates it in an act of consciousness. The target of this criticism is no less than Bergson's case for the intuition of the immediate givens of consciousness against their spatial distortion through intellect or conceptual consciousness. Levinas subtly uses Bergson's preferred language of 'animation' and 'life' to describe Husserl's act of intentional consciousness. Intentionality 'animates' the content of consciousness (the 'adumbrations') or, in an explicitly anti-Bergsonian phrase, Husserl's 'sensations are moments of life and not space' (DH, 14). The theme of life, which will subsequently become omnipresent in Levinas's work, is here introduced as the intimation of a non-intuitive vitalism.

The critique of Bergson is deepened in Levinas's commentary on Part Two of the *Ideas* concerned with the objects of phenomenology. Consistent with his attempt to find a path between intuition and concept, Levinas emphasises Husserl's view of the concept as necessarily incomplete, or, more precisely, incapable of full instantiation. He described such 'inexact concepts' or conceptual equivalents to the Kantian Ideas of Reason as 'Husserl's great discovery' (DH, 19) and immediately in a footnote directed this discovery against Bergson. The implications of transferring the incomplete structure of the Kantian idea to the concept – a move that Kant never explicitly entertained – are considerable. The spatio–temporal limits of appearance that meant that the totality required by the ideas of reason could never be attained are here discovered in the understanding itself. Concepts no longer serve, as they did for Kant, to organise the spatio–temporal intuitions presented to them, but space and time are present in the concepts themselves as their finitude or incompleteness.

In terms of the critique of Bergson, the temporal character of intuition is not seen to be opposed to the distorting spatiality of the concept, but is embedded in the structure of the concept itself. Levinas draws out these and other implications in the footnote:

> Through the discovery of the inexact essence as opposed to the exact essence of mathematics, we move beyond the alternative before which Bergson placed us: either consciousness must be studied like space, grasped by the intellect in well-defined concepts, or it must not be studied by the intellect. (DH, 183)

Against Bergson's choice of the analysis of consciousness by means of limited and distorting concepts, Levinas finds in Husserl a third possibility, one that, once again, he justifies in terms of mobility and life. Husserl can help us move beyond Bergson's alternatives, for: 'With Husserl there is a third possibility. Intelligence does not work solely with the help of geometrical concepts – there can be essence without there being immobility and death in it' (DH, 183). The distinction between object and act of consciousness and the notion of inexact concepts are all ways of resisting Bergson's stark alternative between morbid conceptuality and vital intuition. In the work of Husserl, Levinas finds a vital conceptuality, one in which consciousness is mobile and alive.

Not very far beneath the surface of these epistemological and metaphysical considerations is Bergson's preoccupation with justifying the concept of freedom, the culmination of the argument in *Time and Free Will*. Bergson concluded that freedom was allied to mobility and life, and thus with intuition against the spatial immobility and death of conceptuality. By questioning the epistemological alternative, Levinas also puts into question the location of freedom in intuition. Husserl's 'third alternative' of a vital conceptuality seemed to promise an understanding of freedom that is not opposed to the concept, or law, but is realised through it. This becomes more apparent in a third Bergson footnote, this time appended to a discussion of the life and identity of the subject.

Levinas lists a number of problems involving the relation of the I to consciousness in time, the I as personality, and roots them in the question of 'the problem of the constitution of time as duration which is different from cosmic time and whose moments interpenetrate in a relation of intentionality sui generis' (DH, 20). At this crucial moment, Levinas makes perhaps for the first time a gesture that will become standard in Husserlian commentary – the inevitable reference to esoteric unpublished papers and lecture courses known only to the cognoscenti that have nevertheless exercised 'a most powerful influence before publication'. He also, in yet another footnote, acknowledges the resort to the Bergsonian distinction between cosmic time and time as duration by having Husserl 'encounter' Bergsonian theses without knowing his work. Yet the retreat to duration and thus intuition to justify the I and its experience of time points to a problem that persists in the Husserlian 'third alternative' between concept and intuition.

The search for a 'third alternative' to rationalism and Bergsonian intuition directs the entire commentary, which quickly reveals itself as a set of variations on the themes of an intuitive conceptuality and a conceptual intuition.[27] In the first section on eidetics, Levinas refers to Husserl's combination of intellectual and sensible intuition into an extended notion of intuition as 'the essential moment of true knowledge' (DH, 6). This intuition is capable of seeing 'essences and categories in addition to sensuous empirical facts' (DH, 7), a double intuition of object and essence. Such duplication remains unstable, since it presumes to identify the set of relations that link consciousness to objects with those that link consciousness to essences. In Kant, and later in Bergson, the *immediate* intuitive relation of consciousness to its object is contrasted with the *mediated* relation of consciousness to its concepts. In order convincingly to achieve the 'third alternative' of a double intuition it is necessary to address the issue of the relational character of consciousness, a discussion conducted by Husserl in terms of intentionality.

The notion that consciousness is always in relation, that it is always 'consciousness of something', is contained in the term 'intentionality'. In Levinas's reading, intentionality is the fundamental *property* of consciousness: 'Every perception is perception of the "perceived"; every desire is desire of the "desired", etc.' (DH, 13). The 'fundamental property' of consciousness is relational, but in order to be 'fundamental' the relation itself must precede the terms that are related. For Levinas, 'Husserl's great originality is to see that the "relation to the object" is not something inserted between consciousness and the object; it is the object of consciousness itself. *It is the relation to the object that is the primitive phenomenon – and not a subject and an object that would supposedly move towards each other*' (DH, 13). Postulating a fundamental relation would seem a persuasive way of escaping a philosophy based on fundamental essences or qualities, but it quickly generates chronic difficulties which lead first to the doubling and then to the potentially infinite iteration of the moment of intuition.

The difficulties provoked by understanding intentionality in terms of the fundamental relation of consciousness can be both debilitating and productive. This may be illustrated by one of Levinas's own examples: intentionality is not 'a bond between consciousness on the one side and the real object on the other' (DH, 13). By this he means to illustrate not only that the intentional relation is prior to consciousness and its object, but also that consciousness itself is already intentional. Thus, if the 'object' in question is consciousness, then the predicament emerges of the 'fundamental relation' being itself but the relata of a higher fundamental relation. What is worse, this fundamental relation contains nothing to prevent it, in its turn, becoming the relata of another fundamental relation...Levinas was acutely aware of this problem[28] and dedicated his entire reading of Husserl to securing the 'third alternative' of intentionality from the danger of dissolving into a bad infinity.

The key terms in his securing of Husserlian intentionality from endless iteration are 'intuition' and 'transcendence'. The relationship between the three terms is described in the commentary on Part Three of *Ideas*. The hyperbolic movement of intentional consciousness is a sign of its very transcendence, for, to use Levinas's phrase, '*thought is synonymous with thought that transcends itself*' (DH, 21) and so the thought of thought will always transcend its object. Yet it is the very meaning of this excessive quality of intentional thought that becomes the object of phenomenological inquiry: consciousness as relatum has existence as an object but as relation is transcendent or always in excess of itself. In its first mode, consciousness becomes the 'sensible' object of intuition, in its second, the essential object. The move into an infinitely bad iteration is deferred by making this tension within consciousness – which is none other than the form of relation assumed by it – itself the object of inquiry: 'The existence and transcendence of the object are not metaphysically presupposed, as in the traditional position of the problem, but, prior to all metaphysics, the very meaning of this existence and transcendence becomes the object of study' (DH, 21).

Levinas illustrates the radical implications of Husserl's position by comparing the Cartesian 'I think' with the Husserlian 'I think something'. Levinas remarks on the novelty of this supplement to the *cogito*: 'What is new in this [latter] view is that the idea of immanent intuition, whose indubitable character was discovered by Descartes, is here fecundated by the idea that the intentional character of consciousness, the "relation to the object", is its very essence' (DH, 22). Descartes's indubitable inner intuition that joins thinking and being in 'I think therefore I am' – '*cogito ergo sum*' – is here generalised into the ontological 'I think therefore something is', since Husserl's *cogito* is essentially in relation. 'Immanent intuition' now becomes an intuition of transcendence, since it concerns consciousness as an intentional relation that is directed both to itself as *cogitatum* and beyond itself as *cogito*. Through intuition, consciousness has access to intentionality, leading Levinas to the conclusion that 'This intuitive study of intentionality – is phenomenology' (DH, 22). Phenomenology describes the tension in consciousness between intuition and transcendence. Adopting the language of Husserl's *Ideas*, Levinas concludes that the phenomenological · analysis of intentional consciousness 'shows us a *rigorous parallelism* between the noemata and the noeses in all the domains of consciousness' (DH, 23), the latter including, of course, that peculiar domain in which consciousness is both *noema* and *noesis*.

Levinas ends his commentary with a series of questions arising from the turn to an 'intersubjective phenomenology' summarily intimated by Husserl in *Ideas*. The turn to intersubjectivity will greatly complicate the account of intentionality, a development that Levinas finds partly anticipated by Heidegger. Yet, while Heidegger is rarely mentioned in the *Ideas* commentary, and then only tangentially, he is by no means absent. The debt to Heidegger already guiding Levinas's reading of Husserl will only become fully evident in his doctoral thesis published in 1930, but an idea of what Heidegger represented for Levinas at this time can be drawn from his 1931 essay 'Freiburg, Husserl and Phenomenology'.

In this essay the presentation of intentionality has been given an anthropological turn consistent with a particular reading of *Being and Time*. The 'analytic of Dasein' is explicitly presented in terms of a critique of Bergsonian duration and the latter's view of the geometrical character of space. For Levinas, Bergson's error consists in not seeing that geometrical space – the space of the concept – is itself derived from another more vital experience of space – there is opposition within conceptions of space rather than between space and time. Before and beyond geometrical space is an intentional space, one whose description is borrowed from *Being and Time* and which is 'above all an ambience made up of our possibilities of motility, of distancing ourselves or approaching, therefore a non-homogeneous space with a top and a bottom, a right and a left entirely relative to the usual objects that solicit our possibilities of moving and turning' (DH, 36). This human space is prior to abstract geometrical space, and not, as Bergson thought, a derivative of it.

Levinas is able to undercut Bergson's argument for the spatialisation of time by means of a largely anthropological interpretation of intentionality. The first task of phenomenology for him is 'the determination of the true nature of the human', and this is found in the fact that 'what is supremely concrete in man is his transcendence in relation to himself – or as the phenomenologists say, intentionality' (DH, 34). Levinas now takes for granted a broad definition of intentionality, not just as a theoretical experience 'produced on the model of a theoretical object' but also with the affective features 'love, fear and anxiety', which are lent transcendence by the orientation of a consciousness 'directed towards nothingness'. The emphasis on transcendence in terms of nothingness reflects the influence of Levinas's reading of Heidegger, whose presence becomes increasingly oppressive as the essay draws to a close.

After describing the human in terms of transcendence and then identifying this with what the phenomenologists describe as intentionality, Levinas begins to evoke, without any obvious irony, the redemptive religious and political mission of phenomenology. He claims that 'The phenomenological method wants to destroy the world falsified and impoverished by the naturalist tendencies of our time – which certainly have their rights, but also their limits. It wants to rebuild; it wants to recover the lost world of our concrete life' (DH, 36). The work of rebuilding takes on retrospectively an ominous air in Levinas's naïve description of 'the young Germans I met in Freiburg' for whom 'this new philosophy is more than a new theory; it is a new ideal of life, a new page of history, almost a new religion'. The essay ends with a peculiar religious history of phenomenology, featuring a false, non-phenomenological prophet (Spengler), a precursor (Husserl), and then a messianic incarnation of phenomenology in Heidegger. Heidegger is described as the philosopher who, in the philosophical Jerusalem of Freiburg-im-Bresgau, messianically gathers around him all the nations – 'At the seminar, to which only the privileged were admitted, all nations were represented, mostly by professors: the United States and Argentina, Japan and England, Hungary and Spain, Italy and Russia, even Australia' (DH, 38). Levinas's near-messianic vision of phenomenology's mission to rebuild the world and gather the nations together was to be cruelly deflated in 1933, but already in the late 1920s his more considered position on the political implications of phenomenology was already a great deal more ambivalent than 'Freiburg, Husserl and Phenomenology' would suggest, with doubts increasingly gathering around the concept of freedom.

Levinas's report of the philosophical and political intoxication of phenomenology, while not itself necessarily intoxicated, is far from unsympathetic. Yet on the crucial issue of the relationship of intentionality and transcendence his position remains reserved. He is not convinced that the transcendence of phenomenology is necessarily superior to the creative freedom of Bergson. The reading of intentionality in the *Ideas* commentary has nested in it a forceful account of freedom. Opposed to both the voluntarist aspect of Bergsonian intuition and freedom and what Levinas will with increasing confidence identify as the 'fatalism' of Heideggerian ontology that locates transcendence in nothingness, the play between intuition and transcendence in Husserl's intentionality points to a third freedom, not freedom from but freedom with. If the fundamental relation of intentional consciousness is always open to qualification by intentional consciousness itself, then there is evident within it a play between spontaneity and necessity. Freedom is not to be found in pure spontaneity, as in Bergson – a freedom without fraternity – nor denied in fatality, as Levinas suspected in Heidegger; it is instead located in the movement between spontaneity and necessity.

The preliminary outline of the third concept of freedom is not to be found in the *Ideas* commentary, but rather in Levinas's book from 1930, *The Theory of Intuition in Husserl's Phenomenology*. The analysis of freedom in this work would provide the French republican counterpoint to the messianic enthusiasms that Levinas detected and evoked in German phenomenology. Yet the movement of the argument of this book is extremely complex, developing the opposition of Husserl and Bergson initiated in the *Ideas* commentary, but constantly modulating it through the opposition of Husserl and Heidegger and then culminating in the opposition of Heidegger and Bergson on precisely the issue of freedom and transcendence. Emerging from this complex of themes are the fundamental issues of life and death framed in terms of the increasingly urgent confrontation between the concepts of life proposed by Husserl, Bergson and Heidegger.

The defence of conceptual thought against the Bergsonian claim that it brings only 'immobility and death' begun in the *Ideas* commentary is taken further in *The Theory of Intuition in Husserl's Phenomenology*. In the crucial chapter on 'The Intuition of Essences', Levinas voices the worry that phenomenology may itself fall to the Bergsonian critique of conceptuality: 'Following Bergson's critique of conceptual thought, one could think that the eidetic reduction ultimately deforms concrete reality...Does not eidetic intuition freeze a fluctuating and imprecise reality and transform it into something dead and immutable?' (THP, 116). Levinas of course insists – contra Bergson – that there is 'no contradiction between the intellect, which is the power of grasping what is ideal and abstract, and intuition, which is the immediate perception of what is concrete' (THP, 116–17). His first line of defence elaborates a version of the argument proposed in the *Ideas* commentary: the difference between idealised and ideational concepts, the former approximating to the geometrical concepts of Bergson, the latter being incomplete and so containing a reference to finitude and time.[29] However, the defence of ideation through eidetic intuition goes beyond Husserl's own programme of a renewed transcendental aesthetic[30] to a Heideggerian analysis of being-in-the-world which describes 'space, time, sounds and colours' as they appear in concrete life. The defence of eidetic intuition requires that we root its 'inexact concepts' in 'the being of the world of perception in all its exactitude' (THP, 119).

The same means that Levinas used to defend Husserlian intuition against the spectre of Bergson are then turned against Husserl himself. The gentle doubts evident in the closing pages of the *Ideas* commentary are now elaborated into a full-scale, Heideggerian critique of Husserl's theoretical prejudice. While commending Husserl for attaining 'the profound idea that, in the ontological order, the world of science is posterior to and depends on the vague and concrete world of perception', Levinas adds 'he may have been wrong in seeing the concrete world as a world of objects that are primarily perceived. Is our main attitude towards reality that of theoretical contemplation? Is not the world presented in its very being as a centre of action, as a field of activity or *care* – to speak the language of Martin Heidegger?' (THP, 119). Levinas maintained the critique of Husserl's alledged theoretical prejudice long after he ceased to speak the language of Martin Heidegger. Yet, while his attraction to Heidegger's ontological step beyond Husserl is patent, it is not held without reservation.

It is in the final chapter of *The Theory of Intuition in Husserl's Phenomenology* entitled 'Philosophical Intuition' that Levinas's dissatisfaction with Husserl, but at the same time his unease with the language of Heidegger, become most apparent. Once again the problem is established in terms of Bergson, with Levinas conceding that, while the 'Bergsonian antinomy between intellect and conscious life' may have 'some validity',

Husserl's account of 'inexact essences' offers a solution. As seen, Levinas saw the intuition of inexact essences as providing a way to understand 'how the intellect can cover the field of conscious life without making it spatial' (THP, 140). Yet now, at the end of his inquiry, he seems less certain that Husserl can help solve Bergson's antinomy. The philosophical discussion conducted in terms of conceptuality and intuition unravels into a confrontation of life and thought. In spite of his earlier arguments that the 'inexact essences' remain vital, Levinas now seems to concede that Husserl's philosophical intuition does indeed bring with it rigidity and death. If not opposed to life, Husserl's philosophical intuition does little to promote it, since it remains 'theoretical' and governed by a contemplative attitude:

> Philosophical intuition is not, as in Bergson's philosophy or in the "philosophies of life", an act in which all vital forces are engaged, an act which plays an important role in the destiny of life. For Husserl, philosophical intuition is a reflection on life considered in all its concrete fullness and wealth, a life which is considered but no longer lived. The reflection on life is divorced from life itself, and one cannot see its ties with the destiny and metaphysical essence of man. (THP, 142)

The theoretical attitude that leads to such reflective detachment from life serves as a valuable critique of naturalism which would absorb consciousness into life, but bears within it the risk of making life into a theoretical object, with all the Bergsonian objections that this is liable to provoke. The divorce from life is also a divorce from the 'metaphysical essence of man' or the anthropological understanding of transcendence that Levinas finds and prizes in Heidegger.

The closing pages of the Husserl study reconsider the theme of transcendence and its relationship to the questions of being and freedom. By way of conclusion, Levinas recognises Husserl's achievement in 'the identification of the existence of being with the way being encounters life and the role which it plays in life, a role which becomes visible in the constitution of objects', or, in other words, 'the meaning of the very existence of being' (THP, 154). Yet the recognition is two-handed, since it prizes Husserl, not for himself, but for his anticipation of Heidegger. It is 'only Heidegger' who 'dares to face this problem deliberately', who draws the consequences of Husserl's thought 'in a profoundly original manner'. The precise consequence that Levinas sees Heidegger drawing from Husserl is a renewed insight into the traditional problem of transcendence. Following Husserl, Heidegger discovers transcendence to be the way in which 'being encounters life and the role it plays in life' (THP, 154), and thus according it crucial ontological significance.

At what would seem to be the culminating moment of the text, Levinas lines himself up with Husserl and Heidegger to form a 'we' that has 'overcome the Bergsonian antagonism between intellect and intuition' (THP, 155). Yet, almost as an afterthought, the 'we' begins to unravel before the question of freedom. Returning again to the motivating force of Bergson's work – the justification of freedom – Levinas finds something lacking in Husserl and Heidegger:

> Bergson's philosophical intuition, tightly bound to man's concrete life and destiny, reaches to its highest point, namely, the act of freedom. This metaphysical foundation of intuition is lacking in Husserl's phenomenology, and the ties which relate intuition to all the vital forces which define concrete existence are foreign to his thought. (THP, 155)

Levinas had earlier identified Heidegger as providing for phenomenology the missing account of the 'metaphysical essence of man', and it might be expected that he would appeal to it again, at this point, to support the critique of Bergson's location of the 'metaphysical foundation' of intuition in freedom. Indeed, this punctually occurs in the following two paragraphs on historicity indebted to Heidegger, but something has gone wrong.[31] The account of the 'metaphysical essence of man' in terms of historical situation, wherein 'Historicity and temporality form the very substantiality of man's substance', defines 'man' in terms of 'a specific manner of being his past' (THP, 156). The human is defined almost exclusively in terms of the being of the past. This weighs the 'metaphysical essence' of man more towards destiny than towards freedom, an outcome that immediately provokes Levinas to appeal to Husserl for a concept of freedom. The 'freedom of theory' that he evokes against a thinly disguised Heideggerian ' "existential thesis" of the naïve attitude' (THP, 157) is an unconvincing resort that leaves the reading of Husserl with a sophisticated critique of Bergsonian intuition but an implied antagonism between opposed metaphysical foundations or essences: Bergsonian freedom and Heideggerian destiny. At this point he finds only a weak defence of 'theoretical freedom' in Husserl, although he will subsequently discover a more radical freedom in Husserl's notion of 'self-evidence' that he will develop in the direction of ethical alterity.

The implied conflict between freedom and destiny that emerged at the end of *The Theory of Intuition in Husserl's Phenomenology* is framed explicitly in Levinas's writings after 1933. The 1934 article 'Phenomenology' describes the Heideggerian subject as 'no longer the transcendental and purely contemplative consciousness of Kant and Husserl, but a concrete *existence* doomed to death and caring about the very fact of its being' (DH, 39). The weight of being, or sense of destiny, is identified by Levinas not only with the climate of Heidegger's thought but also, in the same year, with the philosophy of Hitlerism. In the enigmatic text from 1936, *De l'évasion*, Levinas explores the possibility of an escape from ontological destiny in terms of Bergson's *élan vital*, or in terms of a monotheistic theology. But before looking at these texts more closely it is necessary to address Levinas's return to the reading of Husserl and the problem of freedom in his 1940 article 'The Work of Edmund Husserl', which might aptly be subtitled 'Anti-Heidegger' and which prepared the way for the new departure of Levinas's thought after 1945.

In the extremely subtle and disciplined reading of 1940, Levinas returns to the problem with which he ended *The Theory of Intuition in Husserl's Phenomenology*. There, as we saw, the perceived lack in Husserl of any account of the 'metaphysical essence' of man led Levinas to Heidegger and, according to his interpretation, the threatened relegation of the theme of freedom. Levinas presented Husserl's defence of freedom in terms of 'theoretical freedom', as a weak expedient. As if to atone for the earlier preference given to Heideggerian throwness (*Geworfenheit*) and destiny, Levinas now discovers a strong account of the metaphysical essence of freedom in Husserl. Departing from the Husserlian 'inexact essence' that he had earlier pitted against Bergsonian intuition, Levinas reveals this to be at the root of the radical phenomenological departures from Husserl:

> For it was Husserl who introduced into the idea that thought can have a meaning, can intend something even when this something is absolutely undetermined, a quasi absence of object, and we know the role this idea has played in Scheler's and Heidegger's phenomenologies. (DH, 61)

The separation of intentional meaning from an intended object that was developed by Scheler in his account of desire, and by Heidegger in the significance of death, is now located by Levinas in the works of Husserl. Yet the quasi absent object is neither the desire of Scheler nor the nothingness of Heidegger that provokes anxiety, but an alterity at the heart of the identity of the intending subject.

Levinas interprets the absence in Husserl in terms of excess rather than privation, a step made possible by an important revision in his understanding of the relationship between intuition and intentionality. This revision was made possible by a re-assessment of the theme of 'self-evidence'. This theme already featured in the 1930 reading of Husserl, but now is given an enlarged role in the exegesis. Self-evidence is what permits a potentially infinite intention to be concluded or made intuitive; it is a mode of situating the intention. Significantly, Levinas emphasises that self-evidence is 'the presence of the object in person before consciousness' (DH, 61), the phrase 'in person' anticipating Levinas's later theme of 'the face' which, too, is infinite and present 'in person'. Intentionality is now interpreted as 'a self-evidence being sought, a light that tends to make itself known' or an infinity that presents itself for intuition. Distancing himself from Husserl's terminology in order to clarify his thought, Levinas describes self-evidence as a 'unique situation' in which 'the mind, while receiving something foreign, is also the origin of what it receives. It is always active' (DH, 61). The unique economy of self-evidence consists in the mind giving to itself and thus receiving an infinity that is paradoxically foreign but also its own; it is actively bestowing even when it is passively receiving. This paradoxical economy makes the mode of bestowing and receiving into a function of temporality – not just the reception of a destiny, but also the bestowal of an infinity or future.

The paradoxes of self-evidence point in the direction of an account of freedom – which, since Rousseau, has operated through the paradoxical modality of autonomy or self-legislation, the giving and receiving of the law. Levinas indeed immediately identifies self-evidence with freedom, but significantly it is freedom that both gives and is given a world:

> The fact that in self-evidence the world is a given, that there is always a given for the mind, is not only found to be in agreement with the idea of activity, but is presupposed by that activity. A given world is a world where we can be free without this freedom being purely negative. The self-evidence of a given world, more than the non-engagement of the mind in things, is the positive accomplishment of freedom. (DH, 61)

With this, Levinas finds at the heart of Husserl's thought a 'liberal inspiration' or notion of being as freedom that was lacking in his earlier reading and in his interpretation of Heidegger. In an anticipation of the face of the other, Levinas describes 'the light of self-evidence [as] the sole tie with being that posits us as an origin of being, that is, as freedom' (DH, 61); it is the infinite 'in person' of the 'foreign' that is within us. It points to a notion of freedom that contains but also exceeds classical accounts of freedom as autonomy, evoking Bergson's excessive, futural freedom but freeing it from the claims of intuitive immediacy.

In addition to identifying Husserlian self-evidence with the intentional mode of freedom, Levinas also uses it to frame a contrast with Heidegger, saying 'Here Husserl's philosophy is radically opposed to that of Heidegger, where man is submerged by existence from the start' (DH, 61). The essay continues to underline this contrast, providing a Husserlian 'metaphysical essence' to occupy the vacancy previously filled by Heidegger. In respect to the concrete facticity of individual consciousness and the constitution of inner time, Levinas concedes that 'in this regard Heidegger's work is revolutionary', only to qualify this concession with a devastating 'unless': 'Unless, that is, we were to understand Husserl to take the ego itself as the moment of an impersonal event to which the notions of activity and passivity no longer apply, we can find in the notion of the *Urimpression*...indications leading in this direction' (DH, 75). From this preliminary qualification of Heidegger's 'revolutionary' contribution, Levinas then pits Husserl against him on the very issue of freedom. First he identifies a (Heideggerian) misinterpretation that inverts the sense of Husserlian sense, and then links this to a critique of care framed in terms of freedom:

> Intentionality, linked to the idea of self-evidence, which has too often been interpreted as an affirmation of the presence of man in the world, becomes in Husserl the very liberation of man vis-à-vis the world. *Sinngebung*, the fact of thinking and bestowing a meaning, intellection, is not an involvement like any other; it is a freedom. (DH, 75)

If we recall that in 1930 Levinas praised Heidegger for his daring response to the questions of 'the way being encounters life and the role which it plays in life' (THP, 154), we can now appreciate the significance of his discovery in Husserl that the encounter of being and life is characterised by freedom and that the role of freedom is to give sense to life. Not only is there no longer any need for phenomenology to resort to the Heideggerian supplement, but the latter is now identified as a perverse departure from the liberal inspiration of phenomenology.

Levinas ends 'The Work of Edmund Husserl' with an extended polemic against Heidegger, which sees him as within and without the phenomenological tradition: he is a tributary of Husserl even though an abyss separates them. The abyss is none other than the irreconcilable distinction between freedom and destiny. Levinas prepares this stark conclusion by first claiming: 'I do not think that Husserl's intentionality, that is, the phenomenon of meaning itself, can be interpreted as Heidegger's *In-der-Welt-Sein*...[which] affirms in the first instance that man, because of his existence, is already overwhelmed' (DH, 85). On the contrary, it is through intentionality that 'man has the power to keep himself in reserve before the world...[it] is an *Ausser-der-Welt-Sein* rather than the *In-der-Welt-Sein* of consciousness' (DH, 87). From this distinction between Husserl and Heidegger, Levinas draws a radical conclusion regarding the relationship between freedom and history. For Husserl, meaning consists in a transcendent freedom, it has 'never been determined by history', and, indeed, 'time and consciousness' themselves issue from freedom or 'the passive synthesis of an inner and deep constitution that is no longer a being' (DH, 87). Freedom, in other words, is a transcendence that can never be thematised; it is beyond ontology, otherwise than being. Unlike platonic transcendence, this version of transcendence is traumatic, emerging from the foreign that lives in the same. Levinas continues by claiming that 'For Heidegger, on the contrary, meaning is conditioned by something that already was', that it is an irreversible product of destiny, a 'vision of existence and the affirmation that existence is irreducible to the light of self-evidence' that Heidegger 'inherits from afar' a formula with which, we shall see, Levinas links Heideggerian destiny with the philosophy of National Socialism.

By the time 'The Work of Edmund Husserl' had been published in 1940, the presentiment had become reality and Levinas was fighting with the French army in a hopeless defence of the Republic against the army of the German National Socialist government. His polemic against Heidegger was intensified by the latter's declaration of allegiance to the National Socialist movement. This confirmed a suspicion that the surrender of the concept of freedom was dangerous, and that philosophy without this concept was vulnerable to becoming an apology for destiny. The analysis of the 'philosophy of Hitlerism' uncovered a deeper complicity of philosophy with totalitarianism in which the former was by no means the victim of the latter. The suspicion of complicity also led Levinas to imagine ways of escaping the Western philosophical tradition, whether using the resources of that philosophy – the foreign that lived within it – or by making an exit from the tradition of philosophy altogether.

Philosophy and National Socialism

In a letter of 28 March 1996 to *Critical Inquiry* that prefaced the translation of the 1934 essay 'Reflections on the Philosophy of Hitlerism', Levinas described the journal *Esprit* in which it was first published as 'representing progressive and avant-garde Catholicism shortly after Hitler came to power'. The journal, for which Levinas was to write consistently until the 1980s,[32] was rather more than this, representing the strand of 'social personalism' developed by Emmanuel Mounier. Mounier claimed that both the style and the content of his thought was provoked by the Wall Street Crash of 1929 and the political tensions that followed it throughout Europe. Instead of continuing to philosophise for an audience restricted to the University, Mounier founded the review *Esprit* in 1932 in order, in true radical tradition, to take the ideas of the *Esprit* group to a wider public. Levinas's essay appeared in the second volume of *Esprit*, and is one of the first philosophical reflections on racism and National Socialism.

Mounier described personalism as less an ideology than a programme of research open to radical Christian, Marxist and, later, existentialist ideas. His own first major work was a study of the Dreyfusard and Bergsonian, Charles Peguy.[33] The themes of personalism agree with the radical republican search for a rethinking of liberty, equality and fraternity

29

based on the view of the 'person' as irreducible to social and political structures. Yet the liberty of the person was also 'situated' with respect to history, and its equality and fraternity were defined in terms of responsibility for the other and before God (an ethico–political development of the injunction of the Sermon on the Mount to love God and your neighbour). *Esprit* in the 1930s was by no means solely a theoretical journal, but was engaged in a critique of anti-Semitism and totalitarianism. It was silenced by the censor of the Vichy regime after 1940.

In a sense, Levinas's publication in *Esprit* in 1934 and thereafter marked his commitment to the tradition of radical philosophical republicanism in which he had been educated. Through Mounier, Peguy and Bergson, the journal was almost a direct continuation of the publicist radical tradition of the early century.[34] Levinas was also coming to terms not only with intensified anti-Semitism but also with the knowledge of Heidegger's endorsement of the Hitler regime. The essay on Hitlerism represents an attempt, on the one hand, to use what he learnt from phenomenology for understanding National Socialist racism, but also to endorse the radical republican tradition and to begin a life's reflection on the relationship between *Being and Time* and *Mein Kampf*.[35]

Levinas's 1996 preface to the Hitlerism essay is a fascinating exercise in anachronism, one of his major philosophical preoccupations. It poises the Hitlerism essay between presentiment and memory by reading the memory of horror back into the presentiment. The 1934 text is remembered in terms of tracing the 'source' of National Socialism's 'bloody barbarism' to a possibility of 'elemental evil into which we can be led by logic and against which western philosophy had not insured itself' (RH, 63). The memory of 1996 insists that the source of National Socialism was in some sense necessary; it did not lie in 'some contingent anomaly of human reasoning nor in some accidental ideological misunderstanding' (RH, 63). There are a number of interesting features evident in this memory of the presentiment of National Socialism. The first is the – for Levinas – uncharacteristic search for a source of the event of National Socialism, the second is the modal description of the source as 'necessary', and the third its description in terms of the theological category of evil. The framework of Levinas's memory in this instance is uncharacteristic for his late work, which builds on a rigorous critique of origins, modality and the indiscriminate use of theological concepts in philosophy, as well as being unrepresentative of the argument of the original essay.

One reason for the uncharacteristic combination of the search for origins and modality of necessity may lie in the difficult intersection of presentiment and memory that is inscribed in Levinas's preface. The 'prophetic tense' that reads the past with a knowledge of the future necessarily transforms intimations into certainties; yet the formal characteristics of the intersection of presentiment and memory are further complicated by this particular crossroads being presided over by the ambiguous figure of Heidegger. In 'As if Consenting to Horror', Levinas remained preoccupied by the possible relation between Hitlerism and Heideggerian fundamental ontology, a relation that he explained in terms of evil. Here too, fifty years later, Heidegger's philosophy is seen as complicit with a strain of Western philosophy that was not 'sufficiently assured' against 'elemental evil'.

The strains of Western philosophy vulnerable to the elemental evil of Nazism are extremely broadly defined by Levinas. Not surprisingly they include Heidegger, whose complicity with elemental evil is 'inscribed within the ontology of being concerned with being' (RH, 63), even though it is Heidegger's reading of 'Western philosophy' and its post-Cartesian development that immediately allows Levinas to locate vulnerability to evil in the post-Cartesian philosophy that regards the subject as 'correlative with being as gathering together and as dominating' (RH, 63). This is exemplified by 'transcendental idealism' and its conception of freedom, and even extended to 'liberalism'. Against the principle of freedom and being as gathering or domination (or 'equalisation'), Levinas seeks protection from elemental evil in the thought of a human dignity emerging from a fraternity in which humans are called by God to responsibility for the 'other man'.

Turning from Levinas's memory to the presentiment itself reveals a rather more complex argument in which the concept of elementary evil, and philosophy's vulnerability to it, play almost no role. The method of reflection that Levinas follows in the essay owes little to theological modes of arguing about evil and a great deal to the fusion of philosophy and sociology pursued by the Durkheimian school. The introductory paragraphs of the 'Reflections' identify the philosophy of Hitlerism as the elaboration of an 'elementary form' (*forme élémentaire*) or re-awakened 'elementary sense' (*sentiment élémentaire*). These elementary forms, rather like the 'elementary forms of the religious life' previously studied by Durkheim 'express a soul's principal attitude towards the whole of reality and its own destiny. They predetermine or prefigure the meaning of the adventure that the soul will face in the world' (RH, 64). The temporal structuring of reality in terms of attitude, destiny and prefiguration that constitutes the elementary form of Hitlerism questions the founding principles of liberal and Christian civilisation. However, Levinas insists at the outset that the conflict between Hitlerism and liberal/Christian modernity involves the entire temporal structuring of reality and not just a logical opposition between 'Christian universalism and racist particularism' (RH, 64). The meaning expressed in this logical opposition 'only shows up fully if we go back to their source, to intuition, to the original decision that makes them possible' (RH, 64). Levinas then proposes to examine the 'elementary forms', 'intuitions' or 'original decisions' that precede the elaboration of the difference between liberal Christendom and Nazism in terms of the logic of universal and particular. For what is at issue between Christian liberalism and Nazism is not universalism and particularism, but a more fundamental difference between their conceptions of freedom and time.

A methodological hesitation is immediately visible in the opening paragraphs of the essay between understanding Hitlerism in terms of concepts such as 'elementary form' and 'elementary sentiment' drawn from Durkheim and Levy-Bruhl's anthropological studies of the origins of religion and logic, and those of 'source' and 'intuition' drawn from Levinas's phenomenological studies. The adoption of both methods, characteristic of this essay, and much else of Levinas's work, proved extremely fruitful. Durkheim and Levy-Bruhl sought the elementary forms of the religious life and of logical thought in the social representations of 'aboriginal religion', and suggested that elaborated modern forms of experience, religious and scientific, could be traced to these elementary forms (as did another Durkheimian, Marcel Mauss, when he traced modern economic rationality to the elementary form of gift exchange). The compatibility of this approach with the phenomenological method is patent – the elementary forms serve as the horizon that exceeds and makes possible otherwise mutually exclusive oppositions. Levinas tries to bring the anthropological and phenomenological methods together by showing the elementary forms of experience – their constitution of past, present and future – that inform Nazism and its Christian and liberal opponents.

For Levinas, Hitlerism is the elaboration of an 'elementary form' of pagan religiosity that stands opposed to an entire monotheistic civilisation. It is this opposition that forms the horizon of the distinction between particularism and universalism. The latter distinction is not fundamental, but only the derived form of a far deeper opposition. The object of the 'Reflections' is to disclose the horizon upon which Christian universalism and pagan particularism play themselves out in terms of the opposition between monotheistic and pagan civilisations. Each has its own way of structuring time, in particular historical time; each has its own understanding of destiny and freedom and both have their opposed 'predeterminations or prefigurations of their adventure in the world'. The argument is consistent with *Esprit*'s programme of a 'popular front' of the monotheistic religions against a revived paganism, a programme that Levinas shared and developed further in his religious essays of the 1930s.[36]

The opening paragraphs of the essay rehearse the argument for freedom, linking the origins of the concept of freedom with monotheism and then suggesting its secular development in terms of liberalism. The 'spirit of freedom' that characterised Western civilisation is contrasted with the pagan concept of fate. The concept of freedom that Levinas evolves has little to do with liberal notions of freedom figured as autonomy and more to do with Bergson's notion of freedom as creative spontaneity. Levinas reads the latter concept of freedom into the monotheistic refusal of fate.

32

The 'elementary form' of monotheism is 'a feeling that man is absolutely free in his relations with the world and the possibilities that solicit action from him. Man is renewed eternally in the face of the Universe. Speaking absolutely, he has no history' (RH, 64). The 'feeling' or 'elementary sentiment' of freedom structures the experience of the monotheist cultures and distinguishes them from the submission to fate and destiny that Levinas finds in paganism.

The 'elementary form' or sentiment of paganism is an experience of time that is 'irreparable', a 'fait accompli'. Instead of being free of the past and of history through the experience of constant renewal, the pagan experiences history as 'the most profound limitation' and lives with the sense of being 'swept along by a fleeting present [that] forever evades man's control, but weighs heavily on his destiny' (RH, 65). Experience is weighed towards an inescapable past that dominates present and future; both present and future are but repetitions of a past that can only be endured. Levinas begins to sketch a contrast between the elementary form revealed in early Greek philosophy and tragedy and that of Jewish and Christian liturgies of redemption. In the former, 'beneath the melancholy of the eternal flow of things, Heraclitus's illusory present, there lies the tragedy of the irremovability of a past that cannot be erased, and that condemns any initiative to being just a continuation' (RH, 65). Against this sense of fate Levinas contrasts a 'true freedom, the true beginning', a version of the Bergsonian view of freedom as spontaneity, a freedom oriented to the present prophetically saturated with presentiments of the future rather than memories of the past.

Levinas regards this sense of freedom as the product of monotheist culture that replaces tragic destiny with a drama of repentance and redemption. Tragedy emerges in a culture whose elementary form or 'burning feeling' is one of the 'natural powerlessness that man experiences in the face of time', an experience exemplified by the tragedy of the Atrides 'who struggle in the grip of a strange and brutal past that afflicts them like a curse' (RH, 65). For Judaism and Christianity, however, the same 'burning feeling...of a radical powerlessness to redeem the irreparable – heralds the repentance that generates the pardon that redeems. Man finds something in the present with which he can modify or efface the past. Time loses its very irreversibility' (RH, 65). Levinas develops this theme through the 'mystical drama' of the Christian passion and the celebration of the Eucharist through which Christianity 'proclaims freedom and makes such freedom fully possible' (RH, 65). The radical freedom of which he speaks not only subordinates the past to the present – challenging 'the flow of moments of a past', but also the present to the future – the freedom of repentance 'does not form a chain', but the freedom of repentance itself can be repented. The repetition is not a bad infinity, but a continuous opening on to the future.

The radical concept of freedom that Levinas develops is an 'elementary form': it is not exhausted by 'political freedoms' but is a 'conception of human destiny' that does not consist in an inescapable fate but rather the 'feeling that man is absolutely free in his relations with the world' (RH, 64). This absolute freedom is vulnerable to becoming an implacable law of freedom, as when the past is 'forever challenged, forever called into question'. Here the infinite repetition of the free act implied in 'forever' threatens to convert freedom into necessity. With this the Bergsonian concept of freedom as spontaneity falls prey to the same antinomy of Rousseau's freedom as autonomy – we are forced to be free, forced to be spontaneous even to the degree of repenting of our spontaneity. Levinas will later qualify the absolute character of his concept of freedom in order to avoid this antinomy, introducing ethical heteronomy into the concept of freedom itself. His post-war description of his authorship in terms of presentiment and ineluctable memory of political horror points to a qualification of absolute freedom with respect to the Shoah, and in spite of his repeated references to Auschwitz as the 'Passion' of European Jewry his relation to this 'strange and brutal past' is more consistent with the experience of tragedy than the Christian mystical drama of repentance and salvation. While he contrasted the 'Passion' of Auschwitz with the 'adventure' of the State of Israel, it is by no means clear that Levinas saw the latter in terms of repentance and the retrieval of freedom. In 1934, however, Levinas's concern to steer freedom in the direction of the ethical was subordinate to the project of deriving equality from freedom and thus defending it from National Socialist notions of racial inequality.

In a line of argument that he will subsequently refine and take further, Levinas uses absolute freedom to criticise any notion of fate – be it natural, historical or the fusion of both in National Socialist racial philosophy of history – and then to justify human equality. In absolute freedom the individual is liberated from both 'natural existence' and the 'vicissitudes of the world's real history' (RH, 66); is liberated, in short, from any determination be it natural (racial) or historical (political or confessional). In this way 'the equal dignity of each and every soul, which is independent of the material and social conditions of people' is due not to a quality possessed by the individual soul or body but to 'the power given to the soul to free itself from *what has been*, from everything that linked it with something or engaged it with something...' (RH, 66). The rooting of equality in the power of freedom, and then this power in the liberatory potential of monotheism – where the claims of the natural and historical world are nothing as compared to those of God – is consistent with Levinas's attempt to revitalise the revolutionary principles of 1789. This is emphasised in 'Reflections on Hitlerism' by the sympathetic critique of liberalism that follows the derivation of equality from freedom.

The core of Levinas's critique of liberalism is found in the claim that 'the liberalism of the past few centuries evades the dramatic aspects of such a liberation' (RH, 66). While it accepts the result of the radical concept of freedom – the separation of human spirit and reality – it replaces the communal drama of repentance and redemption with 'the sovereign freedom of reason' (RH, 66). Liberalism 'locates the ultimate foundation of the spirit outside the brutal world and the implacable history of concrete existence' (RH, 66), but the act of abstracting reason from the struggle for liberation from nature and history detaches it from any direct involvement in communal struggle. Levinas describes the writers of the French Enlightenment or 'the precursors of democratic ideology and the Declaration of the Rights of Man' as *exorcising* 'physical, psychic and social matter'. The Enlightenment establishes the reign of reason by an irrational act of magic rather than through a communal drama of repentance. What is more, the act of exorcism assumes the sovereign power of reason that it is meant to found – it is assumed that reason by virtue of its light is able to 'chase away the shadows of irrationality' (RH, 66). The Enlightenment not only refused any communal struggle of repentance and redemption, it also assumed that victory over darkness was always in its power – that reason was sovereign. In place of the movement of repentance and redemption through the redemptive gift of God, liberalism emphasised the near-magical operation of the sovereign power of reason, or, in Levinas's concise formula, 'in place of liberation through grace there is autonomy' (RH, 66). Autonomy consists in the sovereign imposition of the ideal laws of spirit upon the historical and natural world, but without the communal drama of repentance and without any dependence on a divine other. Yet without this movement of repentance there is no possible basis for fraternity, and liberalism, while emphasising freedom and equality, is left without a strong concept of community. This makes it vulnerable to proposals for 'community' or 'fraternity' opposed to freedom and equality, such as the national, confessional, class and, more ominously, racial fraternities that pervade modernity and are able through their own dramatic narratives of repentance and redemption to exploit the deficit of liberal rationalism.

Already Levinas has partially succeeded in his attempt to show that the logical opposition of Christian universalism and racist particularism is itself a liberal one that can be understood in terms of the opposition between Christian freedom and pagan fate. What distinguishes the liberal experience of an individual's rational choice between different outcomes – the 'logical possibilities that present themselves to a dispassionate reason' – from the 'experience of the possibilities open to him as a series of restless powers that seethe within him and already push him down a determined path' (RH, 66) is not logic, but a commitment to the elementary form of freedom over that of fate. Yet by reducing the significance of the movement of liberation and its dependence on God in favour of an accomplished and sovereign 'spirituality of reason', liberalism once more becomes vulnerable to critiques based on new conceptions of fraternity uncommitted to the values of freedom and equality. With this move Levinas draws close to the personalist critique of liberalism that, with Mounier, stressed the notion of 'situated' freedom in which freedom is passionately engaged in a struggle out of which emerges community.

At this point in the 'Reflections on Hitlerism', Levinas turns to the Marxist critique of liberalism, and its fusion of a class-determined notion of fraternity ('class consciousness') with a materialist philosophy of history. His reading of Marxism, in common with that of Mounier and the personalists, is balanced and subtle, emphasising the equivocal character of Marxist thought and practice. Levinas stressed that Marxism breaks with the monotheist and liberal view of freedom, marking in his view 'the first doctrine in Western history to contest this view of man', and was thus 'opposed not just to Christianity, but to the whole of idealist liberalism' (RH, 66–7). As materialists, Marxists reject the monotheist/liberal metaphysics of freedom and equality, and refuse to regard 'the human spirit as pure freedom or a soul floating above any attachment'. By not subscribing to the 'elementary form' of absolute freedom, Marxist doctrine appears to fall on the side of fate. In it, the 'human spirit' is 'prey to material needs' before which the magical rites of reason are hollow acts: 'as it is at the mercy of a matter and a society that no longer obey the magic wand of reason, its concrete and servile existence has more weight and importance than does impotent reason' (RH, 67). For this reason, absolute freedom – in Levinas's periphrase 'the type that works miracles' – is condemned to insignificance by Marxism. In place of liberal rational magic emerges a materially-based opposition between bourgeois and proletarian class fraternities that are poised in a state of constant, trans-historical class warfare.

After making this very powerful case for Marxism's critique of the elementary form of absolute freedom, Levinas goes on to show that Marxism's break with liberalism 'is not a definitive one'. Its commitment to freedom and equality places it within the Jacobin revolutionary heritage, and perhaps it even exceeds the liberal version of this heritage in the emphasis it places on the communal process or 'drama' of revolutionary struggle. Levinas insists that, in spite of its critique, 'Marxism consciously continues the traditions of 1789' in its refusal of fate and its commitment to freedom through consciousness: 'To become conscious of one's social situation is, even for Marx, to free oneself of the fatalism entailed by that situation' (RH, 67). The dramatic liberation from 'social bewitchment' is not achieved through the magic of a 'sovereign reason' but through a communal struggle of secular repentance and redemption that Levinas considers to be modelled on Jacobinism. Yet Marxism exceeded Jacobinism by reason of the breadth of its universal aspirations: while the

Jacobin struggle created the fraternity of the armed nation, the Marxist class struggle aspires to create the international fraternity of the working class and, eventually, of humanity. So while rejecting the ideal sovereignty of reason, Marxists remained committed to the values of freedom, equality and a class-based notion of fraternity that at least aspired to universal human significance. Marxists thus shared with liberalism a commitment to the sovereign character of freedom, but vested sovereignty in the proletariat's communal drama of liberation through class strugle rather than in the magical operations of abstract reason.

The equivocal character of Marxism with respect to freedom prompts Levinas to reflect on the mutual implication of idealism and materialism. He does so through an extended discussion of the relation of self and body that explains both how liberalism and Marxism can belong to the same tradition of freedom in spite of their differences, and what distinguishes both from a philosophy that would unify politics and biology. Referring to Socrates' discussion in the *Phaedo*, Levinas introduces the classic opposition between ascetic refusals of the body as an obstacle to the spiritual development of the self and the materialist identification of self and body. Then, in a short series of densely argued paragraphs, he re-orients the terms of this opposition, using the phenomenological method to question the horizon within which it is played out. Instead of assuming the Manichean opposition between body and soul, he proposes to examine the intentional relation between them: such an analysis must begin, not by assuming the terms of the opposition, but by reflecting upon the 'feeling of identity between self and body'. Levinas claims, consistently with his account of intentionality, that 'to separate the spirit from the concrete forms in which it is already involved is to betray the originality of the very feeling from which it is appropriate to begin' (RH, 68–9). The personalist stress on the situated character of the self and the Durkheimian view of the elementary forms are here combined with a phenomenological analysis of the *inescapability* of the body that will become significant in Levinas's next work, *De l'evasion*; meanwhile, however, it serves as a corrective for ascetic refusals of the body.

Levinas's insistence upon the intentional analysis of the relation of body and soul is politically as well as philosophically motivated. The idealist rejection of the elementary sentiment of the identity of self and body results in an abstract concept of freedom that is vulnerable to the claims of biology. Reason, because opposed to the body, cannot argue with its claims framed in terms of elementary sentiments rather than rational propositions. Marxism went some way in this direction, with its materialist critique of what Marx called the French Republican 'idealism of politics', but remained within the broader tradition of freedom. Now Levinas points to the danger of the unexamined or even repressed 'feeling for the body' becoming 'the basis of a new conception of man' (RH, 69). Unlike Marxism, this new 'elementary form' has no residual commitment to the values of freedom and equality, but stresses a biological conception of fraternity – 'race'. Levinas offers a vivid description of this elementary form that shows how rigorously it overturns the revolutionary values of freedom and equality:

> The biological, with the notion of inevitability it entails, becomes more than an *object* of spiritual life. It becomes its heart. The mysterious urgings of the blood, the appeals of heredity and the past for which the body serves as an enigmatic vehicle, lose the character of being problems that are subject to a solution put forward by a sovereignly free Self. Not only does the self bring in the unknown elements of these problems in order to resolve them; the self is also constituted by these elements. Man's essence no longer lies in freedom, but in a kind of bondage [*enchainment*]. (RH, 69)

From the description of the elementary form of biological fate opposed to freedom, Levinas moves to a specific analysis of the National Socialist racist philosophy of history. The 'communal drama' identified in the Marxist narrative of class and universal human liberation is now cast as the drama of the struggle for survival between alleged biological races.

Levinas evokes a connection between the National Socialist critique of liberalism and Heidegger's concept of authenticity, before moving on to an intense reflection upon its political implications. According to National Socialism, 'the forms of a modern society founded on the harmony established between free wills seem not only fragile and inconsistent but false and deceitful' (RH, 69). The rhetorical triumph of spirit over body, rational will over passion, now appears hollow, the 'work of forgers'. Before the hypocrisy of a liberalism that proclaims freedom and equality without fraternity, National Socialism emphasises an abstract, biologically-founded fraternity. The critical procedure is analogous to that of Marxism, but instead of founding fraternity in the universal class it vests it in the particular and murderously exclusive race. It opposes to the deceits and inconsistencies of rational modernity a 'concretisation' of spirit, making it authentically present in a racial fraternity or 'society based on consanguinity' (RH, 69). The ideal of a racist politics is, accordingly, to be understood as an inversion of liberalism. By refusing to understand freedom and the spirit in its intentional relation to the body, liberalism provokes an equally abstract but inverted privileging of the claims of the body – more precisely 'blood' – over freedom and spirit. The concept of absolute freedom outlined earlier has both a dignity and a danger: dignity in its freedom from natural and historical determinations but danger in that this freedom can also negate itself (an inverse movement that Levinas will later describe in terms of 'idolatry').

Levinas hints at a link between the Nazi diagnosis of the inauthenticity of modernity and the critique of inauthenticity and *Das Mann* in Heidegger's *Being and Time*. In modern liberal societies it appears as if sincerity and authenticity are no longer possible, and 'Civilisation is invaded by everything that is not authentic, by a substitute that is put at the service of fashion and of various interests' (RH, 70). Yet to respond to the ersatz civilisation with an appeal to the authentic runs the risk of advocating 'degenerate forms of the ideal' – in this case, the fusion of the fraternities of nation and race. Levinas stresses that the resulting 'Germanic ideal' while seeming to promise authentic 'sincerity and authenticity' does so at the price of freedom and equality: the ideal is made concrete in the 'community of blood' which cannot be chosen or willed and from which there is no escape. The sovereign freedom of reason is qualified by the 'concrete being' of a community of fate 'linked by birth'. In racism, the priority of the body over the spirit is total – the self cannot escape the body in which it finds itself – it cannot freely elect its identity, it cannot renew itself through a drama of repentance and redemption, but its present and future condition is already fated.

The repudiation of freedom in favour of racial fraternity requires, paradoxically, that the ideal of racism be universalised. It has to be true, and true for everyone, because otherwise it would become one option among many that may be freely chosen and renounced according to the tenets of liberal freedom. Yet the essence of racism is that racial identity is universal and inescapable, the ultimate source of all truth and action. Thus racism as a total metaphysical doctrine must become militant and 'strive towards the creation of a new world' (RH, 69). Levinas has effectively overturned the liberal claim that racism is a particularism by showing that it must be universal. He resorts to a questionable reading of Nietzsche to show how universality can be compatible with racism.[37] He takes Nietzsche's analogy between Zarathustra's descent from the mountain and the doctrine of eternal return as a descending stream as an example of a 'basic modification in the idea of universality' (RH, 69) in which 'universality must give way to the idea of expansion, for the expansion of a force presents a structure that is completely different from the propagation of an idea' (RH, 69). The character of this expansion is colonial – the expansion of a force creates a structure of masters and slaves – those who exercise the force and those who are subjected to it. There emerges a universal order, but one governed by war rather than politics – in Levinas's words, 'Nietzsche's will to power, which modern Germany is rediscovering and glorifying, is not only a new ideal; it is an ideal that simultaneously brings with it its own form of universalisation: war and conquest' (RH, 70–71). Although Levinas's analysis of National Socialism is one of the most perceptive and prescient written during the 1930s, not even he could imagine an expansion characterised not only by a colonial but also an exterminatory logic that would incarnate the universal by destroying whatever was deemed not to belong to it.

Levinas concludes by insisting that the threat of National Socialism and the philosophy of Hitlerism should not be underestimated. The National Socialist movement was more than a grotesque political adventure or opportunistic manoeuvre, and its racist philosophy represented not just German national particularism, but a *total* movement that sought to put into question 'the very humanity of man' (RH, 71). In retrospect, Levinas's judgement was uncannily accurate; it may be claimed that he, alone among his philosophical contemporaries, understood the philosophy of Hitlerism and the intentions of National Socialist politics, even if he underestimated its murderous potential.

In the course of his discussion of militant racist universalism Levinas contrasted the expansion of a force with the propagation of an idea. The contrast is developed in terms of the stark distinction between Talmudic tradition and the Führer cult. The former intimates a community that is both free and equal. An idea is given a 'unique accent' in its transmission, while also becoming a 'common heritage'. It creates a community of equals in which 'the person who accepts it becomes its master as does the person who proposes it. The propagation of an idea thus creates a community of "masters";' it is a process of equalisation' (RH, 71). Levinas aligns the Talmudic ideal of the emergence of truth through the tradition of discussion among equals – the community of masters – with the 'universality of an order in Western society', so linking freedom, equality and the fraternity of Talmudic discussion with the democratic order. This renewed sensitivity to Jewish thought and appreciation of its past and potential contribution to Western thought and politics was the prelude to a period of intense reflection on Jewish themes that would be interrupted by the war and then resumed alongside his post-war philosophical work. In it the Talmudic discussion of justice promised a community – 'Israel' – that would contrast with the colonial and exterminatory logics of racist universalism.

Guide for the persecuted

Given the millennial history of mutual misrecognition between Athens and Jerusalem, Levinas's care in pronouncing upon the place of Judaism in his philosophy and of philosophy in his Judaism is entirely understandable. In his post-war writings he deliberately published his philosophical work and his Talmudic commentaries with different publishers (see RB, 62). However, such acts of demarcation are to be set against a continual traffic between philosophy and Judaism in his work, evident from the turn to the prophetic tradition for a revitalisation of ethics to the political reflections prompted by the wars of the State of Israel. More fundamentally, the mobilisation of the question of Jewish identity by anti-Semitic movements focused attention on the philosophical and cultural investments in the concept of identity itself. What enabled this concept to play such a pivotal role in motivating and justifying an unprecedentedly violent project of persecution? During the 1930s the philosophical reflection upon the origins and the uses of 'identity' became inseparable from the experience of the ways in which this concept had been mobilised as an emblem of persecution.

During his studies at Strasbourg, Levinas did not break with his Lithuanian Jewish background, but neither did he consider it as having a programmatic or 'consciously acknowledged influence' on his philosophical studies. He subsequently described his relationship to the Jewish tradition as 'never like in relation to an object, but rather like to my own substance'. This way of describing the place of Judaism is not itself without ambiguity. The invitation to understand it in terms of an ontological difference between Judaism as an ontic object of study and as a 'substance' or ontological mode of being cannot be accepted at face value from Levinas. Of all twentieth-century philosophers he did more to put in question not only Heidegger's ontological difference but also any appeal to the 'proper' or to 'substance'. The involvement in Judaism that he describes is neither one of scholarly detachment nor existential absorption. Rather, the 'substance' that is 'mine' is experienced as a perplexing trauma, especially when that 'substance' has been made into an object of persecution by others. Indeed, the idea of Judaism as an essence or 'substance' was not remote from National Socialist racial definitions of Judaism, but the latter is far from Levinas's notion of identity understood in terms of a being internally divided between self and stranger.

The predicament of persecution is, to say the least, capable of provoking extreme perplexity. At its extremes it can provoke rejection by the victim of the persecuted identity or an intensified and militant commitment to it. It can also force a questioning of the grounds of identity and 'mineness', not only questioning a particular mode of being but the entire way of thinking about being. Levinas's writings of the mid-1930s work through the perplexities of persecution, not only those of the experience of persecution, but also of philosophical perplexities provoked by Heidegger's siding with the persecutors. *De l'evasion*, published in the *Recherches Philosophiques* of 1935 and a series of essays published in *Paix et Droit* in the latter half of the 1930s, represent a sustained philosophical and political exploration of this perplexity.[38]

The title of the 1935 *Paix et Droit* article, 'The Actuality of Maimonides', underlines the contemporaneity of the theme of perplexity. Levinas's reflections on the twelfth-century rabbinic and Aristotelian philosopher Maimonides – codifier of the *Mishnah Torah* and author of *The Guide for the Perplexed* – make central the question of the relationship between philosophy and rabbinics and the possible responses to persecution. The relationship of Maimonides' *Guide* to the dominant

Aristotelian philosophy of his period was paralleled in Levinas's relation-ship to Heideggerian phenomenology. At one level, his perplexity arose from the incompatibility between his philosophical fascination with Heideggerian thought and the political commitments of its author. At another level the object of perplexity was one of the relationship between Judaism and its erstwhile persecutor Christianity. The advent of the mili-tant paganism of National Socialism potentially changed the terms of engagement between them, making a reconciliation possible, perhaps even necessary for survival.

With respect to the perplexities of philosophy, the beginnings of a confrontation with Heidegger made in the 'Reflections on Hitlerism' were developed further in *De l'évasion*. The latter marks both a stage in the development of Levinas's thought and a break with what went before. The confrontation of Bergsonism and phenomenology is developed further, but in the context of a radical critique of the major theses of Heidegger and, for the first time, of Western philosophy as a whole. *De l'évasion* – written, Levinas observed in 1981, 'on the eve of the great massacres' (DE, 7) – firmly aligns Western philosophy with ontology, seeing Heideggerian ontology as its fatal summation. It also links ontology with paganism and an inability to escape 'fatality' – a term increasingly synonymous for Levinas with racism. Against the fatalistic paganism of ontology, Levinas urges the Bergsonian theme of radical freedom, confirming its relation to monotheism, but also its implication in and consequent frailty before the claims of ontology.

The explicit and embittered critique of ontology in *De l'évasion* testifies to the extent that Levinas had distanced himself from Heidegger since 1933. It also betrays a certain desperation before the total claims of ontology, a sense of the inescapability of being. Even the radical gesture of Bergson, Levinas concedes, is but an inflexion of fundamental ontology. And for him too, in spite of his critical target, the method of analysis remains indebted to Heidegger's analytic of *Dasein*, beginning with a description of the main theme of the analysis – desire for escape – and proceeding through a description of the affective states that attend it. While each of the eight numbered sections of *De l'évasion* attends to the analysis of a particular aspect of escape, all are informed by the problem of the radical escape from being and its philosophical discourse. The voice of *De l'évasion* is trapped and confined not only within philosophy but also within the being of fundamental ontology.

The book opens with a despairing description of the conflict between being and human liberty, modulating this conflict into one between 'Western philosophy' and ontologism. From very early in the first section it is evident that the latter conflict is but a ruse internal to philosophy, since the struggle with being is for the sake of a stronger and more comprehen-sive concept of being. The object of the ontological wars is western

42

philosophy's ' ideal of peace and equilibrium that presupposed the sufficiency of being' (DE, 69). Even the most radical attempts to escape being are only directed against 'the horror of a certain definition of our being and not of being itself' (DE, 71). The aim of these introductory comments is not only to put into question Heideggerian ontology, but also what had until recently served as a possible alternative, Bergsonian radical freedom. This now is identified as a particularly remorseless version of ontology: adopting the language of Bergson's *Creative Evolution*, Levinas writes 'The philosophy of *l'élan creator* while completely breaking with the rigidity of classical being, does not free itself from its prestige, for beyond the real it can only perceive the activity that creates it' (DE, 72). Bergsonian metaphysics is now regarded by Levinas as but an internal modification of ontology, replacing being as substance with being as activity. He continues:

> The propension towards the future 'ahead of itself' contained in the *élan*, marks a being devoted to a path. The *élan* is creative, but irresistible. The accomplishment of a destiny is the mark of being: the destiny is not completely traced out, but its accomplishment is fatal. (DE, 72)

Thus even Bergsonian creative freedom is ontological and its trajectory almost inconspicuously marked by fate. It is impossible to escape being by a simple translation of being into becoming, since the latter itself is but another ruse of being.

With the consignment of Bergson to the ranks of the ontologists, Levinas has prepared the way for a thorough reconsideration of metaphysics. His method, outlined in the final paragraphs of the first section, has three basic steps. The first is to 'grasp in all its purity' a concept of 'exit' that is 'inassimilable to renewal and to creation' (DE, 73). The postulate of an exit freed from investments in being is then, in a second step, considered to be constituted 'by a need for *exendance*' (DE, 73). Exendance, or to use a later term 'excess', marks an exit from being that is without definite trajectory and guided only by the need to escape:

> Thus being does not solely appear as the hurdle to be overcome by free thought, nor the rigidity that, inviting routine, demands an effort of originality, but as an imprisonment from which it must try to escape. (DE, 73)

The exit from being is not motivated by the desire for a new being, but solely by the need to escape. In order for this 'need' to be understood (and not itself become another ontological principle), Levinas must propose a third step which is the analysis of identity, in particular that of *Dasein* or *l'homme*. Although Levinas describes human identity as dualistic, this dualism is not to be understood logically as a tautology or contradiction, but as a dramatic tension. Identity itself is formed out of the dramatic unfolding of this tension:

> In the identity of the self, the identity of being reveals its nature as enchained, for it appears under the form of sufferance and invites an escape. Thus the escape is the need to exit from oneself, that is to say *to break the most radical, the most irremisable enchainment, the fact that the self is itself.* (DE, 73)

The analysis of the affects provoked by the sufferings of the drama of the self offers a way into an analysis of the escape from being and from identity. Reserving the analysis of 'the ontological character of nothingness and eternity' – that is, the full critique of Heidegger and being for death – for another time, Levinas begins his analysis of affects in Section III with an analysis of the affect of need, moving in Section IV to pleasure, to shame in Section V and to nausea in Section VI.

Informing these analyses is the audacious attempt to 'renew the ancient problem of the being of being' in the wake of Heidegger's own renewal of the same problem in *Being and Time*. Turning to his contemporary culture characterised by increasingly confident fascist and National Socialist movements, Levinas asks whether modern philosophy's preoccupation with the 'being of being' is not

> the mark of a certain civilisation installed in the *fait accompli* of being and incapable of escape. And in these conditions, is *excendance* possible and how can it be achieved? What is the idea of happiness and human dignity that it promises? (DE, 74)

The diagnosis of a link between ontology and fascism and the three questions of *excendance* – is it possible, how is it to be achieved and what is its idea of happiness and human dignity – may be taken as programmatic for Levinas's future work, and in particular the location of *excendance* in the face of the other. In *De l'évasion*, however, Levinas had not yet taken this particular step out of ontology, although he had prepared the way for it through an analysis of the excessive character of need and its implications for the understanding of affects such as shame and nausea.

The beginnings of a sensitivity to the significance of alterity are visible in the analysis of nausea. On the whole, the argument is directed to showing that the experience of nausea marks a 'limit situation where the uselessness of action is precisely the indication of the supreme instant from which one can only exit' (DE, 90). Nausea is the affect provoked by driving to its limit the dramatic tension between being and the excessive need to escape. Levinas adds, almost parenthetically, that the experience of nausea – the predicament of needing to escape but being incapable of doing so – is modified by the 'presence of the other' that objectifies the experience according to the social norm of illness. In the terms of his later work, the 'other' enters the drama of the self as a 'third', or spectator, whose gaze changes the aspect of experience.

In the final section of *De l'évasion* Levinas confirms the connections between ontology and totalitarianism that he had indicated at the outset of his analysis of the affects of the dramatically divided self. First of all, Levinas uses a similar term – *principe élémentaire* – to that used to describe the basis of Hitlerism in terms of the 'being' that founds ontology. The echoes of 'Reflections on Hitlerism' continue to resound in the assessment of philosophical idealism. In 1934 he had pitted liberal idealism's concept of spirit comprising freedom and autonomy against Nazi celebrations of natural fate and necessity. While still aware of the frailty of liberalism – its vulnerability, as in the case of Bergson, to becoming another ontology – he now prizes it for its 'primary inspiration' which is 'to seek to exceed being' (DE, 98). Even if inconsistent and vulnerable, this aspiration to escape being constitutes for Levinas 'the value of European civilisation'. Against it, Levinas aligns ontology and thus Heidegger with National Socialist barbarism, claiming that 'Any civilisation that accepts being, the tragic despair that it brings and the crimes that it justifies, deserves the name of barbarism' (DE, 98). Ontology is thus implicated in the fatality of modern paganism, its despairing racial philosophy of history and the crimes that it will commit in its name.

The possibility of a monotheistic 'popular front' against the revived paganism of National Socialism intimated in 'Reflections on Hitlerism' is further developed in the essays for *Paix et Droit*. The conclusion of *De l'évasion* saw the dignity of European civilisation to consist in the ability to escape being characteristic of the monotheistic religions. Monotheism offered a means of escape from being and ontology, but a monotheism not understood as a religious confession, but as the 'elementary principle' of European culture. In the essays from the mid-to-late 1930s Levinas shows himself to be one of the few philosophers to take seriously the claims of National Socialism to break with this tradition and to inaugurate a new millennial Reich.

In the 'The Actuality of Maimonides' (1935) Levinas describes his historical moment as one that has put into question 'the essence itself of our existence as much as Jews as men' (EP, 142). The source of these fears is the political and cultural mobilisation against monotheism:

Jewish–Christian civilisation has been put into question by an arrogant barbarism installed in the heart of Europe. With an unparalleled audacity, paganism has lifted its head again, reversing

45

values, confusing elementary distinctions, blurring the limits of the profane and the sacred, and dissolving the very principles according to which until now it has been possible to re-establish order. (EP, 142)

The evocation of a culture in dissolution continues with a description of the growing crowd of those seduced by the demagogy and the political adventurism of National Socialism – never, Levinas observes *a propos* of Maimonides, 'has the crowd of the perplexed been so numerous' (EP, 142). Hence the actuality of Maimonides in defining anew the Jewish mission of opposing paganism by bearing witness to the transcendent: for it was he who, with 'genial lucidity', distinguished between a thinking of the world and of that which exceeds it.

Paganism, on the contrary, '*is a radical impotence to exit from the world*' and its morality 'nothing but the consequence of this fundamental inability to transgress the limits of the world. The pagan is imprisoned in this self-sufficient world, closed in on himself' (EP, 144). The immanence of paganism is also applied to its perceived enemies, and it is for this reason, in 'The Religious Inspiration of the Alliance', that Levinas describes 'Hitlerism' as 'the hardest test – incomparable test – that Judaism has had to endure'. Nazism converts the Jewish mission to bear witness to the transcendent into an expression of the immanent category of race, making Judaism a biological rather than an existential condition. Anti-Semitism adds to traditional Christian anti-Judaism a biological ineluctability: 'the affront in its racist form adds to humiliation a poignant taste of despair. The pathetic fate [*sort pathetique*] becomes a fatality. One can no longer flee it. The Jew is inseparably welded to his Judaism' (EP, 144). And yet, at this point, for Levinas, the essence of Judaism is precisely the questioning before God of any identity or place in the world. The perplexity provoked by casting this election in terms of biological fatality is almost overwhelming.

Against the closure of paganism Levinas urges the theme of 'escape', but now, in contrast to the account in *De l'évasion*, the theme is given a political and cultural figure in 'Israel' and the Church. Nazi racist definitions of Judaism, while being scientifically absurd and 'unworthy of refutation',[39] have forced 'with a hitherto unequalled insistence a re-examination of the Jewish essence and its history among the nations' (EP, 145). Levinas contributes to this re-examination with a reflection on the work of the Alliance and its commitments to the principles of the French Revolution and the emancipation of Judaism. This conception characterised an 'epoch when the principles of '89 [liberty, equality, fraternity] penetrated the political and moral life of the peoples and acquired the self-evidence of common sense' and when 'assimilation passed for an easy solution' (EP, 145). This confidence was questioned by both Zionists who regarded it 'as a betrayal of Jewish nationalism' and by anti-Semites who condemned it as 'hypocrisy'. In the mid-1930s, Levinas did not subscribe to the programme of assimilation, nor to Zionism, and certainly not to racial definitions of Judaism, but admits that racism and the reality of National Socialism has forced the rediscovery of the 'gravity of being Jewish' (EP, 145). Levinas argues instead for a rethinking of the significance of the diaspora – namely, a commitment to the 'principles of '89' without the renunciation of the Jewish mission nor the identity that accompanies it. Later he will argue for a close historical relationship between the prophetic mission of Judaism and the principles of liberty, equality and fraternity, while refusing to accept any notion of fixed identity that might offer an exclusive figure for fraternity.

The exit from the ghetto made possible by the principles of '89 did not necessarily entail the dissolution of Jewish identity in the diaspora. While the diaspora entailed the renunciation of a Jewish political destiny as a nation-state, it nevertheless maintained a religious significance that escaped but also enriched secular political categories. Against attempts to force a return to the ghetto in Nazi policies of segregation, the Judaism of the diaspora remains tied to the religious mission of Judaism to bear witness to the transcendent. Levinas makes the powerful claim that 'to forget the religious essence of the diaspora is to betray the meaning itself of Jewish history, to deny a difficult legacy that is admirable for the resources of love and renunciation to which it lays claim' (EP, 145). Levinas describes the Judaism of the diaspora as 'active resignation' and sees in it an essentially religious phenomenon with political implications, the latter exceeding any aspiration to found a state based on the national or religious fraternity of the Jews.

The redefinition of Judaism impressed upon it by anti-Semitism also required the rethinking of the relation between Judaism and Christianity. Levinas had few illusions concerning Christian anti-Judaism, but saw the shared monotheistic heritage of the two religions as the basis for an alliance against revived paganism. He begins the article 'To Fraternise without Conversion' (1936) with the optimistic claim that 'the antagonism between the monotheistic religions has reduced since the Hitlerism menace to their common patrimony' (EP, 148). The attempt by Christianity to benefit from the political assimilation of the Jews by conversion has been put in question by anti-Semitism – indeed, Levinas was even able to say with chilling accuracy what few Christian theologians were prepared to admit, namely that 'racist anti-Semitism has long condemned the ancient dream of the Catholic church: the conversion of Israel' (EP, 149). Thus National Socialism, while forcing a rethinking of Jewish identity in terms of race and announcing the end of the modern project of assimilation, also marked the end of the millenial project of conversion. The murderous rigour of National Socialism based on an implacable racial definition of Jewish identity paradoxically made possible a rethinking of the significance of the diaspora and a renegotiation between Judaism and Christianity.

In the article 'The Spiritual Essence of Anti-Semitism (according to Jacques Maritain)' (1938), Levinas is even more emphatic about what Judaism and Christianity share. Beyond the historical fact that Christianity emerged from Judaism, Levinas discerns a closer link that 'consists in their shared vocation: Israel and the Church being completely in the world, are yet strangers in the world, putting the world that seems to contain them constantly into question' (EP, 150). From this estrangement the two religions share a common metaphysics and morality, an insecurity in the world and an inquietude. The antagonism between them on the issues of the recognition of Christ's divinity and grace have nothing in common with the antagonism of both to pagan anti-Semitism; the members of both religions – as strangers in the world – are equally threatened by its pagan masters.

Perhaps the supreme point of Levinas's hopes for a Jewish–Christian resistance to National Socialism was also the point of maximum despair of such an alliance – the death of Pope Pius XI and the election of the politically ambiguous, if not worse, Pius XII. In an obituary for Pius XI – 'A Propos of the Death of Pope Pius XI' (1939) – Levinas for the last time before the Second World War conceded that National Socialism had allowed Jews to recognise the Church's mission to oppose the paganism of the world. Levinas described how the 'event of racism in Germany and the prestige it acquired internationally appeared to the Jewish consciousness as the apotheosis of everything that is the antipode of Judaism'. He continued with the implacable insight that, 'in spite of all the analyses of the economic, political and social causes of National Socialism in the light of which the racial persecutions are but an accident in the torments of the modern world, the Jews have the obscure sentiment that Hitlerism was a call to their vocation and their destiny' (EP, 152). In the face of this oppression, both Christianity and Judaism can understand their common heritage in the opposition to paganism.

Finally, on the very eve of the war, Levinas places himself as an outsider before the symbols of Christianity and paganism. He passes beside the cross, and does not go towards it. Nevertheless, 'in a world increasingly hostile that fills itself with *swastikas* our eyes often look to the cross with the straight and pure arms' (EP, 152). It is at this point that the horror of National Socialism ceased to be a presentiment and became reality. For with the publication of the obituary and the 1940 vindication of Husserl's concept of freedom and phenomenology against Heidegger, Levinas was forced into silence. In 1945, after years in a German prisoner of war camp, he began the mourning of the horror.

2

THE POST-WAR POLITICAL

The consequences of National Socialism

Upon the outbreak of the Second World War Levinas was mobilised and served as an interpreter with the French 10th Army, before being captured on active service at Rennes. Designated a Jewish prisoner of war (POW), he was sent to a special POW camp separated from other French prisoners but protected from the SS under the terms of the Geneva Conventions.[1] Levinas described his years in the camp as a 'parenthesis' during which he and his fellow prisoners felt 'no longer part of the world' and, confronted with the racism of the guards and local Germans, no longer even part of humanity. 'We were the condemned and contaminated carriers of germs.'[2] In the intervals between forced labour in the forest, Levinas read Hegel, Proust and the authors of the French Enlightenment, but without enjoying any of the sense of the intellectual community described by Ricouer in his memories of the Stalag.[3] The metaphoric 'prison of being' intimated in *De l'évasion* had become reality, and it was under these conditions of detachment from the world haunted by rumours of the death camps that Levinas began to write *Existence and Existents*, completed after his liberation and return to Paris.[4]

The experience of National Socialism provoked a fundamental re-working of the philosophical categories that Levinas had inherited from phenomenology, most urgently those inherited from Heidegger. The experience of the camp put severely in question Heidegger's concept of *Dasein*, which emerged, strangely changed by Levinas, in the *il y a*. It also forced a critical re-examination of the entire philosophical tradition that culminated in Heidegger and had proved itself to be barely immune to complicity with the totalitarian movements. Levinas's inquiry thus departed from a critique of phenomenology and quickly arrived at a critique of the Western philosophical tradition that preceded it. Levinas suspected a connection between the centrality of the question of being in this tradition and its vulnerability to totalitarian politics. However, as the implications of this critique unfolded during the 1950s, it turned away from a rejection of 'Western philosophy' and gradually assumed the shape of a retrieval of those moments in the philosophical tradition that

xceeded the limits of being. These moments came to be articulated in
terms of infinity, the other and the good.

The consequences of National Socialism for Levinas's thought extended
beyond the immediate horrors of the implementation of its racist political
programme. Throughout the late 1940s and early 1950s, Levinas's political
reflections focused upon the long-term political consequences of National
Socialism. The first of these was the re-invention of Jewish identity following
the racially motivated and pitilessly executed mass murder of European
Jews. Central to this reinvention and its most visible manifestation was the
founding of the State of Israel in 1948. Levinas, we shall see, held a complex
position with respect to Zionism and the State of Israel, but was consistent
in linking the foundation of the State with the broader question of Jewish
identity after the Shoah. The second major political consequence of National
Socialism was the fragmentation of the unity of the anti-Nazi Allies and the
formation of a Cold War political made up of competing blocs and characterised by an uneasy stand-off in weapons of mass destruction. There was
for Levinas a clear relationship between the consequences of National
Socialism for Jewish identity and for world politics, a relation that he sought
to define and redefine in his post-war writings.

In attempting to understand and develop a position with respect to
these consequences of National Socialism, Levinas was forced to transform
the philosophical categories that he had inherited. This work was already
in train as a consequence of his intimations and direct experience of
National Socialism, as well as in his working-through of the Heideggerian
legacy, but was intensified and given added urgency by the unfolding of
the consequences of the Shoah and the Second World War. The question of
Jewish identity could no longer be framed within received notions of identity, but required that identity itself be fundamentally rethought, while the
Cold War required a reconsideration of received notions of war, violence,
history and politics. The confrontation of the philosophical tradition with
the consequences of National Socialism issued in the transformation of
philosophical and political thought systematically worked through in
Totality and Infinity and *Otherwise than Being*.

The haunted peace

As a work of the parenthesis that was Levinas's direct experience of
National Socialism, *Existence and Existents* (1947) is suspended between
presentiment and mourning. A forced guest of the government once enthusi-
astically welcomed and supported by Heidegger, Levinas extended the
struggle with the ghost of his old teacher to the phantasms of German
Idealism and 'Western philosophy'. The distance Levinas had already taken
from Heidegger during the 1930s was sharpened by the bitter experience of
German hospitality that had 'none of the generosity which the German term

es gibt is said to contain' (DF, 292). Levinas described his escape from the *es gibt* that comprised the Stalag, Heidegger, German Idealism and 'Western philosophy' in terms of a diversion of the ontological difference between Being and beings in the direction of 'the horrific neutrality of the *there is*' and the existents that survive it. The latter 'are on the path which leads from existence to the existent and from the existent to the other, a path that delineates time itself' (DF, 292). The path leading out of the Stalag marked the recovery of time from the parenthesis in which it had been stalled, allowing history to recommence. But this new beginning, a post-war history, proved to be haunted by the memory of a political horror that exceeded the capacity of successful mourning.

The scale of the work of mourning provoked by National Socialism was immense, more demanding even than Levinas's worst presentiment. The scale of murder and suffering for which the German government was responsible put in question the very structures of meaning and value that informed German and European culture. Prime among these was the tradition of philosophy, now under suspicion and perhaps itself finally dead and an object of mourning. Levinas later asked repeatedly how it was possible for a culture steeped in idealist philosophy such as Germany to tolerate and even to welcome National Socialism; how could it be that the last Kantian in Nazi Germany was a dog?[5] Even more ominously, the question of anti-Semitic violence was addressed not only to Germany, but to Europe and to Christendom as a whole. With individual exceptions, the cross bowed to the swastika, leading Levinas to abandon his pre-war ecumenical position and to ask how 'Hitler's exterminations...were able to take place in a Europe that had been evangelised for fifteen centuries'.[6] His response differed in important respects to those offered to the same questions by Lukács in *The Destruction of Reason*, who answered in terms of the irrationalism he saw as endemic to German thought and culture, and Adorno and Horkheimer in *Dialectic of Enlightenment*, who answered in terms of the bureaucratic abstract rationality of the modern state and culture. Levinas sought responsibility in the concern with being that characterised Heidegger's thought, German Idealism and the tradition of 'Western philosophy' from which they emerged.

What may initially appear as Levinas's own questionable fidelity to Heidegger's phantasmal object 'Western philosophy' in fact constitutes an important link between German Idealism and the Christian tradition of philosophy that adopted Greek thought and its ontological prejudices while excluding important aspects of its biblical and rabbinic heritage. The obsession with the question of existence – whether that of God, the world or the soul – occluded those considerations of prophesy, justice and goodness that Christian philosophy might have drawn from biblical, rabbinic and other philosophical sources. It is through the recovery of the ethical concerns of these texts and the exploration of their political implications that Levinas staged the work of mourning for philosophy and for the ontological concept of the political (the focus on the Republic or public *thing*) to which it lent meaning and legitimacy.

The path out of the Stalag that led from existence to the existent and then to the other describes the trajectory of Levinas's two major works of the Second World War and the immediate post-war period, *Existence and Existents* (1947) and the lectures *Time and the Other* (1947). With them Levinas achieved a preliminary working-through of his presentiments and experience of horror, establishing the conditions for future work. While he regarded *Existence and Existents* as the continuation of his pre-war work – 'a reprise under another guise of *De l'évasion*' – it was one intensified by the experience of the *Dasein* of internment 'unbearable in its indifference. Not anxiety but horror, the horror of an endlessness, of a monotony deprived of meaning'.[7] The precise path followed by Levinas winds through a series of Bergsonian 'modalities', or recoils from the horrific anonymity of being. The result is a series of modal transitions plotted with almost Hegelian precision, all of which add up to a derivation of time and freedom from the analysis of physical exertion pioneered by Bergson's *Time and Free Will*. Throughout, Levinas's path is guided by the diversion of Heidegger's ontological difference, and, increasingly, of the ontological investments of the tradition of 'Western philosophy'.

The diversion of ontology in *Existence and Existents* that was forced by the encounter with National Socialism marks the beginning of Levinas's inability to forget the 'experience' of the non-assimilability of political horror. The horror of *il y a* is intricately bound to haunting, to the dead who cannot be forgotten – *il y a* is the continual 'presence' of the murdered awaiting justice. The pressure of this responsibility lends urgency and rigour to the refusal of any ontology that would privilege the projects and the acts of the living. From this emphasis on the trauma of a haunted being, Levinas begins a work of mourning that weaves together a political mourning of the dead – the difficult freedom of Jewish identity in the Diaspora and the State of Israel – with a mourning of the tradition of philosophy and its discredited concepts. The outcome is not a rejection of ontology, but, as Levinas explained in his preface, the development of the theme of the *ex-cendance* of being proposed in *De l'évasion* but now linked unequivocally with the good. Levinas extends his ironic diversion of the Heideggerian discourse of forest-paths[8] to a mountaineering metaphor, giving excendance and the good 'a foothold in being' and justifying ontology in so far as the *ex-cendance* of the good justifies 'why Being is better than non-being' (EE, 15).

The matrix of this work was the fragment *il y a* written in prison, published in 1946 and, ostensibly 'incorporated' in Chapter Five of *Existents and Existents*. In reality the fragment was and remains inassimilable, and served to generate the layers of text that enclose it and the escape attempt ventured in the lectures *Time and the Other*, as well as the commentaries that now enclose them. Levinas described the fragment *il y a* as a departure from the Heideggerian climate of thought, and its force governs the extended diversion of the ontological difference that takes place in the text. The change of climate involves the deeper scrutiny of the political and ethical concerns of the 1930s. The problem of the relationship between freedom and community is engaged at almost all levels in this extremely complex and stratified text. Looking both backwards and forwards, *Existence and Existents* criticises Heidegger's *Dasein* and *Mitsein*, but also Bergson's view of freedom as creativity. Out of a bitter critique of such fatal communities of destiny as Nazism and the doubt whether communities can be established on the unqualified freedom of the individual emerges the 'other' – promising an ethico–political community founded neither in fatality nor in freedom, but in a qualified or difficult freedom.

The fragment *il y a* written in the prison camp and published in *Deucalion* in 1946 is a text of the most extraordinary density. It weaves together themes and preoccupations of the 1930s such as the confrontation between Heidegger and Bergson and the reflection on Durkheim and the Durkheimian school, but with a new sensitivity to Hegel, the insistent presence of Shakespeare and a sensitivity to the sombre themes of murder, horror, insomnia and the night. The saturated effect of the layering and interweaving of these texts and themes in a few pages is justly described in terms of a change of climate. Some idea of its significance can be gained from analytically separating the themes, but the effect of this text and its reverberations through the writings of the 1950s rests on its obscure, irreducible density.

The first line of thought that may be traced through the text is an absolute resistance to Hegel and Hegelian dialectic. Studying Hegel in a German POW camp clarified Levinas's opposition to an entire style of philosophy and what might be regarded as its political consequences. Nevertheless, Levinas took from Hegel the discipline of argumentative transition, but only to subvert Hegelian speculation.[9] Although Hegel is not named, the entire fragment is directed against the premises of speculative dialectic: negation, movement through contradiction, the speculative result. Yet this is not an impossible surpassing of Hegel, for Levinas's anti-Hegelian operation is less the overcoming of Hegelian dialectic than its deflation.

The deflationary operation is evident from the opening of the fragment that imagines a reversion to nothingness. A similar scenario can be found at the beginning of Hegel's *Science of Logic*, but with Hegel the reversion situates itself in a broader movement or history that identifies 'nothing' as a reflective determination of being. Levinas agrees with Hegel that the act of reversion to nothingness is an event, but not one that opens a history in the fashion of Hegelian speculation, but rather one that deflates it. The reversion to nothingness with which the fragment opens shunts any possible beginning into a parenthesis, thus blocking any subsequent speculative movement.

Following the suspension of the speculative beginning, Levinas goes on to deflate Hegel's scenario of subject and substance. The *Phenomenology of Spirit* and arguably the *Science of Logic* are structured around the mutual recognition and misrecognition of subject and substance in which being and nothing form determinate moments. Yet in the fragment *il y a* the event of nothingness – none other than the 'there is' – is detached from the movement of subject and substance: it 'is not the indeterminateness of a subject and does not refer to a substantive' (LR, 30). The 'there is' is insulated from the mutual charge of subject and substance: it is 'impersonal, anonymous' and so not subject, and it is 'depth' and so not substance (for Levinas what 'lies under' – *sub stans* – is but more depth; we can never arrive at the bottom or 'substance'). Levinas hastens to add to the speculative pairing of subject and substance the, in Hegelian terms, abstract determination of subject and object: the 'there is' deflates both oppositions and cannot offer 'the starting point for a meditation which broaches being in general' (LR, 30).[10]

Levinas's subsequent 'development' of the event of nothingness consists in deflating the opening move of Hegel's *Phenomenology of Spirit*, which departs from the indication of 'this' and 'that' towards a universal or abstract notion of something. Levinas cannot accept this opening transition, without which Hegel's spirit would remain stalled in immediacy, bluntly asserting his opposition: 'There is no longer *this* or *that*; there is not "something"' (LR, 30). The attempt to gain some dialectical momentum from the event of nothingness remains stalled: 'there is' 'is not the dialectical counterpart of absence and we do not grasp it through thought' (LR, 30). Not only can 'there is' yield no dialectical movement, but the non-movement cannot be thought, thus refusing another central tenet of Hegelianism, namely that the absolute can be thought.

The event of nothingness squanders the 'power of the negative' that is the driving force of Hegelian philosophy. Levinas is careful not to endorse the negation of negation, for this would lead to a dialectical 'result' that confirms Hegelianism; rather, he diverts negation into an iterative circuit of the eternal return of botched negations. The event of nothingness returns 'in the midst of the negation that put it aside, and in the powers to which that negation may be multiplied' (LR, 31). While Hegel would deploy negation in order to move beyond being and nothingness, producing a result ('becoming'), Levinas sees it as a field of forces that neutralises itself; in this circuit of negation, each negation is negated by a more powerful one which ensures stasis. After reading Hegel, Levinas could understand the significance of his own *De l'évasion* – for the deflation of Hegelian speculative dialectic is but the recognition that the negation of the negation does not produce a result – there is no escape from the event of nothingness, there is no exit from 'there is'.

These opening anti-Hegelian moves are complemented by the synthetic closing argument of the fragment. For Levinas, Hegel's attempt to think nothingness as the logical contradiction of being assumes that the event of nothingness produces a result: 'one starts with being, which is content limited by nothingness' in order to move to a new, enriched content. Yet the vindication of history towards which Hegel's dialectic swiftly moves is arrested by Levinas's insistence upon the neutrality of 'there is' – nothing is not 'the limit or negation of being' as it is in Hegel, but an 'interval or interruption' (LR, 35). The deflation of Hegel will prove one of the most important consequences of Levinas's fragment and the body of thought that it generated, for putting into question the metaphysical bases of Hegelianism is to question one of the most powerful and pervasive philosophical and political discourses produced in the modern West. But simply to make abstract gestures against Hegel would, as Derrida insisted in 'Violence and Metaphysics', confirm Hegelianism; yet Levinas does more than this.

While the refusal of dialectical negation is a powerful objection to Hegelianism, even more devastating is the claim that the event of nothingness cannot be thought. Levinas is not content to assert this denial, but develops it through a catena of poetic metaphors that Hegel would regard as pre-philosophical 'picture thinking' linked with the phenomenological analysis of mood derived from Scheler and Heidegger. These analyses contribute another layer to an already stratified and complex text. For the first, Levinas seems to figure being and nothing in terms of such classical metaphors of speech and silence, light and darkness, void and plenitude, continuity and rupture. Yet this is done, not in order to retail a classical structure of metaphor with its origins in Greek philosophy, but in order to disfigure such structures through the event of nothingness. The 'event of nothingness' does not speak, but nor is it silent – it murmurs. It is not light or darkness, but shadow; not void nor plenitude but full of nothing; neither continuous nor interrupted but not-uninterrupted. The ambiguous character of the 'there is' disfigures not only the metaphorical structure but the philosophy itself that has depended on these metaphors as the supplement to its conceptuality.[11] Levinas does not only recognise the dependence of philosophy on rhetoric, but exploits this dependence through disfiguring first metaphor and then the conceptuality that is parasitic upon it. The disfigured metaphors are rhetorical weeds that litter the 'thought' of 'there is' and prepare through their 'ambiguity' for the arrival of an analysis of its moods.

Levinas's analysis of the mood of insomnia has become a *locus classicus* of modern thought, comparing the 'there is' with 'the monotonous presence that bears down on us in insomnia' (LR, 32). However, the full elaboration of this analogy and the introduction of the important theme of vigilance is deferred to the later text *Time and the Other*.[12] In the fragment, insomnia is mentioned in passing and is not the most important mood for the analysis of 'there is'. The important moods whose analysis gives access to the event of nothingness are menace, insecurity and, above all, horror. The exposition moves from the ambiguity of the event of nothingness to 'the menace of the pure and simple presence of *there is*', and through it to the deprivation of security and shelter, finally to arrive at the key mood of the fragment, horror.

Horror is the focal mood of the fragment, described in terms of murder and the normality that seems to succeed it: 'horror is the event of being that returns in the heart of this negation [murder] as though nothing had happened' (LR, 33). Levinas summons *Macbeth* to figure horror: the negation of murder does not lead to a result, as if through a dialectical logic of sacrifice, nor does it simply drop out of history, forgotten, but continues to trouble the survivors and condenses being 'to the point of suffocation' and 'drawing consciousness out of its retreat'.[13] Horror emerges from the impossibility of mourning or forgetting the murdered; that is, working successfully to incorporate them in a history or allowing them to become irrelevant to it. The horror of the event of nothingness is figured in terms of the murdered who cannot depart and therefore are forced to return; in short: 'the haunting spectre, the phantom, constitutes the very element of horror' (LR, 33). The fragment is governed by the horror of surviving and being haunted by the return of the spectres of the murdered – or, the same put otherwise, of being unable to mourn or forget them. Horror is the mood that attends an ineluctable but impossible mourning – the inability either to forget or to work through the event of nothingness that is murder; an impossibility of alleviation that is 'the condemnation to perpetual reality, to existence with "no exits"' (LR, 34), the condition of *there is* where it is impossible to allay the ghosts.

In the wake of the discussion of horror, the earlier anti-Hegelian allusions are given retrospective weight: speculative thought is the thought of successful mourning, or finding a historical justification for the murdered and the sacrificed. Speculative thought would find historical meaning for the dead of the Second World War, making their negation our result: Levinas however resists this logic.[14] It is surely no coincidence that the analysis of horror in terms of impossible but ineluctable mourning is followed by a critique of Heidegger, the thinker whose National Socialism Levinas could neither forgive nor forget and whom he repeatedly discussed in terms of horror.

Levinas here questions Heidegger's focus on the mood of anxiety in his analytic of *Dasein*, and links this to the tension between Heidegger and Bergson that had preoccupied him during the 1930s. The horror of the survivor differs radically from Heidegger's mood of anxiety for one's own death: 'there is horror of being and not anxiety over nothingness, fear of being and not fear for being' (LR, 34). The horror of the vigil, of having to be after, to survive or live on, after the murders exceeds for Levinas the anxiety for being in the face of nothingness. In the case of the former, the event of nothingness – *there is* – has already happened and been survived. The mood of anxiety gives way to mastery, to authenticity or a being that 'is grasped and somehow understood' even in its nothingness; the mood of horror, however, seems infinite – a 'perpetuity of the drama of existence, necessity of forever taking on [the] burden' (LR, 34).

The impatient dismissal of Heideggerian anxiety contrasts with the sympathetic reading of Bergson that immediately follows it. The latter's argument against the concept of nothingness in *Creative Evolution* is explicitly owned by Levinas as an 'inspiration' for *there is*; he notes that, when Bergson 'shows that the concept of nothingness is equivalent to the idea of being crossed out, he seems to catch sight of a situation analogous to that which led us to the notion of the *there is*' (LR, 34). Yet Levinas quickly parts company with Bergson on the status of the event of nothingness. In an inverse recapitulation of the Cartesian *cogito*, Bergson argued that to universalise nothingness – to negate all of being – nevertheless leaves a 'residual entity', namely the consciousness that performs the nihilation: 'it would at least remain as an operation, as a consciousness of that darkness' (LR, 34). For Bergson this proves the impossibility of complete negation and renders 'the concept of nothingness illusory' (LR, 35). Levinas resists the conclusion while accepting the premise: the 'obliteration' of being – to introduce a term that will have a future in Levinas's aesthetics – does not leave a residual consciousness but only the repeated event of annihilation. The nihilation of nihilation does not leave a residue or produce a result but offers only the occasion for more acts of nihilation. The event of nothingness – *there is* – assumes a density which is not that of a dense object whether residue or result, but the pressure of a climate or the charge of a force-field.

As the fragment moves towards its close with the gravity of *there is* outweighing Heideggerian anxiety, another dimension of analysis opens up in retrospect. This involves the earlier discussion of Durkheim and Levy-Bruhl's sociologies of the sacred. What emerges retrospectively is the realisation that, throughout the essay, Levinas is describing a fallen world – a pagan world located not before but *after* Revelation. A link emerges between the anthropology of pagan religion and the deliberate reversion to paganism of National Socialism discussed in 'The Philosophy of Hitlerism'. Levinas establishes a contrast between Durkheim and Levy-Bruhl around the concept of the sacred. For Durkheim, the sacred invests the collective representations of a given society, undergoing a process of transposition moving from 'the "still" impersonal God from which will one day issue the God of advanced religions' (LR, 33). For Levy-Bruhl, the sacred and profane are collapsed in the concept of participation – there is no process of separation that distinguishes the two realms but only their ineluctable mingling. The sacred haunts the profane and provokes a mood of horror in the neutralisation of subject and substance, precluding any

Durkheimian emergence of personality: 'the existence of one submerges the other, and is thus no longer the existence of the one' (LR, 32). In this description of pagan religion, observes Levinas, 'we recognise the *there is*' (LR, 32).

While Durkheim's separation of the sacred and profane opens the possibility of personality and transcendence, Levy-Bruhl's collapse of the two terms into each other 'describes a world where nothing prepares for the apparition of a God' (LR, 33). The horrific condition in which Levinas recognises the *there is* 'leads us to the absence of God, the absence of any being' (LR, 33). Levinas immediately describes this condition in terms of the anthropological past – 'Primitive men live before all Revelation, before the light comes' (LR, 33), but it is clear from all that has gone before that it also applies to those who live after Revelation, after the light was extinguished. The post-war world that Levinas evoked in the fragment and the texts it generated was one that came after a return to paganism. The philosophy and politics of Hitlerism had recreated the condition of pagan anonymous being and had marked the epoch as one of enormous crime. Levinas's fragment from the camp – written in one of the 'bubbles of the earth' that he cites from Shakespeare – is thus a preliminary assessment of the legacy of the National Socialist descent to paganism.

The complexity of the fragment emerges from the weaving together of these various themes, all of which add up to a weighty indictment of political horror. The fragment in its evocation of a fallen world provokes the search for exits. In the two texts that emerged around it – *Existence and Existents* and *Time and the Other* – Levinas explored two diverse routes out of the Nazi epoch that were questionably compatible. The bleak rigour of *Existence and Existents* deepens the analysis of the fragment in pursuit of an 'ex-cendence' from within ontology, while *Time and the Other*, while repeating much of the descent, also intimates an otherwise than being in ethical alterity. The two texts anticipate Levinas's two major texts, *Totality and Infinity* and *Otherwise than Being*, and with them the reflection on the political possibilities of the horror of the *there is* of the post-war world.[15]

In *Existence and Existents* Levinas elaborates upon the themes adumbrated in the fragment. The diversion of Heideggerian ontological difference, and thus the change of intellectual climate, is immediately engaged in the opening chapter, 'The Existent and the Relationship with Existence'. In a manner reminiscent of his work of the early 1930s, Levinas distances himself from Heidegger by citing Bergson's scepticism about 'nothingness' and the insignificance of death. However, the premise of Levinas's reduction of the significance of nothingness and death is not the affirmation of an *élan vital*, but rather the description of the anonymity of being that characterises *il y a*. This is part of a broader turn from a Heideggerian concern with *Dasein's* stance towards being to the modes or hypostases through which being is endured. The enduring of existence precludes any active stance towards it, or any struggle for the continuation of being: the subject is haunted by existence and does not have the luxury of assuming an active stance with respect to it.

In the second chapter, 'The Relationship with Existence and the Instant', Levinas explores one particular attempt at a stance towards being that is neither Heideggerian nor Hegelian-Marxist. The active stance towards being informing the project of labour that characterises the entire Hegelian–Marxist tradition is reversed by Levinas and viewed in terms of the mode of endurance described as fatigue. The experience of forced labour severely qualified the Hegelian–Marxist tradition's view of the relationship between freedom and labour central to the thought of French Hegelians such as Kojève and Hypolite, and ominously by the SS in their motto 'Arbeit macht Frei' placed above the entrance to the concentration camps. It is also, we shall see, an equation central to the ideology of the Zionist founders of the State of Israel, who contrived a cult of freedom through labour. Levinas implicitly questions the role played by labour in the Marxist interpretation of the conflict between master and slave in Hegel's *Phenomenology of Spirit*. In this reading, the labour of the slave is the promise of the future – relating to nature through labour, the slave achieves recognition through the creation of a world; becoming a proletarian, the slave also becomes capable of freedom, despite having lost the struggle to the death with the master. The master, meanwhile, in refusing recognition and not labouring, can only consume and so loses the capacity for freedom. The future will be the reprise of the battle of master and slave to the death, but now as the struggle for the proletariat to complete its creation of a world by the full attainment of freedom.

Although not in an SS-administered camp – Levinas was imprisoned by the *Wehrmacht* – the conditions of forced labour, while not murderous, were sufficient to make Levinas reject the historically deferred equation of work and freedom assumed in the Marxist interpretation of Hegel. Through an analysis of fatigue ostensibly indebted to Bergson but put to very different use, he questions the world-creating outcome of work. Forced labour does not create a world, but only a fatigue that ruins what world there is. Levinas discovers in fatigue – the numbness that succeeds hard labour – a 'lag that occurs between a being and itself'.[16] It gives rise to no result, neither world nor nothingness – but a lag or interval – fatigue grants an understanding of being as parenthesis. Numbness does not have potential, it does not mark an active stance towards being, for it is but a gap or lag that follows an event.

Levinas assumes a series of masks in order to analyse fatigue and work. He first evokes a Heideggerian analysis that would situate effort 'within the system of our occupations of the day' (EE, 30). In this way, effort and *day   vs   night -*

Baudelaire

fatigue can be put to work within an horizon of freely elected ends: 'If there is constraint and servitude in effort, it would seem that constraint can only be external to it; it would lie in the extent that the goal to be reached would be incumbent on our will' (EE, 30). The constraint of work becomes a voluntary renunciation of freedom for the purpose of realising an end, and so to creating a world. Here work is a freely adopted stance that is lent meaning by the horizon of freedom that makes up the world. Levinas, however, takes a step further, and argues that there is no horizon of freedom, but only endurance: 'the instant of effort contains something more; it reveals a subjection which compromises our freedom in another sense' (EE, 31). The commitment revealed by work is not that of a freely adopted stance directed to future goals, but the endurance of an impossible heritage. For Levinas, work is not directed towards a future goal but is directed by a past involvement: he writes 'human labour and effort presuppose a commitment in which they are already involved', concluding from this that it is not a task or project, but a predicament – 'We are yoked to our task, delivered to it' (EE, 31). With this anticipation of the later theme of the 'immemorial past' Levinas inverts the direction of labour, making it less a task than a predicament and thus breaking the connection between work and freedom.

Levinas amplifies the point that work is not necessarily oriented towards a future freedom by a critique of Bergson's *élan vital*. Effort or the creative 'advance over oneself' is always qualified by fatigue or 'the delay with respect to oneself and with respect to the present' (EE, 31). Far from projecting into the future, work does not even arrive at the present – as fatigue it remains extricated in a past whose arrival in the present is always delayed. Levinas's analyses of the temporality of work in terms of fatigue departs radically from the classical analyses of Hegel, Heidegger and Bergson that understand effort as creative or future oriented. By situating work in a parenthesis, lag or delay, Levinas does not only substitute prostration for the upright stance of the worker before being, but also severs the connection between work and freedom. This fundamentally questions the equation of work and freedom central to modernity in its liberal, fascist and socialist variants: all assume work to be directed towards the future and that this future is destined to realise the promise of freedom. As mentioned above, it also fundamentally questions the centrality of work to the ideology of the Zionist movement as it developed in Palestine and later the State of Israel. As will be seen, the valorisation of labour and sacrifice formed what Zeev Sternhell has described as one of, if not the most important 'founding myths of Israel'.[17]

The assumption informing the equation of work, freedom and futurity is the dualism of free action and the resistance of matter. The effort of spirit dedicated to realising freedom by overcoming the resistance of matter assumes the presence of matter, registered in its resistance, and of spirit, registered in its free action. The presence of spirit is, of course, immediately qualified by the futural orientation of the action – were it really present to itself there would be no need for action directed to a future end – but this deficit of, or excess over, presence has always been factored out of the notion of freedom. Freedom is the term used to describe the deficit or excess over the present, but the state of incomplete presence may be more profoundly rooted than is evident in the concept of freedom. Levinas thus calls for a closer analysis of the opposition of free action and matter:

> the conception of action which is being presupposed in this image of a struggle with matter is a notion which philosophers have taken as purely and simply given. It is not deduced, that is, its place in the economy of being is not marked out philosophically. (EE, 32)

Levinas carries forwards the topological 'marking out' of the place of the opposition of matter and spirit in the 'economy of being' by means of an analysis of the *durée* of effort. Explicitly following Bergson, he contrasts the *durée* of effort with the *durée* of play or of a melody. The latter is 'essentially a continuity', while the former is a series of interruptions: 'during the duration of the work, the effort takes on the instant, breaking and tying back together again the thread of time. It struggles behind the instant it is going to take on; it is then not, as in the case of a melody, already freed from the present it is living through...' (EE, 33). The experience of delay – fatigue – marks the place of effort in the 'economy of being'. It is effort that interrupts the neutral and anonymous *il y a* by configuring it in terms of discrete moments, but moments with a peculiar character – 'In the midst of the anonymous flow of existence, there is stoppage and a positing. Effort is the very effecting of an instant' (EE, 34). The step of identifying effort with the interruption of being leads to the preliminary conclusion that the moment of the present in which free action and matter are supposed to conduct their struggle is itself not present: 'the present is the apparition, in the anonymous rumbling of existence, which is at grips with this existence, in relationship with it, takes it up' (EE, 34). It is important to note that the present is an 'apparition' or a haunting and then that the ghost that appears is no less than 'the first manifestation, or the very constitution, of an existent, a *someone* that is' (EE, 34). We shall see that the subject for Levinas at this stage is in the peculiar position of being a ghost that is itself haunted, as perhaps all apparitions must indeed be.

The present as an apparition in anonymous existence ruins any dialectical project that would promise any future outcome to a present struggle. In the phantom present the terms of a potential dialectical contradiction co-exist in an arrested paradox. The paradox is evident in the accumulating juxtaposition of freedom and necessity characteristic of 'free labour' – 'a spontaneous effort, an irrevocable, irredeemable commitment' (EE, 34) – juxtaposing spontaneity with effort, commitment with irrevocability (inability to go back) and irredeemability (inability to go forwards). Neither the master nor the slave will exit enriched by the experience of this dialectic: 'It is then not in the relationship a man who labours has with the matter he fashions according to his will, nor with the master who forces him to work, that the sense of effort and the stamp of a freedom or a subjection it may manifest is to be sought' (EE, 34–5). The entire scenario of the Hegelian dialectic and the experience of modernity that it figures is put in question by Levinas; work is not a source of meaning or freedom, whether in the present or in the future. Meaning, indeed, does not consist in establishing a relation, whether with an object or with an other, but in surviving the lack of relation.

Clearly this 'almost self-contradictory moment of a present that tarries behind itself' is not the site of a productive dialectic, but one which undoes itself, not giving a result but remaining stalled, evoking at best the 'peculiar form of forsakenness' or perpetual mourning that consists in the sense of being always in its past. The fatigued inhabitant of this phantom present remains confined to perpetual parenthesis – it is 'a being that is as it were no longer in step with itself, is out of joint with itself, in a dislocation of the I from itself, a being that is not joining up with itself in the instant, in which nonetheless it is committed for good' (EE, 35). The allusion to Hamlet's declaration that – 'time is out of joint' – is but one of the constant allusions to Shakespeare in Levinas's work of this period.[18] The condition of Hamlet deferring action in the haunted present of the court of Denmark is an apt likeness for the stalled dialectic that Levinas is describing at this point. Yet *Hamlet* also shows that the parenthesis is unstable, and may tip towards catastrophe – in Hegelian terms an outcome, but certainly not a result that enriches the protagonists, or one that they can even hope to survive.

Levinas nevertheless concedes that the *durée* constitutive of work can act as a hypostasis of anonymous existence.[19] The apparition of the subject is 'nonetheless an inscription in existence', one whose very hesitation or delay allows the event of hypostasis to take place:

> the time lag of fatigue creates the interval in which the event of the present can occur, and if this event is equivalent to the upsurge of an *existent* for which *to be* means *to take up being*, the existence of an existent is by essence an activity. (EE, 35)

With this passage Levinas clarifies much of the action of the second chapter, but also describes a limit to his concept of being. His critique of Hegel and of Heidegger focused upon their fixing the generation of meaning in terms of relation – whether the relation to nothingness, to death, or to the object or to the master. Levinas, on the contrary, joins Bergson in locating meaning within modality – the hypostasis or act of 'taking up being'. The scenario of meaning, however, remains suspiciously confined to the Kantian table of categories, moving from those of relation to those of modality. And while Levinas on several occasions transcends this framework, the recourse to a Bergsonian, modal definition of meaning – fortified in the 1950s by Delhomme's elaboration of this moment – is always in the wings.[20] The limitations become most evident in the formulaic distinction between the modal 'saying' and the qualitative 'said' that organises the contents of *Otherwise than Being* and can be said to compromise the radical philosophical and political implications of that work.

Meanwhile, in *Existence and Existents*, Levinas moves to make hypostasis or the modal understanding of existent the 'fundamental situation' of the existent. The 'fundamental situation' is beyond any dialectical relation characterised by negation. It is 'the activity of inactivity', but not understood as a paradox or contradiction in which activity negates inactivity, but as the modal 'movement in rest' – 'it is rest inasmuch as rest is not a pure negation but the very tension of a position, the bringing about of a *here*' (EE, 36). The occupation of a 'here' – the taking up of a situation – is never static, but always part of an economy of forces. The hypostasis or the modal 'taking up realised in labour' is both situated in a 'world' – in Levinas's words it 'takes on a new destiny in the world' – and transcends it; which provokes the question of the 'relation' between fundamental situation and world. This is addressed with great care in the pivotal Chapter Three of *Existence and Existents* entitled simply 'The World'.

Levinas opens his discussion of the world with a syncopated critique of Heidegger and Husserl. In pursuit of a source of excess that will ensure *ex-cendence* Levinas proposes, against Heidegger, that the fundamental 'relation' to the world is not care, but desire. Aligning desire with the modal operation of intentionality – but not in 'the neutralised and disincarnate sense in which it figures in medieval philosophy and in Husserl' (EE, 37) – Levinas goes in search of a source of *ex-cendence* that is nevertheless in the world. He refuses to be restricted by Heidegger's intensification of Husserlian intentionality, one that puts the object 'at our disposal', seeing this as remaining within an understanding of 'the world as what is given to us' (EE, 37). Instead of regarding the world in terms of its givenness to a theoretical or practical intentionality, Levinas approaches it in terms of a desire that is in excess of its object. By severing the traditional link between desire and lack, Levinas is able to complicate its temporality and abandon the traditional desiring scenario of lack–effort/possession–satisfaction. This scenario was central to understanding the relationship to the world in terms of work, where desire is understood in terms of the expenditure of effort in the pursuit of satisfaction under conditions of lack.

By regarding desire as excessive, Levinas is able to escape the dialectical lack–effort/possession–satisfaction scenario along with the understanding of economy and the political that it brings with it – namely war for the possession of scarce resources. By looking at the relationship to the world in terms of desire as excess he can claim not only that the desirable is 'prior to the desire' but that it is also distanced from it in 'a time that is ahead of me' (EE, 39). The exercise of desire consists in the expression of excess: as the object of excess cannot be known before its expression – for then it would not be excessive – the economy of desire has to be understood in terms of the movement excess–expression–creation. The expression of a prior excessive desire and its subsequent confirmation in creation makes sense of the 'position of the desirable, before and after the desire' (EE, 39). It also confirms the new sense that Levinas attributes to the 'givenness' of the world. The world is given in an excessive intentionality that is not directed towards a given object, but that exceeds all given objects; the expression of this excessive intentionality changes its objects and confirms itself in the creation of a new world.

In his later writings Levinas will illustrate this excessive intentionality by the Cartesian notion of the infinite and by the ethical relation to the other. In his discussion of the world in *Existence and Existents* he focuses upon the latter. The main site of *ex-cendence* – the excess over and subsequent re-creation of the world – is located in the 'relation' to the other. What is crucial in this 'relation' is the movement between the excessive break with the world prompted by the other and the re-creation of the world following the expression of excess. Levinas describes this movement in terms of the event of a break with the world and the inclusion of such events in the world by means of civilisation: 'the events that break with the world, such as the encounter with the other, can be in it and included in it by the process of civilisation, by which everything and everyone is given to us with no equivocation' (EE, 39). Excess breaks with the givenness of the world but in its expression creates a new givenness that in turn may be exceeded. The other, who in the world is 'not treated like a thing, but is never separated from things' (EE, 39), exemplifies this movement. The encounter with the other is always excessive, and so cannot be treated as an encounter with an object – but it can be expressed as if the other were given among other objects.

The ambiguous position of the other in and outside of the world allows Levinas to propose a number of distinctions regarding the relation to the other. The other as given in the world has a 'social situation' comprising their rights, prerogatives and the institutions through which they are given to us. Although 'in the world the other is an object already through his clothing' (EE, 40), this object character has been created out of an excessive relation to the other. At this point Levinas takes a fatal step whose implications will unfold in his subsequent work. Instead of inquiring into the 'processes of civilisation' through which the excessive relation is recreated in terms of the givenness of objects, he instead focuses on the contrast between the given world of others and the excessive relation to the other in nudity. He claims that:

> the relationship with nudity is the true experience of the otherness of the other – were the term experience not impossible where it is the question of a relationship that goes beyond the world. Social life in the world does not have that disturbing character that a being feels before another being, before alterity. (EE, 40)

Yet this contrast of intimacy and public life must itself be explored and fully described; if not, there is a danger of confining excess to an allegedly authentic intimacy and consigning public life to the administration of thing-like others. Such a parcelling-out of the movement of excess and its expression threatens to obscure both the role of the political in intimacy, and of excess in politics.

In *Existence and Existents*, Levinas continues to transform the ambiguity of the other – within and beyond the world – into a contrast between social life and intimacy. In the former the relationship to the other is accomplished through given institutions whose 'givenness' Levinas indicates by the shorthand term 'the third'. In the world the relationship with the other is accomplished 'through participation in something in common', or between that which is given to all. In social and political life 'persons are not simply in front of one another, they are along with each other around something' (EE, 41). The problem is that Levinas insists that even in this case the excessive face-to-face relation to the other is preserved – but the way in which it is preserved is not fully explained. It would seem that the original face-to-face relation is preserved in pockets of 'decency' or ethical supplements to the political. What is more, Levinas himself then insists that relating through a third thing makes the other into a thing; more accurately into 'a phantasm' (EE, 41).

The other is always excess, but it seems as if this excess can only be considered in terms of the authenticity of intimacy, in which the other exceeds desire, and the inauthenticity of the phantasm in which the other is simply elsewhere. In both cases, excess is figured in the non-presence of the other, but in the one this is a token of authentic desire, in the other of a social I 'that is incapable of laying itself bare' (EE, 41). In neither case – clothed or naked – can the other lay itself bare, since then it would lose its excessive character and become an object. Such a transformation of a productive ambiguity into an opposition of the authentic and inauthentic contains the potential for dogmatism or worse.

At this point Levinas returns to Husserl and Heidegger, praising the phenomenological reduction of the former for separating the reflection upon the world from being in the world, and the latter for separating 'the notion of the world from the notion of a sum of objects' (EE, 42). Heidegger is immediately criticised for an 'ontological finality' that includes objects 'in the care for existing, which for him is the very putting of the ontological problem' (EE, 42). Levinas regards this 'ontological finality' as transforming 'everything given in the world' into a tool and accuses it of failing to recognise 'the essentially secular nature of being in the world and the sincerity of intentions' (EE, 42). The excessive notion of desire developed earlier is now used to undermine Heidegger's 'ontological finality' – in the expression of desire 'the bond with care is relaxed' and action is motivated by excess rather than need. Levinas discerns a concept of need in ontological finality itself, referred to now as a shadow cast over the expression of desire:

> It is in times of misery and privation that the shadow of an ulterior finality which darkens the world is cast behind the object of desire. When one has to eat, drink and warm oneself in order not to die, when nourishment becomes fuel, as in certain kinds of hard labour, the world also seems to be at an end, turned upside down...Time becomes unhinged. (EE, 45)

The 'secular nature of being in the world' and its sincerity of intentions comprise the moments of enjoyment freed 'from the instinct to exist' and in which we 'go sincerely to the desirable and take it for what it is' (EE, 44). Such moments, which for Heidegger would be inauthentic evasions, are for Levinas hypostases marking 'the possibility of extricating oneself from anonymous being' (EE, 45). He singles out Marxism as the leading example of a philosophy situated within the 'sincerity of intentions' – 'the good will of hunger and thirst, and the ideal of struggle and sacrifices it proposes, the culture to which it invites us, is but the prolongation of these intentions' (EE, 45). This reading of Marxism, beyond its 'alleged materialism', is informed by a complex understanding of the world in which excess, enjoyment and the escape from anonymous being are made concrete in the experience of breathing, hunger and thirst that are remote from any simple idealism or materialism.

In his ensuing reflection on freedom, Levinas makes explicit the implied relationship between the 'sincerity of intentions' and escape. Sincere enjoyment might appear as inauthentic, as an escape from consciousness of being, but it is precisely this character of escaping being that relates it to freedom. Yet this is not an idealist freedom from the world, but a way of being in it:

> In this world where everything seems to affirm our solidarity with the totality of existence, where we are caught up in the gears of a universal mechanism, our first feeling, our ineradicable illusion, is a feeling or illusion of freedom. To be in the world is this hesita-

tion, this interval in existing, which we have seen in the analyses of fatigue and the present. (EE, 50)

Freedom is by definition excessive, and the desire for freedom – the 'ineradicable illusion' – when expressed will *create* the conditions for freedom in the world. The hesitation or parenthesis in existence is here a product of excess, of freedom, and differs from the parenthesis in existence or the 'unhinging of time' in the 'shadow of ulterior finality' to be found in care. The parenthesis in existence permits the 'sincerity of intentions' or an enjoyment of existence without the shadow of care – it permits an understanding of the world 'as an ever revocable attachment to objects in which the non-commitment in being remains' (EE, 51). This revocability or hesitation refuses any rootedness in being – it will be described in terms of the nomadic world, figured by Abraham – yet it is not inauthentic, not fallen, but concrete and sincere:

> Our existence in the world, with its desires and everyday agitations, is then not an immense fraud, a fall into inauthenticity, an evasion of our deepest destiny. It is but the amplification of that resistance against anonymous and fateful being by which existence becomes consciousness, that is, a relationship an existent maintains with existence, through the light, that both fills up and maintains the interval. (EE, 51)

The parenthesis or hesitation offers an opportunity for light both to maintain and to fill it – light here figuring the work of excessive desire, that maintains and fills the interval. This movement is directed against authenticity and the tenets of National Socialism implicitly aligning excessive desire and revelation as well as linking both to 'resistance' – a term which, especially in 1947, still carried a high political charge.

The description of freedom that ends the chapter on the world concludes with a contrast between Heideggerian 'ontological finality' – consistently linked with National Socialist 'destiny' – and a new 'ontological adventure'. The ontological adventure consists in the opening and maintaining of an interval or parenthesis in existence – 'in the midst of being, the possibility of detaching oneself from being' (EE, 50) – the same excessive state as the 'illusion of freedom' that can lead through its expression to creativity. The bringing together of freedom and the ontological adventure in terms of excess marks an original development of themes proposed by Bergson, and – consistent with the lesson Levinas learnt from Bergson – it is a concept of creative freedom distinct from one that emphasises negation of the world, privation and nothingness. In this chapter Levinas has prepared a concept of the world founded in freedom as the expression of excess rather than the overcoming of need and privation through labour. The sketch of a new concept of the world ends by looking forward to an absence of world that is not its negation – what Heidegger in *The Origin of the Work of Art* called 'earth' and what Levinas calls 'the elemental'.

The chapter on the 'elemental' entitled 'Existence without a World' comprises two sections, one on aesthetics (subsequently elaborated in the 1947 essay 'Reality and its Shadow') and the other a version of the *il y a* fragment. Levinas finds in art another site of alterity, but this time situated in terms of objects. The site of art is characterised by the same interval and hesitation already uncovered in the 'ontological adventure' – indeed, the work of art joins in this adventure by giving 'the character of *alterity* to the objects represented which are nonetheless part of our world' (EE, 53). The alterity of the work of art is provoked by the diversion of intentionality which, instead of achieving a perception, 'gets lost in sensation itself, and it is this wandering about in sensation, in *aisthesis*, that produces the aesthetic effect' (EE, 53). The diversion of intentionality into sensibility produces another sense of interval, in effect a transition from the luminous, filled and maintained interval of the world to a world of the *il y a* or neutral being, but one that is after the world rather than before it. The *il y a* in art is punctuated, and instead of the intervals of the world it offers 'formless proliferation' or a dissemination of the *il y a*, transforming it from a medium to a scatter of points. The obliteration of intentionality by the work of art enables a transition from the world of light to the *il y a*, but this now features as a shattered world and a shattered existence. The parenthesis opened in the hypostasis of freedom is not closed, but fragmented, bearing witness in art to a world that is ruined. This conclusion of the section on the work of art leads into the section on the *il y a* or horror that was the matrix of the entire work.

Time and the Other explores many of the themes touched upon in *Existence and Existents* but is oriented towards escape through ethical alterity. In the lectures, Levinas is explicit about the resistance to Hegelianism that had become the burden of his thought: 'The dialectic these developments may contain is in any case not Hegelian. It is not a matter of traversing a series of contradictions, or of reconciling them while stopping history. On the contrary, it is towards a pluralism that does not merge into unity that I should like to make my way and, if this can be dared, break with Parmenides' (TO, 42). The break is ventured by way of analysing the place of the other in the various concrete figures of sociality.

Levinas distinguishes his position from the collective unity of Marxism and the individual unity of existentialism. Levinas seeks a community that is not made up of existential individuals, bound by ideology or labour or by Durkheimian professional associations. At the heart of this rethinking of community is time. Once again, Bergson points the way for Levinas with his 'notion of *élan vital*, which merges artistic creation and generation in the same movement – what I call "fecundity"' (TO, 92), but reproaches it for its pantheism. Instead, Levinas concludes: 'I have tried to find the temporal transcendence of the present towards the mystery of the future. This is not a participation in a third term, whether this term be a person, a truth, a work, or a profession. It is a collectivity that is not a communion' (TO, 94). However, the nature of this collectivity that is not a communion or a unity required a further critique of the limits of ontology and an exploration of its ethical complement and alternative.

The critique of political ontology: towards *Totality and Infinity*

The work of mourning the victims of National Socialism brought with it a fundamental re-orientation of the Western philosophical tradition, turning it from ontology and the question of being towards ethics and the questions of the good and the just. The re-organisation of the ontological investments of Western philosophy had considerable implications for Levinas's political thinking, an outcome consistent with the conviction that the ontological concerns of Western philosophy were related to the emergence of the totalitarian political during the twentieth century. The philosophical writings of the 1950s that culminated in *Totality and Infinity* were thus dedicated to a fundamental critique of political ontology. This critique was driven not only by the direct experience of National Socialism, but also by the consequences of the Second World War and above all the emergence of the thermonuclear truce of the Cold War. The intersection of the critique of ontology with reflection upon the post-war political was evident not only in his essays written for political/philosophical journals such as *Esprit* but also in those written for more austerely philosophical journals such as the *Revue de Métaphysique et de Morale* and *Revue Philosophique de la France et de l'Étranger*. The essays testify to the subtle interplay in Levinas's work of the 1950s between reflection on the post-war political and the emerging ethical re-orientation of Western philosophy.

Levinas's most explicit reflections on the significance of the Cold War were published in *Esprit* and continue the line of inquiry opened in the 'Reflections on Hitlerism' published in the same journal in 1934. The 1956 essay on 'The Spirit of Geneva' uses the meeting of the superpowers in Geneva as an occasion to reflect on the philosophical underpinning of the Cold War geo-political.[21] The continuity with the 'Reflections on Hitlerism' is evident in the critique of paganism that characterises both essays, but in 1956 paganism is linked to the technology of nuclear warfare. The definition of paganism in terms of subjection to expansionary natural forces proposed in the 'Reflections on Hitlerism' is re-adopted in the 'Spirit of Geneva', except that now Levinas substitutes physical, nuclear forces of atomic weaponry for the biological forces that defined race and race war in the earlier essay.

The inhuman biological race war that characterised the National Socialist political has now become the inhuman nuclear war between the superpowers. The powers released by nuclear technology no longer possess any human significance beyond their potential to destroy human life. The apparent struggle between the capitalist and socialist systems for world domination is regarded by Levinas as a war of shadows that exemplifies an historical predicament in which 'human conflict has lost all meaning without the struggle having come to an end' (IH, 161). The development of atomic technology is understood by Levinas to mark the end of human history: 'the release of atomic energy has precisely taken the control of the real away from human will. This is exactly what is meant by the arrest of history' (IH, 161). Not only does human struggle no longer possess any meaning or direction, but its lack of orientation signifies a fundamental transformation of the political. It is a transformation that, at this stage in his thought, Levinas takes to mark the end of a certain human history and he beginning of an inhuman history. Levinas extends the line of thought opened in the 'Reflections on Hitlerism' by regarding the inhuman in terms of a regression to the animal. Later, in the audacious essay of 1961 'Heidegger, Gagarin and Us', the inhuman character of technology is understood in terms of the divine inhuman, or the promise of a universality that closes a human history based on territory and place while opening the possibility of a new human history organised around the nudity of the face of the other.

In 1956 Levinas describes the link between the arrest of history and the transformation of the political by means of the concept of the 'third'. While the 'third' usually signifies for Levinas the political as opposed to the 'second' or other of ethics, the 'third' serving as shorthand for the impersonal institutions of legal and political judgement, here it denotes precisely the inhuman. Levinas writes of the summit negotiations that 'The third partner here is not the third man. It does not assume human form, they are forces without faces. Strange return of the natural powers...' (IH, 161). The 'forces without faces' will return again in the 1960 *Esprit* article 'Principles and Faces'; in both cases they signify the same forces of fatality that drove the racial struggle described in the Hitlerism essay. In 1934, human struggle was overshadowed by a struggle between the inhuman biological forces of race; here human struggle is overshadowed by the inhuman scale of the destructive forces released by nuclear energy.

By locating the moment of the political in the inhuman, Levinas is forced to redefine the political. At this point in his work he proposes a contrast between a 'human' and a 'cosmo' political, regarding the latter as a technologically advanced return to prehistory. Under the reign of the human political, when the 'third' was the 'third man', the inhuman was already present but not all-encompassing:

From the inhuman, so prodigious in those centuries, still came the human. The human relations that made up the social order and the forces that guided that order, exceeded in power, efficacy and in being those of the forces of nature. The elements borrow from us through society and the state onto which they add their own meaning. (IH, 162)

In this phase of history the encounter of the human and the inhuman was governed by the third of the human social order. In it the humanised 'world' was the condition for meaningful human action, even for deadly conflict; the human remained the horizon of history, and even in conflict there persisted, however occluded, the sentiment of responsibility for the other human. In this phase of history, the human horizon of events offered 'an invitation to work for a better world, to believe the world transformable and human' (IH, 163).

In the 'Spirit of Geneva' Levinas comes close to acknowledging that the moment for such a politics has now passed. In the epoch of inhuman history,

For the first time social problems and the struggles between humans do not reveal the ultimate meaning of the real. This end of the world would lack its last judgement. The elements exceed the states that until now contained them. Reason no longer appears in political wisdom, but in the historically unconditioned truths announcing cosmic dangers. For politics is substituted a cosmo-politics that is a physics. (IH, 164)

The reduction of human politics to an inhuman physics or cosmo-politics is accompanied by an abdication 'on both sides of the iron curtain' of responsibility in favour of achieving a balance of uncontrollable forces. Both National Socialist bio-politics and Cold War cosmo-politics surrender a political situated within a human horizon for a calculus of implacable inhuman forces before which humans are deprived of their wisdom, agency and ultimately their responsibility.

In the article of 1960, 'Principles and Faces', Levinas extends the themes of 'The Spirit of Geneva' by introducing a further element, also intimated in the Hitlerism essay. In the light of his philosophical critique of ontology begun after the war and continued during the 1950s, Levinas now openly insists on a complicity between the Cold War political and 'Western philosophy'. The exposure of the ontological commitments of 'Western philosophy' and the ethical re-orientation of philosophy undertaken in the writings of the 1950s and culminating in *Totality and Infinity* are here linked with the theme of the abdication of political responsibility by the parties to the Cold War.

Rather wickedly, Levinas takes the occasion of a speech by the then General Secretary of the Soviet Communist Party, Nikita Khrushchev, to show that the speech, far from being just propaganda, was in fact a contribution to Western political metaphysics. He suggests that it should be located within 'the implicit or explicit metaphysics that the political thought of the West lives off' (IH, 166). Fully consistent with his political position in 1956 and the philosophical turn from ontology to ethics during the 1950s, Levinas argues that 'the West suddenly appeared to depend upon the perpetual postponement of the consequences flowing from its own principles' (IH, 167). With this claim Levinas entertains the possibility that a human political may still be possible, but one organised around the postponement of the consequences of its founding ontological principles. This postponement may take a number of forms, all basically guided by the alternative between a deferred political ontology or a politics that renounces the 'metaphysics on which the political thought of the West depends' and begins to elaborate a politics beyond ontology, one otherwise than being. Following his experience with the political judgement of the State of Israel, Levinas will finally articulate a notion of prophetic politics in which the totality of the political and institutional structures of the Western political are disrupted and diverted by a prophetic voice sounding from the ethical responsibility for the other.

The title of the 1960 essay – 'Principles and Faces' – promises a confrontation between ontological principles and the ethical face-to-face. The political consequences of the ontological principles of the West were already shown in the 'Reflections on Hitlerism', notably in the reduction of being to the conflict of forces and the link between reason and universality. Already in 1934 Levinas had shown that the combination of ontological force and universality was potentially explosive; now in 1960 he underlines the necessity for postponing their fusion. Fascism is cited as an example of the imperfect fusion of force and universality, with the force of the nation remaining particular; National Socialism, by contrast, combined force and universality in the concept of race. Levinas now argues that Soviet Socialism marks another possible fusion of force and universality: the worker is both the source of the force of productivity and of political universality, and the fusion of the two in the universal history of the class struggle between the productive and the unproductive offers another political realisation of the desire for totality that emerges from the principles of Western philosophy.

In his reflections on how most effectively to postpone the fusion of force and universality, Levinas returns to the alternative between particularism and universalism that he criticised in the 'Reflections on Hitlerism'. As then, he refuses to accept the terms of a choice between 'the particularities of tradition, family, country, corporate group' and the 'millennial quest for universality', and remains reluctant to pit one claim to universality against another. He now recognises that in order to rethink the political it is necessary to put in question the entire opposition of universality and particularity by asking '*Is there not a universality other than that of the state and a freedom other than objective?* Difficult reflections for they must go further than one thinks. Well beyond Marx and Hegel. They lead perhaps to putting into question the deepest foundations of Western metaphysics' (IH, 168). This would, of course, be Levinas's project in *Totality and Infinity*, one that had been prepared in the philosophical writings of the 1950s, in the writings on the 'difficult freedom' of Judaism as well as here in the reflections on the Cold War. The putting into question that is evoked involved no less than the articulated opposition to the ontological constitution of the modern political. The formulation of an ethics of alterity is thus inseparable from the critique of political ontology.

Levinas hints at the presence of the ethical even at the heart of political ontology in his interpretation of Khrushchev's visits to the West as satisfying the 'ethical necessity for humans to see behind the anonymous principle the face of the other human' (IH, 169). The possibility of an ethical surplus breaking through the totality of political ontology had become central to Levinas's political philosophy and had been prepared philosophically in a number of essays representing important stages on the way towards *Totality and Infinity*. In 'Freedom and Command' (1953), 'The Ego and Totality' (1954) and 'Philosophy and the Idea of Infinity' (1957), Levinas systematically puts into question the foundations of Western metaphysics and the political structures raised upon them. Extending his initial philosophical response to National Socialism to the post-war political he begins in these essays the project of an ethically qualified political ontology that would be systematically developed in *Totality and Infinity*. The critique of Heidegger is extended to the Western tradition as a whole, but with a view to recuperating those ethical moments in it that were otherwise smothered by ontology.

Levinas's essay 'Freedom and Command', published in the *Revue de Métaphysique et de Morale* in 1953, has several intersecting lines of argument which develop previously explored themes and prepare new ones. The essay begins by taking up again the concept of resistance proposed in 1947 and extending it by means of a distinction between the resistance of an 'independent reality' to the will and the 'resistance of a different order'. The distinction is elaborated through an analysis of labour and war which repeatedly returns to a reading and defence of Plato's *Republic* which, for Levinas, is 'obsessed by the threat of tyranny'. Levinas's reading is conducted in terms of an intersection between Plato's Republic and Hegel's master and slave dialectic – thus bringing together the themes of tyranny, war and labour.

Tyranny has 'unlimited resources at its disposal', including the destructive work of obedience. This means that obedience is not freely chosen, but becomes an inclination; the creation of a 'servile soul is not only the most painful experience of modern man, but perhaps the very refutation of human freedom' (CP, 16). This observation develops the earlier critique of the National Socialist view of destiny, and revives the earlier defence of freedom. Levinas contrasts tyranny with a state founded upon freedom: 'Freedom consists in instituting outside of oneself an order of reason, in entrusting the rational to a written text, in resorting to institutions. Freedom, in its fear of tyranny, leads to institutions, to a commitment of freedom in the very name of freedom, to a state' (CP, 17). Levinas then further specifies the conditions of this commitment or command: 'it must be an exterior law, a written law, armed with force against tyranny' (CP, 17). There then arises the classical problem, stated by Rousseau in *The Social Contract*, that the institutions of freedom 'become in a certain way alien to the will...the freedom of the present does not recognise itself in the guarantees it has provided itself against its own degradation' (CP, 17). This introduces into freedom the problem of time, here in the guise of degradation, but also more generally in the exteriority of freedom to itself expressed in the anachronism of freedom always being ahead of its own law.

Levinas then moves to reflect upon the tension between freedom and work, an important moment in his analysis if he is to continue his resistance to the Hegelian–Marxist claim for the universality and liberatory potential of work. Previously, Levinas's critique of work was couched in terms of fatigue; now it is identified with violent action: 'Action on things, work, consists in finding the point of application where the object, by virtue of general laws to which its individuality is completely reducible, will submit to the workers' will' (CP, 18–19). Work, or the domination of things, assumes an 'informed reality', with the object of work becoming a particular case of a universal concept. Levinas now begins to develop a critique of the Hegelian master/slave dialectic as proposing a model of sociality based on the two modes of recognition: war and work. Levinas objects that recognition is not possible through war, which is but the clash of forces. For him, 'War is not the collision of two substances or two intentions, but an attempt made by one to master the other by surprise, by ambush' (CP, 19); such a bid for mastery does not involve recognition but only violence akin to that applied to objects in work: 'The other becoming a mass is what describes the relationship of war, and in this it approximates the violence of labour' (CP, 19). The anti-Hegelianism of 1947 has been extended into the heart of the master/slave dialectic, now revealed as a violent collision of forces rather than a play of recognition and misrecognition.

Folded into the analysis of labour and war is the contrast with a relation to the other as a *tode ti* or the 'individuality of a thing' (CP, 19), which is described in terms of the face. The *tode ti* cannot form part of a system of categories nor can it serve as an example of a form (neither Hegel nor Plato) – the face 'has a meaning not by virtue of the relationships in which it is found' (CP, 20); it expresses without reserve – there is no idea or substance behind the face to be expressed, for 'A face does not expose, nor does it conceal an entity'. The *tode ti* of the face as substance resists being brought into a system – the encounter with a face is imperative – governed by the commandment 'Thou shalt not kill' – and remains outside of all categories.

Levinas draws a number of important conclusions from the discovery of the face. The first is that the face marks an exteriority that is nevertheless an object of experience – external to experience but also within it. Second, the face, in Husserlian terms, is 'prior to all *Sinngebung*', a critique of Husserl that is extended into one of Heidegger – 'creation is the fact that intelligibility precedes me' or the contrary of *Geworfenheit* in that the bestowal of meaning succeeds the encounter with the face of the other. It is on the basis of this analysis that Levinas returns to Plato and the critique of tyranny. He reveals this critique to have many objects: critique of literal tyranny, tyrannical religion and the tyranny of incantatory art. Against all of these sites of tyranny/idolatry – in which the individual is violently subordinated to a universal – Levinas proposes the non-tyrannical but transitive relation that might be called religion, the non-violent situation where 'one speaks to the other' in a 'face-to-face'.

The essay from the following year, 'The Ego and the Totality', also published in the *Revue de Métaphysique et de Morale*, develops many of the themes of 'Freedom and Command' but with a focus not on freedom as such but on the 'situation of being simultaneously a position in the totality, and a reserve with respect to it or a separation' the reserve indicated by 'exteriority'. The essay departs from the philosophical naturalism that had preoccupied Levinas since 1934, namely a philosophy that begins with biological life. There is a movement from the consciousness of biological life (pursuit of nutrient) to exteriority. This movement is not driven by a being-for-death – this is the result of the inability of the organism to adapt to exteriority. Rather, Levinas argues that there is a relation to an exteriority which is not death or absorption into exteriority. It is possible to be within totality and at the same time beyond it, an insight crucial to any attempt to develop an ethically qualified political ontology.

The essay is also interesting for its discussion of the spectral 'third party' who is 'both present and absent' (CP, 39) and its critique of what Levinas regards as the naturalistic foundations of psychoanalysis. Levinas comments that 'To rise above the totality and acquire consciousness of justice, one must get out of the ambiguous discourse of psychoanalysis which is inevitable as long as thought is part of the system it is to take in (CP, 42). This exit from totality requires 'a being that is not in the system, a transcendent being' (CP, 42). With this, Levinas returns to the theme of the face and then to some closing comments on money as a 'third'. For

Levinas money dissolves naturalism, since it is a 'universal power of acqui-sition, and not a thing one enjoys' (CP, 45). As the possession of the power of possession, 'money presupposes men who have time at their disposal, who are present in a world which endures beyond momentary contacts, men who trust one another and form a society' (CP, 45). Money 'points to a new justice' that might 'save us from economy, that is, from the human totality' (CP, 45). Like technology, money liberates humanity from the potential tyranny of dyadic relations of possession, although as a third it bears its own risks. These thoughts will later be developed into the impor-tant discussion of commerce in *Totality and Infinity*.

The key to the excessive character of exteriority was elaborated in terms of the concept of infinity in 'Philosophy and the Idea of Infinity', published in 1957 in the *Revue de Métaphysique et de Morale* and later added to *Discovering Existence with Husserl and Heidegger*. Here Levinas develops the earlier critique of Heidegger and National Socialism on a number of different levels, taking up themes from previous work and intimating connection which would emerge more clearly in subsequent writings.

The essay opposes two conceptions of politics and philosophy, one based on totality expressed in terms of internally opposed forces and one arising from an immanent but unthematisable infinity. The first position is another variation of the critique of naturalism developed in the 1930s. Once again, as in the essay of 1953, naturalism is described as a tyranny which possesses and reduces the singularity of the other. The result is a state of war, a confrontation of forces and skills dedicated to the end of reducing the other to the same.

Levinas sees Heidegger's *Dasein* as an example of this state of war. This is a crucial step for it allows Levinas to see in Heidegger's neutral Being the capacity for war. The 'neutrality of Being' offers a 'way of access to each real singularity through Being, which is not a particular being nor a genus in which all the particulars would enter, but is rather the very act of being...' (CP, 51). One consequence of this understanding of being is an inversion of the possession of freedom in which 'man is possessed by freedom rather than possessing freedom' (CP, 51). Either way, what is important is the concept of possession, which Levinas would dispossess of its privileges.

Levinas extends this argument to claim that 'Heideggerian ontology subordinates the relation to the other to the relation with the neuter, Being, and it thus continues to exalt the will to power, whose legitimacy the other alone can unsettle, troubling good conscience (CP, 52).' There follows a critique of Heidegger's attitudes towards technology and National Socialism summed up in the claim that 'when he deplores the orientation of the intellect towards technology, he maintains a regime of power more inhuman than mechanism' (CP, 51). First of all, he repeats his critique of obedience to tyranny which he described in 1953 as 'modern tragedy?' but now addressed specifically to National Socialism:

'it is not sure that National Socialism arises from the mechanist reification of men, and that it does not rest on peasant enrootedness and a feudal adoration of subjugated men for the masters and lords who command them' (CP, 52). Such enrootedness is described as an 'existence which takes itself to be natural', a 'pagan *existing*'. Levinas not only identifies this naturalism at the root of Heidegger's thinking of being and his inversion of the possession of freedom, but also extends it to the entire Western tradition of possession. He writes 'this earth-maternity determines the whole Western civilisation of property, exploitation, political tyranny and war' (CP, 53), and sees in it the 'pretechnological power of possession effected in the enrootedness of perception' (CP, 53). What emerges in the essay is an analysis of tyranny framed in terms of the analyses of the links between property, obedience and paganism that may be undone by a liberatory global technology.

Levinas does not try to escape from the fate of tyranny through evoking the states of nausea and fatigue, but tries to create a new set of thematic links encompassing infinity, externality, justice and the other. In this essay he begins by discovering in Plato and Descartes intimations of a radical concept of infinity – infinity is not a content which can be contained in thought but one which necessarily exceeds it. Levinas here mobilises his established critique of Husserl and intentionality: 'The intentionality that animates the idea of infinity is not comparable with any other; it aims at what it cannot embrace and is in this sense the infinite' (CP, 54). Not only does the thought of infinity have the peculiar property that it '*thinks more than it thinks*', but the thinker of this thought '*is more than himself*', a surplus expressed in the formula of '*more in the less*' (CP, 54). The peculiar and unique intentionality of which Levinas speaks is thus beyond ontology while pointing to a moment of excess immanent to ontology itself.

The intentionality 'animating' infinity is that of the relationship with the other – 'The idea of infinity is the social relationship' (CP, 54). The other cannot be integrated into the identity of the self, unlike an object of which 'the I makes of its theme, and then its property, its booty, its prey or its victim' (CP, 55). Infinity arrives with the 'absolute resistance of the other', not the resistance of an opposed force (which would be a state of war between two proprietors) but a 'resistance which has no resistance', an ethical resistance in which '*I am no longer able to have power*' (CP, 55) and which 'puts a stop to the irresistible imperialism of the same and the I'. The self is both dispossessed and disempowered by the resistance of the other, an important development of the theme of ethical resistance already adumbrated in 1947 and again in the 1953 'Freedom and Command'.

Levinas now explores some of the implications of his understanding of infinity at greater length. First he locates the thought of infinity with respect to desire and time. Infinity is futural and excessive; it is a thought 'which thinks more than itself'. As futural it is aligned with desire, but not a desire issuing from indigence and need, nor one based on lack. It is a desire which forever puts itself into question, keeping open its future and, as such, not capable of being satisfied – it does not follow from a lack that might at some point be filled: 'The true desire is that which the desired does not satisfy, but hollows out. It is goodness. It does not refer to a lost fatherland or plenitude, it is not homesickness, it is not nostalgia. It is the lack in a being which *is* completely, and lacks nothing' (CP, 57). This desire puts itself in question (the 'hollowing out'), and does not pursue a lost authenticity (as Heidegger) or a promised land or utopian freedom.

What is this hollowing out? It seems to consist in the Talmudic ethos of questioning. Levinas brings desire and infinity together with freedom and perpetual questioning in an account of justice, or, more accurately, of living a just life. Freedom is not realisable, cannot be brought to plenitude, but is always 'hollowing out' its claims to power and possession before the face of the other. The questioning is thus:

> The life of freedom discovering itself to be unjust, the life of freedom in heteronomy, consists in an infinite movement of freedom putting itself ever more into question. This is how the very depth of inwardness is hollowed out. The augmentation of exigency that I have in regard to myself aggravates the judgement that is borne on me, that is, my responsibility. (CP, 58)

This view of freedom changes the nature of philosophy: the questioning proper to philosophy is not dialogue, 'the fortunate meeting of fraternal souls that greet one another and converse', but the 'exposedness of my freedom to the judgement of the other' (CP, 59). Levinas draws out the implications of this changed view of philosophy by claiming that 'if the essence of philosophy consists in going back from all certainties towards a principle, if it lives from critique, the face of the other would be the starting point of philosophy. This is a thesis of heteronomy which breaks with a venerable tradition' (CP, 59). Here Levinas proposes a radical separation of the concept of freedom from that of autonomy, a link almost taken for granted in the modern tradition of ethical and political thought and shared by thinkers as diverse as Rousseau, Kant, Hegel, Marx and Nietzsche.

The 'difficult freedom' at which Levinas arrives in 'Philosophy and the Idea of Infinity' was more fully developed in *Totality and Infinity*. Yet the presentation of such fundamental concepts of Western thought as freedom, desire, infinity and possession has already been significantly inflected. The continued focus on freedom that characterised these essays and the possibility it opened of an ethically qualified political ontology in *Totality and Infinity* would itself subsequently be put in question by Levinas. The motivation for this questioning was the sustained post-war reflection on Jewish identity, and in particular the implications posed for it by the founding of the State of Israel. The problem of the relationship between Jewish identity and its formulation in terms of political ontology – the State of Israel – preoccupied Levinas for much of the post-war period and forced a more radical approach to the understanding of the limits of the political.

'Being Jewish'/'Being Western': towards *Otherwise than Being*

Levinas's inquiry into the philosophical origins of National Socialist racism, begun in 1934, was resumed with urgency immediately after the Second World War. The critique of his own phenomenological formation was accompanied and driven by the need to rethink the relationship between being and identity in the specific case of Jewish identity. The National Socialist racist identification of what it meant to be Jewish was part of an implacable political ontology. Being Jewish was a racial classification of an essence or state of being imposed by the National Socialist state and then driven to its last murderous conclusion; in Nazi eyes the ontological condition of racial identity made them frame the so-called 'Jewish Question' in terms of global race war. Levinas's critique of ontology, beginning with phenomenology and extending to the Western philosophical tradition, attempted to destroy the philosophical premises of the Nazi 'Jewish Question'. His philosophical development of a new notion of identity contributed to the rethinking of Jewish identity as much as the painful reflection upon Jewish identity after the Shoah lent urgency and shape to the philosophical critique.

The crisis in Jewish identity following the experience of forced identification and mass murder under the National Socialist government and its satellite regimes provoked a reconsideration, not only of what it meant to be Jewish, but of what it meant to *be*. One of Levinas's first essays published after the war – 'Etre Juif' – opened an inquiry that he would pursue throughout the 1950s and 1960s under the title 'Difficult Freedom'. The essay was published in a special issue of the journal *Confluences* (1947: 15–17) dedicated to the theme 'Bilan Juif'. The collection was a reflection on the historical and philosophical implications of the mass murder, and was for Levinas an opportunity to reflect on being Jewish in the specific sense of Jewish identity and the more general implications of Judaism for the understanding of being. The essay takes issue with assimilation in the narrow sense of the social and political assimilation of Jewish citizens in the modern nation-state and more broadly in the assimilation of Judaism to ontology or being in general.

The essay marks a crucial transition between Levinas's work of the 1930s and what was to come during the 1950s. The reflection on assimilation emphasises the Christian character of the concept of being in the modern world. Christianity imbues the modern state, prompting Levinas to observe that 'Perhaps the most striking characteristic of Christianity is its capacity to become the religion of the state and to remain such after the separation of church and state: to furnish the state not only with its legal festivals but also all the framework of daily life'.[22] Social and political assimilation in the narrow sense is thus an assimilation to a crypto-Christian polity. However, more than this, Christianity has also in Levinas's view governed the broader ontological understanding of being in terms of presence that informs modern science and philosophy. Levinas explains this in terms of the difference between Judaism and Trinitarian Christianity. In the latter, the emphasis on the person of the Son entails that being as presence is privileged, with the incarnate Son of God present among us now – 'God himself is brother, that is to say, he is contemporary' ('Etre juif', 259). For Judaism, Levinas claims, God is the Father who is always in the past – 'being' understood in terms of presence is not central for Judaism in the way that it is for Christianity. Being Jewish cannot easily be approximated to being, but always refers beyond it to what Levinas will later call the 'immemorial past'.

Levinas sees the unassimilated quality of being Jewish as one of the sources of anti-Semitic hatred, evoking his thoughts on Hitlerism to claim that the freedom which not being in the present brings with it is the source of National Socialist anti-Semitism. In passing, Levinas criticises Sartre's 'Anti-Semite and Jew' for its critique of essentialism; the question of essence or otherwise assumes an understanding of being as present to which Judaism does not conform, for 'being Jewish' brings the weight of the past to the present, making it almost insupportable were it not for liberation that comes with it, for 'its originality consists in breaking with a world without origin and simply present' ('Etre juif', 263). Judaism is thus accorded the metaphysical vocation of being otherwise than the Christian state and also otherwise than the notion of being as presence that is founded in the doctrine of the incarnation. With this essay Levinas, for perhaps the last time, explicitly brings together the question of Jewish identity or the place of Judaism in being, the critique of ontology and the possibility of a politics that would exceed that of a still-Christian state. Subsequently these paths of inquiry will diverge, with their basic direction however remaining consistent with the questions of 'Being Jewish'.

Although it was published before the proclamation of the State of Israel, while reticent, 'Being Jewish' about Zionism, already suggests that Jewish identity involves much more than membership of a nation or citizenship in a nation-state. It also involves more than a confessional allegiance, the notion of Jewish identity carefully developed by reform Judaism during the nineteenth century. While these alternatives were problematic, they certainly did not justify, in Levinas's eyes the surrender of Jewish identity through assimilation. Faced with diverse conceptualisations of racial, political and religious identities and the dissolution of identity in assimilation, Levinas sought less the re-invention of a Jewish identity than a questioning of the notions of being and identity itself in the wake of the Jewish experience of the horrors of forced identification.

Nevertheless, the re-investigation of identity provoked by the crisis in Jewish identity did not, and perhaps could not, follow a consistent line of development. For the reformulation of Jewish identity depended not only on the philosophical re-working of the concept of identity but also on the vicissitudes of post-war history. Being Jewish was a historical predicament inseparable from the legacy of the European Civil War and the global struggles of the Cold War and of decolonisation. This was evident in the unresolved tension in Levinas's work of the 1950s between the demands of history and those of philosophy. Predictably, the task of redefining Jewish identity was given greatest urgency during the difficult early years of the State of Israel, during which Levinas's political judgement of the aspirations and the achievements of the new state were far from consistent.

One consistent pattern informing the essays that make up *Difficult Liberty* is generated by the tension between 'Being Jewish' and 'Being a Westerner'. Levinas did not share the wholly understandable rejection of Europe by Jewish youth who had suffered so much at its hands. Indeed his writings immediately following the foundation of the State of Israel are thinly coded warnings against the political ontology informing Zionist ideology. The beautiful memoir of Léon Brunschvicg – 'The Diary of Léon Brunschvicg' – published in 1949, a year after the foundation of the State of Israel, presented Brunschvicg as an exemplar of the European, and by implication the non-Zionist Jew. Levinas urgently wishes to 'remind Jewish youth who, after their recent experiences, may have had enough of Europe – its "Western culture", its "Christian humanism", or whatever – how much civilisation was embodied in this European Jew' (DF, 39). The source of his urgency is precisely the foundation of the State of Israel and the near-contempt in which it held the Diaspora. While admiring the '[Zionist] youth that aspires to the simple life on a soil that is worked and defended with self-sacrifice and heroism', Levinas warns against 'simply forgetting...two thousand years of participation in the European world, culminating not just in Auschwitz but also in a personality like Léon Brunschvicg' (DF, 39). The defence of 'Being a Westerner' exemplified by Brunschvicg is linked to an unequivocal critique of being exclusively Zionist; yet it does not quite add up to a defence of Brunschvicg's 'assimilation' nor to a condemnation of Zionism.

Yet the figure of the assimilated Brunschvicg is not intended to pose an alternative Jewish identity to the Zionist farmer/soldier, but forms part of a complex identity whose historical contribution should not be forgotten in the re-invention of Jewish identity. Levinas writes 'the basic toughness and straight-forwardness that helped to conquer Palestine should not remain the final virtues of a renewed Judaism. Perhaps we should derive from the Diaspora something more than the qualities of farmers and soldiers' (DF, 39). The renewal of Judaism and Jewish indentity will not be satisfied by the formation of the State of Israel, but will also require the retrieval of elements from the Western tradition. For Brunschvicg and his generation, these were the victories of Dreyfus and 1918, perceived as victories of reason over injustice.

Levinas recommends Zionist youth learn from Brunschvicg not only a commitment to the values of truth and justice, which are for him both republican and Talmudic values, but also a way of remembering and properly mourning injustice. Brunschvicg's generation 'remembered less the fact that such an injustice [the Dreyfus Affair] had been possible in a civilised age than the triumph recorded by justice. This memory marked them' (DF, 43). Levinas establishes a subtle parallel between their memory of the victory of justice, rather than the defeats of injustice, and the Allied victories of 1945 that may be said to 'demonstrate that in history, vice is ultimately punished and virtue recorded', adding that 'we do not wish once more to bear the brunt of this demonstration' (DF, 45). Rather than give Hitler a posthumous victory by regarding Auschwitz as the truth of the Diaspora, Levinas wishes also to remember the defeat of National Socialism; for implied in the parallel are the questions how will the survivors be marked by the experience of the Shoah, and will the post-war generation remember only its extreme injustice or also the eventual victory over it?

Brunschvicg's memory of the victory of truth and justice contributed to the serenity of his and his generation's identity; a quality that 'lay in justice and not in the will to power...moral conscience rather than in the horrible prestige of the Sacred' (DF, 43). Instead of being marked by the memory of injustice, of having an identity marked by suffering and horror, Brunschvicg's memory of the victory of truth and justice permitted a 'profoundly successful form of assimilation' that 'proceeded not from betrayal, but from adherence to a universal idea to which he could lay claim outside of any particularism' (DF, 43). What Levinas here calls universalism will later become the infinite or the prophetic that exceeds particularism; here it forms part of a coherent characterisation of a politics of truth and justice that emerges from an affirmative memory of justice and victory, rather than one of injustice and defeat. It is thus continuous with the attempt to work through political horror that is to be found in the philosophical writings of 1947.

In the context of this essay, the appeal to Jewish youth not to forget Europe takes on a new dimension. Is the politics of Zionism – before and after the Shoah – marked by an exclusively negative presentiment and memory, one made up of violence and injustice? If this is so, then the memory of murder will mark Jewish identity more than the eventual victory over the murderers. What political identity will emerge from being the victim of a Germany that had become 'a metaphysics' in Nazism, or a Russia that had become a 'messianism' with world socialism? The danger, barely intimated here, is that a wholly negative memory might so scar Jewish identity that its State, too, might embody a messianic metaphysics and abandon the prophetic mission of Israel to realise truth and justice and instead to recommence the cycle of violence and injustice. The necessary mourning of National Socialism demands more than the memory of murder, oppression and defeat, but must also extend to the victory over the murderers and oppressors. In 1949 Levinas could only issue a warning in the form of a hope 'that today's Jewish youth, when it sets off for new spiritual and sometimes geographical horizons, does not purely and simply shake the dust of the world it is leaving off its feet. There is gold in that dust' (DF, 45). The millennial history of the Jewish experience in Europe did not only lead to disaster and the emergency exit represented by the State of Israel, but possessed many dimensions and had crucially contributed to the invention of Europe.

By the following year Levinas had characteristically modified his evaluation of the gold of the European tradition. While in 'The Diary of Léon Brunschvicg' the defence of the European tradition and the two thousand years of Jewish participation in it were not distinguished, the essay 'Place and Utopia' (1950) differentiates more sharply between the Jewish and the Christian contributions to 'Europe'. In the place of remembering that Europe meant more than Auschwitz, Levinas now brings to memory the Jewish contribution to European identity. The examination of the differences between Christianity and Judaism in 'Place and Utopia' begins with a stark accusation of the failure of Christianity: 'In the midst of so many other horrors, the extermination of six million defenceless beings, in a world that in two thousand years Christianity has not been able to make better, in our eyes robs its conquest of Europe of much of its prestige' (DF, 99). The failure of Christianity was both spiritual and political. While its utopian rejection of the world could warrant the revolutionary and utopian uprooting of the individual from the secular world, and the renovation of their identity in Christ, it could also endorse their acquiescence in the place in which they and the authorities to which they were subjected themselves found.

In both cases Christian spirituality produces the conditions for political failure, a lesson that Levinas drew from Hegel's exposition of the 'Barbarism of Pure Culture' in the *Phenomenology of Spirit*. In the first case, the utopian rejection of the world is quickly inverted into its affirmation: 'The faith that moves mountains and conceives of a world without slaves immediately transports itself to utopia, separating the realm of God from the reign of Caesar. This reassures Caesar' (DF, 101). By imagining the kingdom of God as eternal and not of this world, the Christian leaves the secular kingdom untouched and unthreatened. The other direction of Christian spirituality, to prefer place over utopia, is a consequence of the rejection of the world: acquiescence in the world of Caesar is accompanied by 'the virtues of being warrior-like and putting down roots, of being a man-plant, a humanity-forest whose gnarled joints of root and trunk are magnified by the

rugged life of the countryman' (DF, 100). Levinas's metaphor for an acquies-
cent Christian culture is more charged than it initially appears. The rustic
virtues of place are always associated for him with the thought of Heidegger,
transforming the critique of place into a coded critique of the Christianity of
his former teacher and its compatibility with pagan National Socialism.[23]
The critique of the tree metaphor is similarly directed at Simone Weill, who
relied on it in her *The Need for Roots*. This direction of criticism was elaborated in Levinas's later essay 'Simone Weill Against the Bible' (1952) which
unfolds his critique of Christianity in more detail (DF, 141). Finally, the
critique of the warrior–farmer image was also integral, as we have seen, to
Levinas's earlier reservations concerning heroic Zionism.

Levinas distinguishes Judaism from both paganism and the Christian
relapse into paganism[24] through a scrutiny of the metaphor of the tree. He
asks 'What is an individual, a solitary individual, if not a tree that grows
without regard for everything it suppresses and breaks, grabbing all the nourishment, air and sun, a being that is fully justified in its nature and its being?
What is an individual if not a usurper?' (DF, 100). Levinas identifies three
possible responses to this predicament: the first is the pagan celebration of
the strength to usurp 'the place in the sun'; the second, the Christian utopian
rejection of the world in favour of the kingdom not of this world; and the
third is 'ethical action' or Judaism. The first response accepts usurpation and
considers it a virtue to be 'a murderer' – one who places the satisfaction of
the self before the life of the other, what Levinas called in 'Being a Westerner'
(1951) 'the biological self [that] cannot dispense with mythology and war'
(DF, 48). The other two alternatives seek ways 'To be without being a
murderer' (DF, 100) or to separate being from the sacrifice of the other, and
so create a *spiritual* rather than a *biological* self but, in very different ways.

Having distinguished Judaism from paganism and Christianity, Levinas
proceeds to outline its salient characteristics. It 'does not choose to flee the
conditions from which one's work draws its meaning and remain here
below' (DF, 100), which is to say that it is not utopian. It has 'chosen action'
and 'the Divine word moves it only as law'. But this is not a law in the name
of whose purity it is necessary to reject the world, for ethical action guided
by this law 'does not tackle the Whole in a global and magical way, but
grapples with the particular. All the same, it cannot efface the given facts of
a problem rather than resolving it. It is historical, it exists in time' (DF, 100).
Ethical action is neither rooted in place nor projected into utopia, but
moving from the historical fact of usurpation pursues the 'difficult task of
living an equitable life' (DF, 101). The avoidance of murder and usurpation
in historically given situations is the lesson of the law, and the casuistic
reflection upon it guides and constitutes a just life.

The outline of a Jewish identity informed by reflection and debate upon
ethical action is another extension of Levinas's thinly disguised critique of
Zionism. The attempt to live equitably according to the law in given histor-

ical situations is 'the proper concern of a just society. It involves making Israel' (DF, 101). Making Israel or living the equitable life does not require the existence of a State – indeed the law, for Levinas, is neither tied to a particular place, nor is it utopian, without place – its proper element is the time of history. The version of Zionism that celebrated Ancient Israel as a sacral site of Canaanite, let alone Hebrew, religion was rejected by Levinas, who spoke of the incomprehension of the spirit of talmudic Judaism that 'today propels a whole young generation who wish to be faithful to notions that are wholly foreign to Judaism' (DF, 100–1). The critique of a Zionism tied to place was accompanied by one of utopian Zionism 'The Bible does not begin the building of an ideal city in a void' (DF, 101). In place of these Zionisms, Levinas proposed a Jewish identity based upon ethical action that oriented itself with respect both to a universal law and to concrete historical situations. This was no less than a Judaism of the Diaspora, a Judaism of the book instead of a Judaism of place or utopia, one in which 'The ethical order does not prepare us for the Divinity; it is the very accession to the Divinity' (DF, 102). This difficult task involves 'the reasoning and the humour of the Talmudists, the overwhelming certainties of the prophets and the virile confidence of the psalms' (DF, 102), in the light of which Levinas concludes 'All the rest is a dream' (DF, 102).

It is unclear at the end of 'Place and Utopia' quite what the 'rest' is – whether it is Christianity and paganism or the Zionist aspiration for a Jewish state. What is already clear is Levinas's commitment to a diasporic Jewish identity located in relation to the book, and the distinction within the book between Talmudic reasoning, prophetic certainty and the messianic 'confidence and virility' of the psalms. His subsequent work will strive to bring together Talmudic reasoning and prophetic ethics, discovering a reasoned ethics capable of guiding 'ethical action' and so contributing to 'making Israel'. Levinas's distinction between 'making Israel' by means of a universal active ethics and by means of political and military action in the Middle East could not, however, be sustained with the rigour of these early responses to the foundation of the State of Israel.

Provoked by Christian interpretations of the State of Israel, such as those of Paul Claudel to which he responded at length and with a certain horrified admiration, Levinas turned to a direct confrontation between his view of Israel and the State of Israel. In the important essay 'The State of Israel and the Religion of Israel' (1951), Levinas reflected publicly for the first time on the distinction between Israel and the State of Israel that remained implicit in his preceding essays

'The State of Israel and the Religion of Israel' begins with an ironic contrast between the 'sublime destiny' of the 'religious privilege' of Israel and the 'earthly joys' of the State of Israel with its 'Jewish uniform or a Jewish stamp' (DF, 216). However, Levinas makes the distinction only to question its terms, namely State and religion. To conceive of an absolute opposition between the religion and the state of Israel would be to understand religion and politics in terms of the Christian distinction between the kingdoms of the world and of God. Instead, Levinas claims that the 'difficult and erudite work of Justice' that characterises rabbinic Judaism[25] is not only above the state 'but has already achieved the very notion of the spirit announced by the modern state' (DF, 217). The spirit of the modern state contained in the trinitarian formula of liberty, equality and fraternity is thus anticipated in the Talmud and elaborated in the principles of rabbinic Judaism, prior to the modern state. Levinas's emphasis on the *anachronistic* character of Judaism is central to the resolution of what would otherwise seem a paradox in which 'The Jewish people therefore achieves a state whose prestige none the less stems from the religion which modern political life supplants' (DF, 217). The pursuit of universal justice by rabbinic Judaism is not anachronistic in the sense that it is rendered obsolete by the structures of the modern state, but because it anticipates and always exceeds the work of the state, a movement particularly evident in the case of the State of Israel.

Levinas supports this audacious conclusion with the equally audacious premiss, drawn from Hegel, that the modern state has incorporated the spiritual aspirations of the kingdom of God. This claim was already implied in the 'Reflections on Hitlerism' where liberalism and Marxism were regarded as secular versions of the originally religious experience of freedom. Freedom along with equality and fraternity constituted the 'spirit' of the modern state. Now, however, the claim is even stronger, with Levinas unrolling a line of argument that begins with the prestige attached to the modern state, then moves through the explanation that 'the sovereignty of the State incorporates the universe', and arrives at the conclusion that 'man recognises his spiritual nature in the dignity he achieves as a citizen' and that the modern State marks 'the coincidence of the political and the spiritual' (DF, 216). In such a state the decline of organised religion is inevitable, since 'set against the universality of the political order, the religious order inevitably takes on a disordered or clerical air' (DF, 217). In this respect, the state of Israel as a modern state would seem to be set in opposition to Israel as an object of religious experience. And yet the State of Israel can only justify its existence as the modern political form adopted by the Jewish people who are defined by their religious experience of the longing for Israel.

Levinas prepares the statement of this paradox by asking if 'it is enough to restore the State of Israel in order to have a political life', and answering that 'Israel' – not the State of Israel – 'asserts itself in a different way' (DF, 217). Levinas argued in 'Place and Utopia' that the assertion of Israel – 'making Israel' – consisted in living equitably according to the law in given historical situations and not in building a city in the wilderness. In that text, Israel was implicitly distinguished from the State of Israel, the one is ethical and the other ontological – but now Levinas concedes a special place to the State of Israel in the making of Israel. By 'bracketing' the territorial claims of the State of Israel – the claim for a place in the sun – Levinas is able to maintain that the State of Israel offers a 'concrete expression' of living equitably according to the law 'in the sordid questions of food, work and shelter'. It is by living equitably in the concrete situation of a new state and not in the Diaspora that 'an Israeli experiences the famous touch of God in his social dealings' (DF, 218). With the foundation of the State of Israel the law does not respond casuistically to situations provoked by pagan, Christian or Moslem histories, but defines and responds to its own historical situation as a nation-state.

What is 'special about the State of Israel' is not the fulfilment of an ancient (messianic) promise of restoration, nor the inauguration of 'a new age of material security', but the 'opportunity' it offers 'to carry out the social law of Judaism' and for the 'Jewish people...to begin the work of their lives' (DF, 218). From the 'horrible' position of the Diaspora, the position of being 'the only people to define itself with a doctrine of justice, and to be the meaning incapable of applying it' (DF, 218) the 'Jewish people' can now, in the State of Israel, establish the conditions necessary to apply its doctrine of justice. The arrival of the theme of history at this crucial point in the discussion of the politics of Israel is notable, and will be examined more thoroughly in Chapter Five. At this point in 'The State of Israel and the Religion of Israel' Levinas begins a reconsideration of the issues of place and territory until now excluded from discussion.

A striking feature of the paragraph discussing the 'special' nature of the State of Israel is the reference to the 'Jewish people'. To accept this designation is to subscribe to a particular and historically specific concept of Jewish identity, namely the basic assumption of political Zionism that the Jews constitute a *Volk* or people/nation. Given the sophisticated concept of identity with which Levinas works, this is not a fully acceptable assumption. It also gives a particularist answer to the question of fraternity in the trinity of liberty, equality and fraternity; the emphasis upon the Jewish people assumes in advance their fraternity as a discrete *Volk*. In spite of these possible concerns, Levinas states that it is the 'Jewish people' who 'crave their own land and their own state' in order to fulfil their historic vocation. Yet this also smuggles in the assumptions that the only possible historical subject is nation-state and that a dispersed 'people' are incapable of history. The latter concerns disappear with the definition of Jewish identity in terms of a *Volk*, but they give rise to new problems. The model of a people occupying land and forging a state also puts in question their justification for doing so. A worry on Levinas's part is evident at the end of the paragraph, when he makes a parallel between the justification for the 'resurrection of Israel' in the 'subordination of the State to its social promises' and the Ancient Israel 'resurrected' in the modern state whose 'presence on the land' was justified by 'the execution of justice' (DF, 218). Implicitly, the justification for the 'presence on the land' of the State of Israel is the subordination of the State to the 'social promises' – but for whom would this serve as a justification?

At this point, instead of returning to the concerns about place and territory voiced in 'Place and Utopia', Levinas diverts his discussion into a critique of ritualism and the re-assertion of his view of Judaism as living equitably according to the law. He sees the problem facing the Israeli political as one of adapting the modern forms of the state to the demand to live equitably, but makes the assumption that such a life is possible in such a state. In an increasingly problematic fusion of rabbinics and Hegelianism Levinas writes:

> Justice as the *raison d'être* of the State, that is religion. It presupposes the high science of justice. The State of Israel will be religious because of the intelligence of its great books which it is not free to forget. It will be religious through the very action that establishes it as a State. It will be religious or it will not be at all. (DF, 219)

His discussion of this passage focuses on the great books and leads into a justification of the relevance of rabbinic jurisprudence to modern institutions and the dilemmas they provoke. Yet the context of ethically justifying a nation-state is left without comment. The essay concludes with a call for a science of justice that will unite the 'Jewish State' (itself a Zionist formula, as opposed to the 'State of Israel' which Levinas used hitherto) and its doctrine. Yet, in all this, something has been forgotten.

The 'action' that establishes the State of Israel would also make it a religious state, one that makes it possible to live equitably. This action assumes that the 'spirit' of the modern state – in Hegelian terms the realisation of freedom – is also the spirit of rabbinic jurisprudence. The foundation of the State and the justification of the 'presence on the land' thus rest on this fusion. Yet what if the demands of living equitably and 'making Israel' exceed the political possibilities afforded by the State of Israel; what if the State behaves unjustly, as did the King in Ancient Judaism? This possibility is explored later by Levinas in terms of the inspiration of prophesy. But at this point Levinas turns away from reflection on the law and the difficult freedom of living equitably, and subordinates ethics to the interests of political ontology – the realisation of rabbinic ethical justice through the institutions of the modern state. This text forgets the other lessons – that the law may challenge the institutions of the State of Israel, or perhaps, in a reprise of Hegel's 'barbarism of pure culture', that the State may issue in a violent inversion of its ethical interests.

Only one year separates the critique of the State of Israel in 'Place and Utopia' and the apology in 'The State of Israel and the Religion of Israel'. Yet between them the two essays represent the extreme points of the range of Levinas's responses to the foundation of the State of Israel. More than simply responses to a political event, Levinas's positions on the State of Israel are symptomatic of a wavering between a modified critique of political ontology and its complete rejection in the name of an ethical prophetic politics. The attempt to reconcile ontology and rabbinics in the justification of the State of Israel is in contrast with the refusal to territorialise Israel and the universal law. In the one case, liberty and equality are realised through the fraternity of the 'Jewish people' giving themselves a state; in the other, the question of fraternity – or ethics – is left radically open in order to preserve its universality.

While the State of Israel represents one response to the claim that talmudic commentary on the law 'already achieved the very notion of the spirit announced by the modern state' (DF, 217), another is the absorption of Judaism into the 'spirit of the modern state'. If the secular modern state is guided by the same spirit of liberty, equality and fraternity that guides talmudic commentary, then commitment to the values of the modern secular state should suffice for universality without resort to the State of Israel. Levinas already hinted at such a position in his memoir of Brunschvicg, for whom the victory of Dreyfus was one for the republican principles of justice and equality rather than for confessional fraternity. However, this position very closely approaches that of assimilation, for, if the values of Judaism are realised in the spirit of the modern secular state, what need is there for a specifically Jewish identity beyond citizenship in a modern state? If, in Levinas's words, modern 'man' recognises 'his spiritual nature in the dignity he achieves as a citizen' (DF, 216), what need is there to supplement this with a particular religious commitment?

The aspiration to achieve universality by means of assimilation to the spirit of the modern state was judged by Levinas nonetheless to have been a failure. In an essay from 1954, 'Assimilation Today', Levinas points to the Dreyfus Affair and National Socialism as shaking 'the material and philosophical foundations on which European Judaism had rested for 150 years' (DF, 255) – foundations established in the Enlightenment and Napoleon's invitation to Jews to become citizens and subscribe to the republican principles of liberty, equality and fraternity. While shaken, these foundations were by no means overturned, for after 150 years 'the men, things and landscapes of the West are a substantially real world for Judaism' (DF, 255). Yet the invitation to assimilate has proved a failure for two reasons. First of all 'it did not put an end to the anguish felt by the Jewish soul' (DF, 255) since, for Levinas, 'every Jew remains, in the largest sense of the word, a Marrano,' (DF, 255), not in the narrow sense of being a Marrano Christian but in the broader sense of being a Marrano republican. In the second place, and linked to the anguish that attends assimilation to the spirit of the republic, assimilation 'did not placate the non-Jews, or put an end to anti-Semitism' (DF, 255). The climate of anti-Semitism that accompanied the republic arose from the definitions of fraternity which, as was shown above, could potentially exclude Jewish citizens.

While the Shoah made the failure of assimilation undeniable, the conditions were nevertheless established for a redefinition of Jewish identity in the Diaspora and a redefinition of citizenship on the basis of the Jewish experience. The Shoah and the foundation of the State of Israel showed the reason for the failure of assimilation to lie in the Christian character of the modern state. Drawing on what he had learnt from Durkheim, Levinas judged that 'Ignorance of the secularised forms of religious life at the heart of the secularised states themselves was the fundamental vice of the philosophy of assimilation' (DF, 256). Levinas now develops a new argument for understanding the relationship between religion and the state, maintaining that 'There exists in fact an element of diffuse religion, halfway between the strictly rational order of political thought and the mystical order of belief, in which political life itself swims' (DF, 256). This elemental religiosity or 'national spirit' has so 'impregnated daily social customs' that it has become invisible. It is the medium for the political, just as the *il y a* was the medium for existence. For Levinas the foundation of the State of Israel gives the example of an elemental religiosity that is Jewish, and this is important 'independently of its significance for the political destiny of the Jewish people' (DF, 257) nameley, for revealing through contrast the otherwise imperceptible Christian character of the secular states. Yet is not Levinas forgetting his own lesson, that part of this 'element of diffuse religion' in the modern state is indebted to Talmudic conceptions of justice, equality and fraternity, and that the composition of the element of modern political life is rather more complex than is conceded in the contrast of Israel with Christian politics?

Levinas insists that the State of Israel makes evident to Jews in the Diaspora the crypto-Christianity of their citizenship – what seemed a secular 'highest spiritual value' is revealed as a form of Christianity. It also gives an explanation for the anguish of the Marrano republican, since it shows that the anguish of the Jewish citizen is well-founded, given the Christian character of the modern state – Levinas goes so far as to suggest that the Marrano in the broad republican sense is also a Marrano in the narrow, Christian sense of the term:

> Jews' entry into the national life of the European states has led them to breathe an atmosphere impregnated with Christian essence, and that prepares them for the religous life of these states and heralds their conversion. The strictly private Judaism that advocated assimilation did not escape this unconscious Christianisation. (DF, 257)

The 'unconscious Christianisation' has now been made conscious by the existence of the State of Israel, making it impossible to return to assimilation in the old sense of putting the apparently universal principles of citizenship in a modern state above those of a particular religious identity.

Levinas's claim that modern states are impregnated with a 'Christian essence' is at once too total a rejection of modern citizenship and a denial of his other claim that rabbinic Judaism anachronistically anticipates the 'spirit' of the modern state. He will argue subsequently for a distinction within these principles between the Talmudic/Christian virtues of justice and equality and the exclusively Christian definition of fraternity that informs the revolutionary principles. He will also argue for a fourth 'political dimension' to the three dimensions of liberty, equality and fraternity in his great essay on Jewish identity and modern citizenship 'Space is not One-Dimensional' (1968), written soon after the Six Days War. However, the position argued then and after goes considerably beyond that developed in the 1950s. Rather than redefining citizenship and the founding values of the modern state in the light of Jewish experience, a redefinition emerging from a reconsideration of the bases of Western thought, he continued in the 1950s to search for a new principle of Jewish identity in the Diaspora that would be neither assimilationist nor Zionist.

In 'Assimilation Today' Levinas comments that 'if we wish to remain citizens of the great Western nations, participate in their values, guarantee the resulting duties, but remain Jews, we have to resolve to follow a new discipline' (DF, 257). This new discipline is the 'revival of Jewish science', already mentioned in the context of Israel but now extended to the Diaspora. It consists in confronting the questions of 'do we still want to be Jews?' and 'do we still believe in the excellence of Judaism?' (DF, 258) by means of study. What this meant was explained in an earlier essay, 'Reflection on Jewish Education', from 1951. The 'existence of Jews who wish to remain Jews – even apart from belonging to the State of Israel – depends on Jewish education' (DF, 265). This entails education in Hebrew and the study of the Talmud, activities to which Levinas deeply committed himself as a teacher and administrator for the Alliance and in his Talmudic commentaries.

The argument for the universality of the spirit of the book – paradoxically conducted in terms of kindling and transmission of fire – is complemented by another form of universality in the 1961 essay 'Heidegger, Gagarin and Us'. Here Levinas synthetically confronts the main themes of his post-war work, the critique of Heidegger and the memory of Nazism, the Cold War and political ontology and the character of Jewish identity. The opening evocation of commonplace fears of technology is prelude to a celebration of its destruction of a pagan sense of place, a vocation that it shares, for Levinas, with Judaism. Levinas writes:

Technology wrenches us out of the Heideggerian world and the superstitions surrounding *Place*. From this point on, an opportunity appears to us: to perceive men outside the situation in which they are placed, and let the human face shine in all its nudity. (DF, 232–3)

Levinas regards Gagarin as the most consequential critic of Heidegger; 'what counts most of all is that he left the Place' (DF, 233) and by living totally uprooted 'beyond any horizon', freed the human from the pagan particularism of place and from the cruelty that attends the distinction of human beings between 'natives and strangers'. The figure of humanity uprooted and a stranger in the world relying on others and offering food, drink, and shelter is one in which 'Man is his own master, in order to serve man' (DF, 233).

Levinas ends by aligning the universality of Judaism with that of technology, opposing both to a pagan sense of place and the Christian integration of place into sacred geography. Judaism, he concludes, 'Like technology, has demystified the universe. It has freed nature from a spell. Because of its abstract universalism, it runs up against imaginations and passions. But it has discovered man in the nudity of his face' (DF, 234). With this, the universality of Judaism and of technology promise an ethics – in Levinas's words, they announce a 'faith in man's liberation' (DF, 231). This liberation follows not from an ontology of place, nor from the subordination of the power of technology to a political ontology of territory, but from the discovery of an ethical universality that is otherwise than being and anachronistically anticipated in rabbinic Judaism.

Israel: between totality and the ethical

Levinas's thought in the 1950s was inseparable from the reflection on the political, specifically the political horror of National Socialism, the Cold War and the question of Jewish identity and the State of Israel. His reflections on the political required a root-and-branch recasting of the philosophical structures that informed the modern political, showing the extreme consequences of political ontology in the National Socialist and Soviet Socialist totalitarian states. The elaboration of a non-ontological philosophy that breaks with the Western tradition and its ontological terminus in Heidegger was driven by the experience of the Shoah and the difficult heritage for Jewish identity that it posed. The development of a critique of ontology both drew from and shaped the redefinition of Jewish identity that Levinas began during the 1940s and 1950s.

It is not surprising that the State of Israel should prove the site for a number of problems in these renegotiations. It provided an answer to the problem of Jewish identity, but one which was entirely complicit with the political ontologies that Levinas was otherwise criticising. On the one hand Levinas sought to defend the State of Israel by recognising in it a radical transformation of political ontology in the direction of a universal ethics, while on the other he rejected any attempt to restrict the thinking and the making of Israel to a place or territory and, by extension, any attempt to reduce Israel to the terms of political ontology. The two responses to the State of Israel closely correspond to the movement of Levinas's two main works – *Totality and Infinity* and *Otherwise than Being* – between the internal critique and retrieval of ontology and the elaboration of an ethics that is otherwise than being and thus beyond ontology.

The two positions are not mutually exclusive, do not obey the law of the excluded middle; they together represent a transformation of the terms of political ontology before the fact of Jewish identity as both diasporic and tied to a nation-state. In his non-ontological rethinking of the political, Levinas will see the Jewish experience of an identity, at once diasporic and tied to a territory, as exemplary for modern political identity in general. His philosophical negotiation of the condition of the Jewish citizen within and beyond political ontology will be extended into a general account of the political. Hence the importance of the two great texts as works of political philosophy considered in the next chapter. The significance of the tension between the sacred history of Israel and the place of the State of Israel in universal history will be considered in Chapter Five.

BETWEEN WAR AND PEACE
The burdens of *Totality and Infinity*

> My critique of totality follows in effect from a political expe-
> rience that we have still not forgotten. (EI, 73)

Totality and war

The significance of working through the experience of political horror by
means of a critique of the concept of totality became gradually apparent
during the 1950s. Yet in retrospect the reasons for this choice of critical
terrain seem compelling: the term 'totality' was sufficiently broad to hold
both the specific political critique of the totalitarian political of National
Socialism and the general philosophical critique of Western metaphysics.
'Totality' was at once the specific term identified by Victor Klemperer, the
philologist of the language of the Third Reich, as 'one of the keystones' of
'everyday Nazi discourse'[1] as well as, and perhaps not coincidentally, one of
the central concepts of modern philosophy, featuring significantly in the
works of Kant, Fichte, Schelling and Hegel. *Totality and Infinity* is a report
on Levinas's investigation of the complicity between philosophical and political totality that began with Heideggerian ontology, then moved on first to
German Idealism and finally to the entire tradition of Western philosophy.

The term 'totality' in Levinas's work of the 1950s aligned a number of
related, but by no means identical, critical trajectories. The most significant
was the claim that Western political thought and institutions depended on
an 'implicit or explicit metaphysics' informed by a notion of totality and
predisposed towards a totalitarian concept of the political. This view
informed Levinas's argument in 'The Spirit of Geneva' that non-totalitarian
politics were only possible as a postponement of the political consequences
of the metaphysical principles of Western philosophy, prime among which is
'totality'. This broad critique of the principle of totality was further aligned
with a number of more specific sub-critiques. The fusion of universality and
force that characterised National Socialist bio-politics and the nuclear
cosmo-politics of the Cold War offer specific examples of political totality to
which may be added the concept of economy adopted from Bataille and

used in Levinas's critique of capitalism to denote the closed 'total' system of possession and exchange. Linked with the latter usage was the use of totality to denote 'objectification', in terms of the translation of freedom into law through institutions and creativity into objects through work.

Apart from grouping together a number of complementary directions of argument, the term 'totality' also possesses some important if equivocal disjunctive properties. In a paradox that Levinas will exploit in an alternative reading of the history of philosophy, the principle of totality is not itself total, but is dependent to a large extent on a relation to its opposite or contrary principle. In order to begin to imagine a non-totalitarian politics it is important not to be duped by the total rhetoric of claims to totality. Accordingly, Levinas repeatedly emphasises the dependence of totality on its opposite, notably in the title 'totality *and* infinity' but also in the chain of related disjunctives made up of the 'same and other' and 'interiority and exteriority'. While mobilising such disjunctive properties, Levinas by no means regards them as the poles of a dialectical movement. Rather, what is 'otherwise' than totality is understood more often in terms of what is immanent to it, what qualifies, checks, displaces or otherwise postpones its operations. Indeed it is often the more subtle disjunctive properties of totality and its other that are taken to characterise the concept of political justice that Levinas pursues beyond totality and totalitarianism.

The concept of totality describes a field of meaning whose character is dependent upon its relationship to its other and the ways in which this relationship is conceded and denied. Yet this should not be understood in terms of a dialectical movement of recognition and misrecognition, but rather as denoting the intrinsic incompletion of totality, the qualification or postponement of its realisation. The 'exterior' thus always qualifies totality and destabilises its claims, since totality must contain all exteriority or forfeit its claim to be 'total'. Totality would seem always to be confined to aspiration, moving towards a realisation that is endlessly deferred by its encounter with exteriority. The view of totality as a constantly frustrated movement can be contrasted with the acceptance of the necessity of movement. From the first perspective the movement from totality towards exteriority attempts the violent identification of totality and exteriority through war. It strives to make exteriority present to totality even at the risk of its destruction. From the second perspective, the movement from exteriority differentiates totality internally and anachronistically disrupts its identity. In this movement totality is dispersed into a pluralism or an anarchy. The movement of ascent from totality to infinity is also the descent from infinity to totality – the first movement is described by Levinas as 'ontology', the second as 'ethics'. What is most important here is the movement or mutual orientation produced by the disjunctive relationship between them, one that Levinas describes as the 'work of justice' and which led ineluctably to the difficult thought of the mutual implication of the wars of ontology and the peace of ethics.

From the outset of *Totality and Infinity* the 'work of justice' is situated between war and peace – it is neither solely the violent identification of the other in the totality of the same nor the peaceful dissolution of the self's claim to totality before the face of the other. While politics as the mastery of social forces is allied with ontology and war, politics as the 'work of justice' is neither ontological nor ethical, neither war nor peace, but describes the movement within the interval between them. This is an important specification, since it opens the space for a political realism within the 'work of justice' which should not be understood as an ethical utopia. The work of justice is as consistent with the acknowledgement of the war implied in peace as the peace implied in war. In short, politics as the work of justice should not be understood as a synthesis of ontology and ethics since it is neither an ethically qualified ontology nor an ontologically qualified ethics, neither the moralisation of the real nor the realisation of the ethical.

From this standpoint, 'politics' describes the movement between ontology and ethics, a movement that can assume many political figures. An all too conceivable politics would consist in the exacerbation of the violence of identification when confronted by the alterity of the other, a totalitarian politics of anti-Semitism. Another politics would find the violence of totality dispersed by the encounter with the other, or even displaced or postponed. What is common to them all is the siting of the political in the movement between totality and the other, thus linking the question of orientation with the work of justice.

Finding the political in the movement of totality and infinity has a number of implications for Levinas's concept of the political. It puts in question any attempt to add a political dimension to the ethical relation; the latter is already implicated in a political movement. It also re-orients Levinas's two main texts, *Totality and Infinity* and *Otherwise than Being*, marking the movement between the texts as a particular siting of the political. Levinas's concept of the political is to be found between the movement from ontological totality to ethical infinity in the first text, and from ethics to subjectivity and sensibility in the second. It is a movement guided by a disjunctive logic that throughout *Totality and Infinity* solicits the ethical within ontology and, in *Otherwise than Being*, the ontological within the ethical. It is the lack of joint between ethics and ontology that opens the space for politics, but which also leaves the character of that space undecidable.[2]

It is within the movement between ethics and ontology, which is also one between war and peace, that Levinas will try to locate the historical meaning of Israel and the prophetic politics that it is called upon to represent. Yet it is by no means a simple movement that can be exhausted by the citation of the political figure of the 'State of Israel' as somehow denoting the ontological realisation of the ethical. The complexity of the movement is evident in the relationship between Levinas's two major texts as well as in the real existing history of the state called Israel. *Totality and Infinity* makes the passage from war to peace by way of a disengagement from ontology and an orientation with respect to ethical infinity, while *Otherwise than Being* rehearses the disengagement from ontology but finds that its presentation of the 'extreme conceptual possibilities' of peace expressed in the new ethical categories of proximity, substitution and the hostage ineluctably recall the themes of ontology and, with them, war. The prophetic politics of justice that would emerge in the dangerous space between ontology and ethics is in neither case free from the risk of war.

From lucidity to vigilance: the questions of *Totality and Infinity*

The question with which *Totality and Infinity* begins – 'whether we are not duped by morality' (TI, 21) – is answered at the end of the fourth and final section of the book, 'Beyond the Face'. There, after giving the formal redefinition of fraternity that he had pursued consistently since the 1930s, Levinas concludes that without 'the infinite time of triumph…goodness would be subjectivity and folly' (TI, 280). That is to say, we *are* duped by morality when morality and goodness are not understood in terms of the 'infinite time of triumph'. Levinas arrives at the latter phrase by means of the analyses of fraternity, the erotic, fecundity and the family that comprise Section IV of *Totality and Infinity*, but informing this analysis is a broader preoccupation with the issue of perpetual peace or the messianic 'infinite time of triumph'.

The link between *Totality and Infinity* and Levinas's earlier concerns is confirmed in the final part of Section IV, 'The Infinity of Time', that rehearses the dual critique of Bergson and Heidegger's notions of time. This critical movement is familiar from Levinas's work of the 1930s and was later described in the lectures *God, Death and Time* by the title 'Inside Heidegger: Bergson'. It is in this context that the 'infinite time of triumph' is disclosed as a 'messianic time' within and beyond history: 'Messianic triumph is the pure triumph; it is secured against the revenge of evil whose return the infinite time does not prohibit. Is this eternity a new structure of time, or an extreme vigilance of the messianic consciousness?' (TI, 285). This concluding question, the answer to the opening question of whether we are 'duped by morality', 'exceeds the bounds of this book' but also repeats its movement between the totality of eternity and the infinity of the ever deferred vigilance of the 'messianic consciousness'.

At issue in the movement between the opening question of morality and the closing question of the messianic is the basic theme of *Totality and Infinity*, namely, war and peace. The messianic triumph consists in the victory of peace over war, but the closing question of the work is one

97

of whether 'perpetual peace' may not itself be in turn another totality that must be subject to the vigilance of the 'messianic consciousness'. This closing question throws light on Levinas's rapid transition in the preface from the question of the deceptions of morality to the question of war. The closing appeal to 'messianic vigilance' is anticipated in the preface in the term 'lucidity'. After posing the question of morality, Levinas continues: 'Does not lucidity, the mind's openness upon the true, consist in catching sight of the permanent possibility of war?' (TI, 21). The 'possibility of war' and the possibility of the 'revenge of evil' that are the respective objects of 'lucidity' and the 'extreme vigilance of the messianic consciousness' at the beginning and end of *Totality and Infinity* are the same, and underline the fact that the question of peace is never far from that of war.

Although they are the same, there is nevertheless a movement between lucidity as 'the mind's openness upon the true' and the 'extreme vigilance of the messianic consciousness' in the face of the possible revenge of evil. It is a movement that figures the transition from ontology to ethics or from philosophy to the religious. In the course of *Totality and Infinity* the horizon of philosophical lucidity is exposed as the ethical command of the other that is the concern of the vigilance of messianic consciousness. The movement between (or within) lucidity and vigilance is accomplished by means of a reflection on the relationship between war, totality, the same and ontology. This movement is shadowed by a set of relations whose outlines are evident even within the philosophical tradition, and whose movement orients peace with respect to the infinite, alterity and the ethical.

While war and peace are the primary objects of Levinas's inquiry in *Totality and Infinity*, his method of analysis demands extended detours along the pathways of ontology, ethics and transcendence. Before following these pathways it may be helpful to consider some of his general comments on the motivation and the method of the work.

One the most revealing methodological comments occurs towards the end of the preface where Levinas situates his work with respect to Franz Rosenzweig and the phenomenological method.[3] With respect to the former he notes that 'We were impressed by the opposition to the idea of totality in Franz Rosenzweig's *Stern der Erlösung*, a work too often present in this book to be cited' (TI, 28). The acknowledgement of a debt to Rosenzweig situates *Totality and Infinity* within the horizon of the latter's 'new thinking' or the extension of the critique of German Idealism and, in particular, Hegel to the 'Ionic tradition' of Western philosophy. Levinas's work will thus, like that of Rosenzweig (but implicitly also that of Heidegger), provide a reckoning with the ontological investment of the Western philosophical tradition – 'from Ionia to Jena', in Rosenzweig's phrase – an investment figured in that tradition's commitment to the concept of totality. However, while indebted to Rosenzweig's 'new thinking', Levinas does not subscribe to its method, which remains immersed in the language and conceptual architecture of classical German Idealism. Instead he pursues the critique of totality by means of the resources bequeathed by Husserlian phenomenology, in particular its method of intentional analysis. While adopting the critique of totality, Levinas's 'presentation and the development of the notions employed owe everything to the phenomenological method' (TI, 28).

The critique of totality is carried out by means of intentional analysis, but Levinas's use of this method must be understood in terms of the radical version of it developed in his phenomenological writings. This involves a form of intentional analysis that is not restrained by the structure of *noema* and *noesis*. Nevertheless, in *Totality and Infinity* the opening moves of Levinas's intentional analysis appeal to Husserlian orthodoxy:

> Intentional analysis is the search for the concrete. Notions held under the direct gaze of the thought that defines them are nevertheless, unbeknown to this naïve thought, revealed to be implanted in horizons unsuspected by this thought; these horizons endow them with a meaning – such is the essential teaching of Husserl. (TI, 28)

Levinas considers himself to depart from this teaching by emphasising the movement of revelation that takes place in the act of *noesis* and that carries it beyond the *noema* that is revealed. This is an excessive movement that can be traced through the method of phenomenological deduction in which

> What counts is the idea of the overflowing of objectifying thought by a forgotten experience from which it lives. The break up of the formal structure of thought (the noema of a noesis) into events which this structure dissimulates, but which sustain it and restore its concrete significance, constitutes a *deduction*... (TI, 28)[4]

Levinas quickly moves to locate the excess described by the phenomenological deduction, first with respect to 'metaphysical transcendence' and then with respect to the ethical. He intends to prove not only that 'ethical relations are to lead transcendence to its term' (TI, 29) but also to show the reason why this is possible, namely because ethics offers a transcendent intention that is not governed by the theoretical opposition of *noesis* and *noema*: 'because the essential of ethics is in its *transcendent intention*, and because not every transcendent intention has the noesis–noema structure' (TI, 29). Levinas's methodological challenge to the primacy of theoretical reason and transcendence entails more than the technical reprise of an aspect of his critique of Husserlian phenomenology. It is indeed essential to establishing the argumentative structure of *Totality and Infinity*. He claims that the 'traditional opposition between theory and practice will disappear before the metaphysical transcendence by which a relation with the absolutely other, or truth, is established and of which ethics is the royal road' (TI, 29). This claim disrupts the pretensions to primacy of both theoretical and practical reason:

> Hitherto the relation between theory and practice was not conceivable other than as a solidarity or a hierarchy: activity rests on cognitions that illuminate it; knowledge requires from acts the mastery of matter, minds and societies – a technique, a morality, a politics – that procures the peace necessary for its pure exercise. (TI, 29)

This passage is important not only for illustrating Levinas's suspension of the difference between theoretical and practical reason, but also for distinguishing his position from any attempt to assert the primacy of practical over theoretical reason. Levinas's suspension of the distinction between theoretical and practical reason self-consciously distances his approach from that of the Heideggerian analytic of *Dasein*. While conceding that technical, moral and political mastery provide the conditions of peace necessary for the pursuit of theoretical reflection, it is clear that this is not the peace sought by Levinas in his analysis of ethical transcendence. Yet this immediately and deliberately puts into question the context of his notion of the political, which is neither a theoretical ideal guiding action nor the routine acts of societal mastery exposed by sociology and empirical political science.

In the preface to *Totality and Infinity* Levinas emphasises the critical aspect of the phenomenological deduction, its function in making possible a critique of totality. However, implied in the method is a reference to an excess that transcends any totality. The character of this excess is explored throughout the text, first by means of the deductive phenomenologies of theoretical philosophy in the 'arid' Section I on 'The Same and the Other', and then through the practical philosophy of everyday life that echoes Heidegger's 'Analytic of Dasein' in Section II on 'Interiority and Economy', followed by the analyses of ethics in Section III, 'Exteriority and the Face', and transcendent ethics in Section IV, 'Beyond the Face'. While it is clear that the excess in question cannot be understood ontologically, it is not the case that it is located in the ethical – the ethical or the relation to the other is but the 'royal road' to transcendence, it is not transcendence itself. This is indicated in the movement from ethics to transcendent ethics in Sections III and IV that Levinas describes in terms of the consummation of infinity.

The character of the transcendence in question is well described in 'The Other and the Others', (Section III, Part C, Section 6), in the context of a discussion of fraternity. After introducing the asymmetry that constitutes responsibility before the face of the other, Levinas goes on to describe fraternity in terms of a plural community of singularities who are not distinguished as differences within a genus but as the kin of a common divine father: 'Monotheism signifies this human kinship, this idea of a human race that refers back to the approach of the Other in the face, in a dimension of height, in responsibility for oneself and for the Other' (TI, 214). What is most significant in this passage is not so much the terms 'oneself' and 'other' but the theme of orientation expressed in such terms as 'reference', 'approach' and 'height'. Fraternity does not so much describe a relationship (community) between two terms as the movement of orientation towards community in responsibility.

The emphasis upon an excessive movement rather than an excessive term (such as 'other' or 'divine') is explicitly endorsed in the following Section 7, 'The Asymmetry of the Interpersonal'. Levinas describes the movement that commits one 'to human fraternity' as speech, or being 'in relationship while absolving oneself from this relation' (TI, 215). The movement between I and other is then described in a rich lexicon of terms, including engagement/disengagement, positioning, presenting and separating. Levinas concludes that it is the movement of orientation expressed in these terms that constitutes transcendence. It is not that the I or the other is transcendent – which would be to oppose a Cartesian position to its inverse – but rather the movement of orientation expressed in terms of relation/non-relation, engagement/disengagement, position, presentation and responsibility. Levinas confirms that the differences between I and the other are not fundamental but 'due to the I–other conjuncture, to the inevitable *orientation* of being "starting from oneself" towards "the Other". The priority of this orientation over the terms that are placed in it (and which cannot arise without this orientation) summarises the theses of the present work' (TI, 215). According to this summary it is the movement of orientation rather than the relation of I and the other that is the locus of transcendence.

The stress upon transcendent movement is consistent with the position of 'extreme vigilance' discussed above. It is not that messianic peace is ever achieved or perhaps even achievable, but rather that we are always orienting ourselves with respect to it; peace is always in the process of arriving. The stress on the approach rather than the condition of peace is also, as Levinas goes on to show, consistent with a critique of ontological totality:

> Being *is* not *first*, to afterwards, by breaking up, give place to a diversity all of whose terms would maintain reciprocal relations among themselves, exhibiting thus the totality from which they

proceed, and in which there would on occasion be produced a
being existing for itself, an I, facing another I... (TI, 215)

Priority is given to the movement of orientation that dissembles itself
in terms of the being and/or of self and other. The process of orientation,
however, does not yield an unequivocal result. The movement can as
easily result in war and the mutual destruction of self and other as in
their fraternal flourishing. Orientation 'leaves room for a process of
being that is deduced from itself [totality], that is, remains separated and
capable of shutting itself up against the very appeal that has aroused it,
but also capable of welcoming this face of infinity with all the resources
of its egoism: economically' (TI, 216). The self embroiled within totality
can orient itself towards a war against the other in a bid to preserve its
identity and resources, or towards a welcoming of the other in a redistri-
bution of its resources and a risking of its identity. The outcomes of
orientation are not mutually exclusive, but are developments that contain
each other and thus call for vigilance. The risk to self and other necessarily involved in managing orientation calls for both lucidity and
vigilance.

Levinas's discussion of the different movements in orientation concludes
with a reference to 'Multiplicity in being, which refuses totalisation but
takes form as fraternity and discourse, situated in a "space" essentially
asymmetrical' (TI, 216). This multiplicity in being emerges from a movement of orientation that can settle neither in absolute alterity nor in
totality. The negotiation of this tension between the movements towards
alterity and totality constitutes the political and the philosophical in the
spaces of fraternity and discourse: it is described as emerging first of all as
'fraternity' and then as discourse. Fraternity – the central problem of
Levinas's political thought – is here given precedence over discourse, the
analysis of which (in terms of 'the saying and the said') has hitherto dominated the reading of Levinas's philosophy.

A further implication of the attention paid to orientation and its directions is that both war and peace, multiplicity and totality, are implicated in
each other. They do not constitute absolute positions, but provisional
orientations fraught with risk. Even, perhaps especially, a political orientation towards fraternity is always in danger of tending towards a totality
such as those of class, confession, nation or race that support claims to
totality by means of the deadly exclusion of alterity. Analogously, a philosophical tradition oriented towards totality can also contain elements of
multiplicity. Levinas points to the latter in a number of places, notably in
the discussion of Plato's idea of the Good, Descartes's notion of infinity
and Kant's appeal to hope. These provide moments in which the ontological tradition exceeds itself. At one point Levinas even speculates that
Plato's notion of the transcendence of the idea of the Good over being

'should have served as the foundation of a pluralist philosophy in which the plurality of being would not disappear into the unity of number nor be integrated in a totality' (TI, 80). However, this tendency was contained by recasting transcendence in terms of the negation of totality instead of regarding it as the multiple processes of 'separation and transcendence which are the themes of this book' and which make up 'the fabric of being itself' (TI, 81).

The disjunction evident in the title of *Totality and Infinity* should be read as both a complement and an opposition. The refusal of Manichean oppositions that characterise Levinas's method and his view of the primacy of orientation over that which is oriented carries over into his reflections on war, peace and the concept of the political. The movement from the lucidity evoked in the opening pages of the book to the messianic vigilance of its close represents a re-orientation of thought from the truth of war underlying the deceptions of morality to the promise of peace. However, as will be seen, war and peace are never far from each other, an insight that is as crucial for Levinas's philosophical view of the political as it is for his political judgement in a hard case such as the State of Israel.

War in peace

Only beings capable of war can rise to peace. (TI, 222)

Totality and Infinity followed more than a decade of reflection on war – the genocidal world war of National Socialism, the Cold War and the wars associated with the foundation and defence of the State of Israel. It is thus not too surprising that it is pre-occupied from start to finish with the issue of war and peace. The text, as Derrida has noted, works according to a rhythmic pulse which joins and separates a number of discrete themes of argument. The overture to these movements is the preface, which introduces the main themes and intimates their variations. These few dense pages exemplify the way in which Levinas expanded and transformed the question of morality and prepared the ground for the introduction of the deductive phenomenological method. They prepare for the extended development of the themes of 'war and commerce' and the 'work of justice' that takes place in the text.

The preface to *Totality and Infinity* describes how war disorients morality. The opening apostrophe to 'lucidity' describes it in terms of the vision of the 'permanent possibility of war'. Lucidity thus consists in the sight of the 'shadow' that 'falls over the actions of men', a shadow that 'divests the eternal institutions and obligations of their eternity and rescinds ad interim the unconditional imperatives', and that 'renders morality derisory' (TI, 21). War is oblivious to any defence of the given institutional and moral orientations of action in terms of their eternal and absolute value. Under the lucid gaze which sees war everywhere, politics becomes the 'art of foreseeing war and winning it by every means', an art which is 'henceforth enjoined as the very exercise of reason' (TI, 21). The lucid detection of the presence of war within the resorts of morality prepares the main challenge of the text, which is to disclose a pacific vigilance folded in its turn within militant lucidity.

From the perspective of the opening paragraphs, politics as the art of war is equivalent to the lucidity of reason, since war is the truth of being and lucidity the 'openness upon the true'. War is described as 'the pure experience of pure being' – the moment when 'the drapings of illusion burn' – a movement of destructive re-orientation: 'The ontological event that takes form in this black light is a casting into movement of beings hitherto anchored in their identity, a mobilisation of absolutes, by an objective order from which there is no escape' (TI, 21). War is thus an omnipresent, ineluctable and *total* movement that tends to destroy both the identity and the alterity that are its vehicles: 'War does not manifest exteriority and the other as the other; it destroys the identity of the same' (TI, 21). Politics according to this definition is allied to the self-destructive work of reason that, using war to overcome war, finds itself implicated in a process of self-destruction – carrying out 'actions that will destroy every possibility of action' – the formal description of Levinas's political critique of nuclear warfare developed in 'The Spirit of Geneva'.

An important stage in the argument for the self-destructive tendencies of war is the postulate of an ineluctable 'objective order' that 'casts into movement beings hitherto anchored' and that 'mobilises absolutes'. Here Levinas understands the re- and dis-orientations of war as expressions of an excess that nevertheless does not 'manifest exteriority'. The transcendence of war is manifest in an immanent drive or force that turns upon itself and is incapable of recognising exteriority. War, continues Levinas, has implications for metaphysics in so far as it 'establishes an order from which no-one can keep his distance; nothing henceforth is exterior' (TI, 21). War, in other words, claims to be total, and yet is driven by the frustration provoked by the pursuit of a total order that remains dependent upon an other or enemy.

After deducing the total character of war, Levinas proceeds to make an important link between war, totality and philosophy. He states that 'The visage of being that shows itself in war is fixed in the concept of totality that dominates Western philosophy' (TI, 21). The face that is assumed by being in war is that of a mobilised objective order, and it is this combination of a wholly immanent yet mobilised objective order that constitutes the dominant philosophical concept of totality. Levinas here is claiming not only that the dominant experience informing Western philosophy is

cf. beginning of AE.

war, but also that philosophy shares with war the tendency to mobilise a rigorously immanent 'objective order' or totality.

Levinas illustrates this claim by returning to his earlier work on Nazism, and in particular its concept of an expansive force whose excess over any totality can only be expressed destructively. In his illustration, individuals are 'reduced to being bearers of forces that command them'; their meaning is 'derived from the totality' and, as bearers of a force expressing a totality unknown to them, they become implicated in a logic of sacrifice in which 'the unicity of each present is incessantly sacrificed to a future appealed to to bring forth its objective meaning' (TI, 22). The object of sacrifice is not just the present, but the identity of the present and of the subject living in the present: the meaning of the subject is relegated to totality – an experience that Levinas will describe by using the Marxist term 'alienation'. Yet, as we have seen, the meaning of war is self-destruction – sacrifice for the sake of sacrifice – a thesis bleakly illustrated in Levinas's example of nuclear warfare. The rational lucidity of philosophy was earlier described as the insight into the permanent possibility of war, an insight which is now shown to be implicated in war, and perhaps even complicit with its perpetuation.

Just over a page into *Totality and Infinity* and the answer to the question of morality already seems evident – given the totality of war, we are indeed duped by morality. 'Moral consciousness' withers before 'the mocking gaze of the political man' who subscribes to the totality of war, seeing and foreseeing it everywhere and guiding his actions by this insight. Even peace is implicated in war: 'The peace of empires issued from war rests on war. It does not restore to the alienated beings their lost identity' (TI, 22). The sacrifices called forth by war are not restored by an armed peace, for peace requires a 'primordial and original relation with being'. We will only cease to be duped by morality 'when the eschatology of messianic peace will have come to superpose itself upon the ontology of war' (TI, 22). With this is announced the theme of the vigilance of 'messianic consciousness' – for eschatology escapes the claims of totality and for this reason is distrusted by philosophers for whom, being outside of totality, it can only appear as an irrational quantity or a matter of faith. Yet Levinas is careful not to replace totality by eschatology, but rather to 'superpose' the latter upon the former, or even, in the cases of Plato and Descartes and Kant, to discover it already nested within ontology.

The 'primordial and original relation' to being is thus contained within ontology while also exceeding it. It is not simply futural, since this would make eschatology compatible with totality – the fear of a 'new structure of time' or realised peace that would be but an expression of the completion of totality. Eschatology is not oriented according to the telos of a given totality, but is 'a relationship with a *surplus always exterior to the totality*, as though the objective totality did not fill out the true measure of being, as though another concept, the concept of *infinity* were needed to express this transcendence with respect to totality, non-encompassable within a totality and as primordial as totality' (TI, 22–3). In eschatology transcendence is manifest as exteriority, a surplus that does not appear in the self-destructive drive to totality, nor in the void surrounding totality, but as its other.

Levinas immediately employs the transcendence of eschatology in a radical revision of any Hegelian philosophy of history that would envisage totality in terms of the gathered past, present and future of history. Transcendence implies that 'beings' are not simply manifestations of the totality from which they borrow their meaning, but 'have an identity "before" eternity, before the accomplishment of history, before the fullness of time, while there is still time' (TI, 23). From the standpoint of eschatology, each moment is in an absolute relation to eternity, not one mediated by history. At each moment, beings 'exist in relationship...but on the basis of themselves and not on the basis of the totality' (TI, 23). Instead of being expressions of totality, beings are now responsible for their actions, and able to give account of themselves. Transcendence or the 'idea of being overflowing history' makes possible

> *existents* that can speak rather than lending their lips to an anonymous utterance of history. Peace is produced as this aptitude for speech. The eschatological vision breaks with the totality of wars and empires in which one does not speak. It does not envisage the end of history within being understood as a totality, but institutes a relation with being which exceeds totality. (TI, 23)

The latter relation will emerge as the orientation prior to the terms oriented discussed earlier – what is significant at this point is Levinas's concession that the eschatological relation does not simply break the relation to totality, but is also capable of *instituting* a new, excessive relation to being. This moment of institution is of course vital for a conception of the political that will exceed the preliminary definition of politics as the art of foreseeing war. Yet this opening onto a new thinking of the theme of institution remains entangled with Levinas's equivocation with respect to ontology. In *Totality and Infinity*, transcendence discloses an original or primordial relation to being occluded by totality; this revised ontology is the key to any reconsideration of political institution, but is by no means affirmed, even in this text.

The problem of an eschatological politics is immediately confronted by Levinas in the guise of a claim that 'Of peace there can only be an eschatology' (TI, 24) – that the 'irrefutable evidence of totality' founded in 'the experience of war' refutes eschatology in the same way as it refutes morality. Does not the salvation of morality by means of an appeal to eschatology simply displace the site of deception, replacing the danger of being duped by morality with that of being duped by eschatology? Levinas concedes this danger with respect to ontology, or that 'apprehension of an object' in which 'the bonds with truth are woven'. War, it seems, is capable of burning away even the drapings of messianic eschatology, revealing it as a 'subjective opinion and illusion'. At this point it would seem as if any attempt to institute eschatology would deliver it to ontology for unmasking by the experience of war. Yet Levinas argues that eschatological peace is prior to war and is more than the end of war; it is a movement of orientation whose transcendence can be translated into the force of war. This is to claim no less than that there is a movement of orientation prior to being, one that from this side of being appears as a primordial relation to being.

Levinas calls as witness for this process of translation the structurally hypocritical character of the civilisation of war. He notes ironically that

> ever since eschatology has opposed peace to war the evidence of war has been maintained in an essentially hypocritical civilisation, that is, attached both to the True and the Good, henceforth antagonistic. It is perhaps time to see in hypocrisy not only a base contingent defect of man, but the underlying rending of a world attached to both the philosophers and the prophets. (TI, 24)

Levinas here points to an instability within totality wherein the world is torn by the incompatible claims for the truth of the ubiquity of war and respect for the good. What he does not emphasise, but what is also revealed in this passage, is a further complication in the position of the eschatological – it would seem that the opposition of peace to war is a declaration of war by peace upon war. In this case, even the peace of eschatology would be hypocritical, affirming war in the act of affirming peace. The significance of necessary violence that is intimated here surfaces immediately in the succeeding discussion of exteriority.

Levinas turns to a closer examination of the 'superposition' of the eschatological upon the ontological. He is careful to insist that he is advocating neither the 'substitution' of philosophy by eschatology or prophesy nor the philosophical demonstration of eschatological theses, but a methodological scrutiny of totality that 'works back' while remaining 'on this side of objective certitude'. He proposes in this spirit to 'proceed from the experience of totality back to a situation where totality breaks up, a situation that conditions the totality itself. Such a situation is the gleam of exteriority or of transcendence in the face of the Other. The rigorously developed concept of this transcendence is expressed by the term infinity' (TI, 24–5). Levinas thus 'works back' to the movement of transcendence provoked by the face of the other, showing how in the concept of infinity it is nevertheless maintained on this side of 'objective certitude'. When expressed immanently in terms of totality, this movement emerges as the destabilising drive of war; when expressed in terms of exteriority the movement is the orientation to transcendence.

What now emerges is that any movement provoked by the face of the other, whether oriented towards immanent totality or exterior infinity, is always violent. At this point in the preface Levinas poses another of the important questions of *Totality and Infinity*, this time concerning the relation between freedom and violence. Levinas asks: 'Would the violence which, for a mind, consists in welcoming a being to which it is inadequate contradict the ideal of autonomy that guides philosophy – which in evidence is mistress of her own truth?' (TI, 25). Levinas indirectly introduces a distinction between the violence directed against freedom and that directed by freedom. In the former, the welcome of the other violates the freedom of the autonomous subject since it arrives from a place beyond its power, while in the latter the free subject exercises violence in the expression of its power. The former violence, which will later come to constitute a call to responsibility, is 'To contain more than one's capacity...to shatter at every moment the framework of a content that is thought, to cross the barriers of immanence' (TI, 27). The containment of excess, termed by Levinas as 'the act of thought', 'involves a violence essentially: the violence of transivity, lacking in the transcendence of thought'. This violence does not 'mean to embrace or to encompass the totality of being in thought', but to shatter any possibility that thought might ever embrace or encompass totality. In the formal terms used by Levinas in the first part of *Totality and Infinity* – 'The Same and the Other' – the first violence is the shattering of the same by the other, while the second is the suppression of the other by the same or the violent subordination of its alterity to a claim to totality.

The notion of the 'act of thought' or the orientation towards the welcome of more than can be contained by the same, is the locus of a number of discrete arguments. Beside the argument for the priority of infinity over totality, of the other over the same, there is a further argument for the priority of production over disclosure. The 'act of thought...also named in its objective form as the "mode of being", "infinition"',[5] is opposed to Heidegger's notion of disclosure: the act of thought is not the disclosure of being but the production of an event. Through this event the 'entity simultaneously is brought about and is revealed' (TI, 26). This argument establishes an important link between violence, the act of thought and responsibility. The act of thought, which is also the 'eschatological vision', violently liberates a subjectivity from totality while also imposing upon it a call to responsibility: 'The idea of infinity delivers the subjectivity from the judgement of history to declare it ready for judgement at every moment...' (TI, 25). At each moment the subject is both judged and called to judge – a complex movement contained in the term responsibility and the 'work of justice' that it calls forth. In the 'act of thought' the subject is disclosed as responsible and in the act of commencing and recommencing the work of justice.

In order to show the 'philosophical primacy' of infinity over totality, Levinas proposes to 'recount how infinity is produced in the relationship of the same with the other, and how the particular and the personal, which are unsurpassable, as it were magnetise the very field in which the production of the infinite is enacted' (TI, 26). There are a number of important transitions nested in this recounting of the production of infinity that inform the structure of the entire work. Levinas begins by telling *how* infinity is produced – the mode of production of infinity involves the relation of same and other, and then describes how this relation – the field of production – is activated, 'magnetised', by the 'particular and the personal'. This entails the methodological progression from the field of philosophical abstraction – the same and the other – to the activation of that field by the concrete relations of the particular and the personal. This movement corresponds largely to that brought forward in the abstract analysis of the infinite relation in Section I, 'The Same and the Other', as well as the analyses of its concrete productions in Sections II and III, 'Interiority and Economy' and 'Exteriority and the Face'. These steps in the argument show the disclosure and the bringing about of infinity.

There is, however, a further important step in the argument that is announced after the discussion of infinition as a mode of being. This is the realisation by the subject of its responsibility before infinity. In this moment, when 'subjectivity realises these impossible exigencies' – realising in the sense of achieving and comprehending – infinity is not only produced but also consummated. In Levinas's words, 'This book will present subjectivity as welcoming the Other, as hospitality; in it the idea of infinity is consummated' (TI, 27). The consummation of infinity – welcoming the infinity of the other – is discussed in Section IV, 'Beyond the Face'. The welcome and hospitality of the other is the consummation of the infinity produced by the violent encounter with the other. In the first stage, subjectivity and its totality are shattered by the advent of infinity by means of the other, then they are reconstructed in the welcome and offer of hospitality extended to the other and the shattering that it brings with it.

The subjectivity intimated by Levinas is far from the sovereign, autonomous subject of modern philosophy inaugurated by Descartes with the *cogito*. The latter became the subject of modern political philosophy – the autonomous property owner who freely exchanges in commerce with other property owners or who creates a polity in a social contract with other free subjects. The paradoxical subject of *Totality and Infinity* does not achieve self-certainty through control over its property – whether its goods, its thoughts or its very self – but is defined by the hospitality extended to the other. With this, Levinas arrives at his critique of disclosure and then his endorsement of Rosenzweig and the deductive pheno-menological method with which we began.

In the preface to *Totality and Infinity*, Levinas announces the main themes of the work and the way in which they will be worked through. Two of these are of particular significance for understanding Levinas's concept of the political. The first is the theme of war and commerce and their relation to the social order. Associated with this theme are the sub-themes of institutions and the limits of freedom and the limits of a particular understanding of the political. The second theme is that of 'the work of justice', which is associated with the 'welcoming of the face' and the eschatological and messianic themes, and which provides the intima-tions of a notion of the just political.

War and the other

> War like peace presupposes beings structured otherwise than
> as parts of a totality. (TI, 222)

The theme of war that dominates the preface to *Totality and Infinity* haunts the remainder of the text. It appears in the first section where it informs a discussion of ontology, freedom and the philosophy of Heidegger and in the second section where it is central to a reflection upon insecurity and habitation. In the third section war is addressed in terms of violence and subjectivity while in the fourth section it appears in relation to a discussion of tyranny and the state. The theme of war can be seen to integrate the various stages and directions of the book, although it is always shadowed by its other, peace and the work of justice.

In the complex and stratified discussion, 'Metaphysics precedes Ontology', in Section I, war is presented as the most significant symptom of an 'allergic relation with alterity' for which *Totality and Infinity* proposes an antidote. But the preparation for this conclusion departs from a general reflection on theoretical philosophy and passes though an inquiry into the relation between ontology and freedom on to a specific critique of Heideggerian ontology. The latter is thus unequivocally associated for Levinas with a philosophy of war.

The opening lines of 'Metaphysics precedes Ontology' move from a view of knowing or the 'theoretical relation' that 'lets the known being manifest itself while respecting its alterity', to one that approaches 'the known being such that its alterity with regard to the knowing being vanishes' (TI, 42). Levinas concentrates on the second movement, regarding it as the dominant trope in Western philosophy, although not, as seen with respect to the Platonic idea of the Good and Descartes's infinite,

110

to the total exclusion of the first movement. He gives the second move-ment – the erasure of alterity – two linked phases. The first phase consists in the nihilistic imperialism of freedom according to which knowing is identified 'with the freedom of the knowing being encountering nothing which, other than with respect to it, could limit it' (TI, 42). The second phase in the eclipse of alterity, presented by Levinas as in some respects a condition for the first, is the neutralisation of alterity by its reduction to 'a third term, a neutral term' such as conceptuality, sensation, or – most significantly for Levinas – Being.

The earlier discussion of the neutrality of Being in terms of the *il y a* are here given a reprise, except that here Being is no longer figured as an anonymous rumble, but as light: 'Being, which is without the density of existents, is the light in which existents become intelligible' (TI, 42). This intelligibility to which is given the name 'ontology' nevertheless obscures alterity – the main function of the neutral light of Being, in other words, is to occlude alterity. Such occlusion is then said to promote freedom and the security of the subject: 'the freedom that is the identification of the same, not allowing itself to be alienated by the other' (TI, 42). The price of the occlusion of alterity or the surrender of exteriority in the name of identity is the renunciation of metaphysical desire and the 'marvel of exteriority' upon which it thrives.

Levinas immediately qualifies the apparent closure of the link between freedom and ontology by maintaining that the philosophical tradition itself 'calls into question the freedom of the exercise of ontology' (TI, 43). The spontaneous exercise of freedom is called into question by ethics, or in Levinas's words 'by the presence of the other', whose strangeness is irre-ducible 'to the I, to my thoughts and my possessions' (TI, 43). The welcome of the other – transcendence – is the calling into question of the same by the other, and by extension the calling into question of freedom, the neutrality of being and their product – the occlusion of alterity. Levinas concludes that 'as critique precedes dogmatism, metaphysics precedes ontology'. However, he immediately returns to the argument by intro-ducing a specification: the *neutral* term is also a *middle* term.

The step from neutrality to mediation is essential for the anti-Hegelian critique of totality that Levinas is here engaging, for being and freedom are linked by Hegel through the concept of mediation. It is mediation that permits their articulation in a system, or 'totality'. However, Levinas does not directly confront Hegel, but instead discusses Socrates, Berkeley and Husserl as preludes to the main object of his critique, Heidegger. Yet, resisting the temptation to move directly to Heidegger, it is important to consider his argument concerning Socrates's teaching, for it is here that the political entailments of mediation and its critique first become apparent.

Levinas characterises Socratic anamnesis in terms of the primacy of the same: 'to receive nothing of the Other but what is in me, as though from

111

all eternity I was in possession of what comes to me from the outside' (TI, 43). The dissolution of the other into the memory of the same inaugurates an understanding of freedom cast in terms of freedom from the heteronomous claims of the other: it is described by Levinas as 'the permanence of the same, which is reason' (TI, 43). Freedom in this light is but the secured sovereign space of the same that 'neutralises' and 'encompasses' the other. In order for the other to be so reduced there has to be a surrender or a betrayal, but the precondition of the yielding of the other to the same is conflict.

Still within the discussion of Socrates, although increasingly tendentious in terms of an historical exposition, Levinas makes a critical move in respect to the 'mediation (characteristic of Western philosophy)' (TI, 44). He considers mediation to be paradoxical in positing a distance or an interval between the terms to be mediated at the same time as abolishing that distance through mediation. Consequently he proposes that mediation be understood as resting upon a 'great betrayal' in which the distance or 'separation' between self and other is owned and disowned. He explains this by an analogy between the same and the other and the slave and the master. This is closer to Hegel than Socrates, and evokes a version of the master/slave dialectic but without the dialectic. He writes: 'As for man, it [the surrender] can be obtained by the terror that brings a free man under the domination of another' (TI, 44). The experience of terror convinces the other, or the 'free man', to betray his alterity by surrendering himself to the domination of the master. This is immediately followed by a definition of 'domination' in terms of the 'work of ontology' as 'apprehending the individual (which alone exists) not in its individuality but in its generality...'. Levinas continues: 'the relation with the other is here accomplished only through a third term which I find in myself' (TI, 44). In this passage Levinas presents the domination of the sovereign I in terms of its reduction of the individual to a genus or third term which is found in the self. Hence domination is not a direct relation, not the direct identification of the other by the self – this would be tyranny – but a mediated relation in which identification is carried out by means of a neutral or third term which is nevertheless to be found in the self. These somewhat formal determinations become important for his discussion of the third and the problem of institutions. For the latter mediate conflict, but in order to equate the other to the same they must assume the standpoint of the self or the neutrality of the third term.

After some discussion of Berkeley and Husserl, Levinas arrives at his critique of Heidegger and of ontological politics. Heidegger's thought is shown to be consistent with the identification of freedom and neutral being that characterises ontology. With questionable justice Levinas considers freedom in Heidegger to denote 'the mode of remaining the same in the midst of the other' (TI, 45). This is due to mediation or the view that Heidegger subordinates 'every relation with existents to the relation with Being', and then imagining that 'freedom comes from an obedience to being' (TI, 45). As we have seen, Levinas finds in Heidegger first the neutralisation of alterity in the neutral third term – Being – and then, through this mediation, the understanding of Being in terms of freedom and obedience – precisely the paradox of legislation described by Rousseau in *The Social Contract*.

The language of Levinas's reading of Heidegger undergoes a subtle transformation in the course of the paragraph, one that is parallel to that deployed in the characterisation of the teaching of Socrates. In it the political entailments of ontology are brought to the foreground. The definition of freedom is couched in terms of the 'autarchy of the I' and ontology itself, 'as first philosophy is a philosophy of power' (TI, 46). The remainder of the discussion now focuses on the meaning of this phrase.

Levinas immediately sharpens the claim that ontology is a philosophy of power by claiming that it is also the philosophy of the state. It is at this point that the argument for the inextricability of state politics and war returns to prominence, along with the critique of the armed peace secured by the state. Against the Hegelian claim that reason, universality and freedom unite in a philosophy of right or the state, Levinas argues that the political peace advocated by the philosophy of power is not secured against war. Ontology 'issues in the State and in the non-violence of the totality, without securing itself against the violence from which this non-violence lives, and which appears in the tyranny of the State' (TI, 46). The state becomes the neutral third term that equates differences in the name of totality: it offers peace, but at the price of the domination of alterity. Here Levinas is transparently questioning the claim of the modern state to realise freedom and equality, showing that the equality in question involves the suppression of differences. The claims for equality may found a kind of peace, but in the name of totality and at the expense of alterity.

The critique of the state is consistent with Levinas's preoccupation with the revolutionary principles of liberty, equality and fraternity. Its development in *Totality and Infinity* does not advocate the utopian rejection of liberty and equality in the name of fraternity, but proposes instead to supplement them with a concept of fraternity as the welcoming of the other. However, before returning to the justification of fraternity, Levinas takes the opportunity to complete his critique of Heidegger.

The reading of Heidegger develops the themes of 'Place and Utopia' and 'Heidegger, Gagarin and Us' considered in Chapter 2 of this book. It consists in a defence of global technology on the grounds that it is able to disrupt place and the paganism associated with it. Levinas argues that, for Heidegger, the freedom that consists in obedience to the truth of being is 'accomplished in existing as builder and cultivator, effecting the unity of the site which sustains space' (TI, 46). This view is consistent with the earlier understanding of the state as providing the unity of the site, or 'totality', that sustains a certain notion of space. This is a notion of space as territory or place that Levinas will later question with reference to the State of Israel, in his essay 'Space is not One-Dimensional'. He now links this notion of space with the destiny of sedentary peoples, making the provocative claim that 'Heidegger, with the whole of Western history, takes the relation with the Other as enacted in the destiny of sedentary peoples, the possessors and the builders of the earth' (TI, 46). The sedentary peoples, as opposed to the nomadic, found their relations to their territory and to the other on possession: 'Possession is pre-eminently the form in which the other becomes the same, by becoming mine' (TI, 46). By not calling into question possession and the same, Heidegger's philosophy is a 'philosophy of injustice' and a defence of tyranny.

The already complex links between ontology, the unity of the site and possession are given a further dimension by Levinas's defence of the liberating effects of world technology and the critique of the idolatry of the possession. The first line of argument is intimated through a critique of Heidegger's casting of technology in terms of the oblivion of being:

> Heideggerian ontology, which subordinates the relationship with the Other to the relation with Being in general, remains under obedience to the anonymous, and leads inevitably to another power, to imperialist domination, to tyranny. Tyranny is not the pure and simple extension of technology to reified men. (TI, 46–7)

Tyranny or imperialist domination extends 'the unity of the site which supports space' to the world – here the earlier discussion of the unstable expansive properties of totality are implicitly linked to Levinas's earlier critique of National Socialism, effecting a link between the philosophy of injustice and Nazi tyranny. Yet this is not the outcome of technology, which Levinas regarded favourably as disrupting sedentary totality. Rather, 'Its origin lies back in the pagan "moods", in the enrootedness in the earth, in the adoration that enslaved men can devote to their masters' (TI, 47). The devotion of the possessed, those who through terror submit to the domination of their master and with this to totality and the masters of that totality, verges on idolatry. It amounts to the renunciation of responsibility – transferring responsibility to the totality – and the implied commitment to war against whatever threatens that totality. It is to privilege the fixed identity provided by the totality – the same – over the constant questioning of identity provoked by the responsibility for the other.

At this point Levinas returns to the themes of war and peace and the need for a philosophy of fraternity. Within the philosophical tradition now linked with the 'sedentary history' of the West, conflicts between the same

114

and the other are resolved by reducing the other to the same through the medium of third, apparently neutral terms, whether in theory 'or, concretely, by the community of the State, where beneath anonymous power, though it be intelligible, the I rediscovers war in the tyrannic oppression it undergoes from the totality' (TI, 47). The war of expansion of the totality or 'unity of the site' against its external other is paralleled by the war against its internal others, those who do not conform to its 'universal' dictates of equality. Against this philosophy of war, injustice and tyranny, Levinas restates 'the effort of this book', which is 'towards apperceiving in discourse a non-allergic relation to alterity, towards apperceiving Desire – where power, by essence murderous of the other, becomes faced with the other and "against all good sense", the impossibility of murder, the consideration of the other, or justice' (TI, 47). Here Levinas poses the alternative of an ethical philosophy of justice that welcomes alterity and the excessive desire that it provokes, seeing in it the possibility of a responsibility for the self and the other otherwise denied.

In his discussion of the occlusion of the other by the philosophical tradition, Levinas distinguished between the theoretical resolution of the conflict of other and same and the concrete resolution of the 'community of the state'. The distinction between the theoretical and the concrete, which informs the very architecture of *Totality and Infinity*, is nevertheless put in question by the general argument for the priority of the movement of orientation over the terms oriented. Yet it persists, and as a residue of the very Platonism that elsewhere Levinas puts in question, it powerfully determines the direction of his argument.

The opposition of the theoretical and the concrete also informs Levinas's view of the ethical alternative to ontological injustice where the theoretical 'effort' to apperceive a 'non-allergic relation to alterity' is given a 'concrete' instantiation. Levinas writes, 'Concretely our effort consists in maintaining, within anonymous community, the society of the I with the Other – language and goodness' (TI, 47). As will be seen, this concrete instantiation begs interpretation. It can be regarded in terms of the fraternal supplement to the liberty and equality of the modern state, and thus linked with a powerful reformist current in republican theory, or it can be regarded as accepting the necessity of the fraternal community to be given a political form, one that is indebted to ontology and tied to a territorial site. The first case is important for understanding Levinas's general notion of the political, the second for the particular politics of the State of Israel. The repetition of the opposition of theory and the concrete will prove increasingly disruptive in Levinas's later thought, producing a split between Israel as a 'utopia of the human'[6] and the violent internal and external politics of the State of Israel.

At this point we move forward to the discussion of possession and habitation in Section II, Part D, entitled 'The Dwelling'. The importance of this discussion lies in Levinas's elaboration of a mode of dwelling that is not necessarily sedentary, not dependent on the possession of a site and thus not rooted exclusively in political ontology. The discussion in 'The Dwelling' is prepared by the comments on enjoyment and labour that conclude Section II, Part C, 'I and Dependence'. Levinas takes up again the critique he had developed during the post-war period of philosophies such as Marxism that are based on a movement of need and satisfaction that assumes scarcity. Labour is not motivated by lack, but by ensuring the persistence of the 'plenitude of enjoyment' against 'the unknown that lurks in the very element it enjoys' (TI, 144). It is the insecurity posed by the future threat to enjoyment rather than the experience of lack in the present that provokes labour,[7] the 'nothingness of the future' opening an 'interval of time in which possession and labour are inserted' (TI, 146). This view of the motivation of labour has a number of important consequences for Levinas's concept of dwelling and for his understanding of the political.

The first consequence involves an acknowledgement of the 'force' of Marxist views of the importance of labour, albeit from a 'different perspective'. Marx's distinction between work – driven by scarcity – and labour as an expression of human 'species being' is not entirely remote from Levinas's purposes. But for him the 'proletarian condition...in which need prevails over enjoyment' is but a limited case (TI, 146). For Levinas, enjoyment of labouring in freedom, thus 'ensuring oneself against life's uncertainty', is the normal condition from which the proletarian condition diverges. Indeed, he sees the latter condition as closer to Heidegger and 'the absurd world of *Geworfenheit*' in which being thrown into a situation of need prevails over the enjoyment of freedom.

As earlier, in the critique of Marxism developed in the 'Hitlerism' essay, Levinas proceeds to a defence of freedom. Enjoyment is aligned with freedom, as is insecurity regarding the future. However, in *Totality and Infinity* Levinas's argument does not end here, but proceeds to an ethical derivation of enjoyment: 'The passage from instantaneous enjoyment to the fabrication of things refers to habitation, to economy, which presupposes the welcoming of the Other' (TI, 146). From this premiss Levinas opposes two understandings of exteriority – one based in lack, the other in excess. The first exteriority consists in troubling the moment of enjoyment by the 'heterogeneity of the world', the negation of enjoyment represented by material constraint and lack. The shock of encountering this exteriority negates the freedom of the I, which thus discovers its extreme dependence upon the material world. This shock contrasts with that of the second exteriority, that of the encounter with the infinity of the other, that enriches freedom by separating I and the material world and opening an interval of time for possession and labour.

The encounter with the other preserves freedom from dissolution in material scarcity or self-destructive anxiety for the future. It opens an 'extraterritorial' space and time (Levinas refers always to 'extraterritoriality'), not specifying its spatial or temporal characters that allow for displacement and postponement. The future thus 'arises in its signification as a postponement and a *delay*', allowing for the 'mastery of the future' through labour and habitation (TI, 150). As a form of labour and habitation emerging from 'extraterritoriality', this occupation of space and time is not sedentary but nomadic. Nevertheless it remains an *occupation*, even if it is founded on the encounter with the other which defies the rules of formal and dialectical logic.

Levinas immediately emphasises that this is not a utopian celebration of a nomadic perpetual peace. The ethical statement that 'The welcoming of the face is peaceable from the first, for it answers an unquenchable Desire for infinity' is immediately qualified by the observation that 'War itself is but a possibility and nowise a condition for it' (TI, 150). While contingencies of struggle for scarce resources may be warlike, the labour and habitation informed by a freedom enriched by the infinity of the other is essentially pacific. But it should be noted that, even for the latter, war remains a possibility. The peace occasioned by the relation to the other does not rule out war, even though war is not of its essence.

The capacity for war is explored in the remainder of Section II. The argument is complex and perhaps, in the final analysis, Levinas holds back from exploring its full consequences. The most salient line of argument in Part D moves between material exteriority and the exteriority of the other. The I in its dwelling is under menace – its present possession is marked by 'consciousness of danger, fear, which is feeling par excellence' (TI, 166). Yet it is through the relation with the other that future time is granted, leaving the I as a 'being that is threatened, but has time at its disposal to ward off the threat' (TI, 166). Thus the 'relation with the other, with infinity, metaphysics' offers the time for labour, but also for overcoming obstacles, opposing other forces and 'forestalling danger' – in other words, for waging war. Yet the other, while opening the space for labour, habitation and war, at the same time throws all of these into question. The other 'paralyses possession', allowing me to 'free myself from the very possession that the welcome of the home establishes' (TI, 170–71). The other demands generosity – that I give away my possession and admit the other to the home – but also negates the murder that the threat to possession might provoke.

The other makes possible the time of labour and possession while also putting it into question. It makes possible the time of war while forbidding murder. This is because the other teaches the I, showing it to be implicated in a totality of opposed forces. Through this teaching, the I 'discovers itself as a violence, but thereby enters into a new dimension' (TI, 171). Levinas takes several precautions to ensure that the other cannot be considered to be on a war footing with the I that it has made and now challenges. The other is above totality, not within it; the other is 'fundamentally pacific', not another freedom to oppose mine; its 'alterity is manifested in mastery that does not conquer, but teaches' (TI, 171). Its teaching is essentially moral, putting into question violence and substituting the word for war in a 'primordial dispossession, a first donation' (TI, 173). Yet there is need for more argument to sustain the claims that this dispossession is not an act of war, that we are still not duped by morality, or that the conditions of welcoming the other and making the donation are not themselves a possession that must be defended by war.

The question of necessary war is explored further in Part C, where Levinas contrasts the totalities of state and market with a pluralism born of the 'separation' occasioned by the relation to an other. This pluralism is defined by a 'social relation' which combines the relation with the other (*autre*) and with others (*autrui*), but in an excessive manner that refuses any closure in totality – 'an objectivity posited in the impossibility of total reflection, in the impossibility of conjoining the I and the non-I in a whole' (TI, 221). The social relationship, however, should not be assumed to be one of peace; indeed Levinas notes immediately that the 'foundation of pluralism' – the relation with the other – 'while maintaining [the terms that constitute a plurality] against the totality that would absorb them, it leaves them in commerce or in war' (TI, 221). The detailed discussion of war and commerce that now ensues develops the point made in Section B regarding the possibility of war that is opened by the encounter with the other.

Levinas begins by insisting that war and commerce are derivatives of the relation to the other, and not themselves the 'primordial form' of plurality. He states unambiguously that 'War and commerce presuppose the face and the transcendence of being appearing in the face' (TI, 222). Before exploring this claim directly he disqualifies a competing, Hegelian, definition of war that would identify violence with the outcome of the limitation that attends a totality. Violence does not consist in the limitation of the one by the other, since this 'is conceivable only within a totality where the parts mutually define one another' (TI, 222). Even in those cases of antagonism, the antagonistic forces remain capable of combining into a totality. The reason for Levinas's careful separation of violence from antagonistic relations within a totality lies in the importance he gives to his definition of peace. He is not satisfied with defining peace as the absence of violence, claiming unequivocally that 'the exclusion of violence by beings susceptible of being integrated into a totality is not equivalent to peace' (TI, 222). This is because totality 'absorbs the multiplicity of beings, which peace implies' – beings reduced to identity by becoming parts of a totality may be pacified but are not capable of peace, for 'Only beings capable of war can rise to peace. War like peace presupposes beings structured otherwise than as parts of a totality' (TI, 222). The bleak rigour of

Levinas's argument for the mutual implication – or to use his later term the *intrigue* of war and peace – is a key element in his attempt to redefine freedom in terms of time and alterity.

The theme of the postponement of the worst is central to Levinas's political thought. Here, too, peace is understood as the postponement but not eradication of war – 'there is' war. But in order to secure a convincing concept of peace it is necessary to establish a correspondingly implacable concept of war. War is thus cast as the 'supreme risk' in which 'The calculations that make possible the outcome of a play of forces within a totality do not decide...' (TI, 223). This risk is then tied to freedom, which Levinas again detaches from any relation to totality. For him freedom is not granted by a totality but is the outcome of the relation to the other, giving rise to the paradox of 'a being independent of and yet at the same time exposed to the other' (TI, 224) that opens the possibility of both war and peace.

The opening for war and peace is constituted by the temporal character of the being exposed to and yet independent of the other. For, in the situation of war and before 'the inevitable violence of death it opposes its time, which is postponement itself' (TI, 224). Levinas continues by defining freedom in terms of this postponement. Since the possibility of war is omnipresent for such a being, it remains 'primordially' exposed to violence – 'Violence does not befall it as an accident that befalls a sovereign freedom. The hold that violence has over this being – the mortality of this being – is the primordial fact. Freedom itself is but its adjournment by time' (TI, 224). From this discovery of freedom in postponement, Levinas then moves to a horrific phenomenology of war.

Levinas begins by describing the implications of freedom as postponement of violence for the body. He describes corporeity as 'the mode of existence of a being whose presence is postponed at the very moment of his presence. Such a distension in the tension of the instant can only come from an infinite dimension which separates me from the other, both present and still to come, a dimension opened by the face of the Other' (TI, 225). The freedom of postponement that is made possible by the other is also capable of provoking war, and in war the exposure to violence is, for Levinas, literally infinite. For, in war, 'violence does not aim simply at disposing of the other as one disposes of a thing, but, already at the limit of murder, it proceeds from unlimited negation. It can aim at only a presence itself infinite despite its insertion in the field of my powers. Violence can only aim at a face' (TI, 225). From the depths of this violent murder of the infinity in the other, Levinas looks in three directions, two of which emphasise the theme of responsibility.

The first is the direction of the radical account of freedom, here viewed not as a 'freedom *within* totality', the Hegelian freedom which would 'reduce freedom to the status of an indetermination in being' (TI, 225), but

as tied to infinity. To bear this freedom, to live in the perpetual postponement of suffering the worst, is a heavy responsibility. Perhaps even heavier
is the responsibility of living in peace with the other. On this second path
Levinas describes the other as fallen into 'the hands of forces that break
him' – perhaps your or my hands? In this case the transcendence of the
other 'is manifested positively in the moral resistance of the face to the
violence of murder. The force of the Other is already and henceforth
moral' (TI, 225). From this resistance rises the possibility of peace through
the work of justice – the 'ethical epiphany' of the face that *demands* a
response adds to the freedom manifest in the postponement of suffering
violence the postponement of perpetrating violence.

The postponement of suffering and perpetrating violence points
towards a peace or work of justice that cannot be included in a totality.
The burden of the asymmetries is borne as responsibility, one which is
absolved by its translation into a totality. The divestment of the burden of
responsibility is achieved 'in an order in which the asymmetry of the interpersonal relation is effaced, where I and the other become interchangeable
in commerce, and where the particular man, an individuation of the genus
man, appearing in history, is substituted for the I and for the other' (TI,
226). Here is a reprise of the reduction of alterity to totality already seen
in the section on enjoyment. With it the claims of totality are acknowledged in the identification of the I and the other. But the comforts of
commerce are once again undermined by the ubiquity of war. Even
commerce involves the postponement of death and violence; its anonymous exchange of equivalents has nested within it war or the 'contention
with the invisible' that defers the moment of violence:

> Struggle must not be confounded with the collision of two forces
> whose issue one can foresee and calculate. Struggle is already, or
> again, *war*, where between the forces that confront one another
> gapes open the interval of transcendence across which death
> comes and strikes without being received. The Other, inseparable
> from the very event of transcendence, is situated in the region
> from which death, possibly murder, comes. (TI, 233)

The exchanges of commerce and the anonymous political order of the
state remain on a war footing, haunted by the menace of ineluctable
violence – suffered and perpetrated – but haunted also by the ethical
promise of peace in the work of justice.

Peace and the 'work of justice'

Levinas's 'work of justice' is presented at the close of *Totality and
Infinity* as the contrary to the 'work of the state'. But the contrast is

ubiquitous, and is prepared earlier in the distinctions Levinas makes between justice and its traditional partners in Western political theory, the 'true', 'being' and 'freedom'. By separating the work of justice from its subordination to discourses of the true, of being and of freedom, Levinas is able to translate his ethical critique of morality into a political theory. He achieves this translation by means of an alignment between justice and divinity that would be further analysed in *Otherwise than Being* and its paralipomena. The conditions for this development, however, were established already in *Totality and Infinity*.

One of Levinas's first critical specifications of the concept of justice consisted in separating justice from its Platonic subordination to truth. In his discussion of Plato in Section B, Levinas insists that 'Society does not proceed from the contemplation of the true; truth is made possible by relation with the Other our master. Truth is thus bound up with the social relation, which is justice' (TI, 72). Thus justice does not follow from the truth, from the adequation of act as fact with the idea, but in the relation with the other that for Levinas provides the condition for truth. In a characteristic inversion, it is not the idea that is revealed in discourse, but the discourse with the other that reasons the need for the idea.

Levinas is even more insistent in separating the concept of justice from that of being, carefully distinguishing his position from that of Heidegger. He casts himself as 'radically opposed to Heidegger who subordinates the relation with the Other to ontology...rather than seeing in justice and injustice a primordial access to the Other beyond all ontology' (TI, 89). Levinas also refuses to subscribe to any of the political implications or alleviations that follow from the attempt to prioritise the ontological over the ethical, namely the subordination of the other to a shared being (racist or nationalist thinking) or the competition with the other for the enhancement of one's own being (Nietzsche) or the sympathetic absorption of the other's differences (Scheler). In his words:

> The existence of the Other does not concern us in the collectivity by reason of his participation in the being that is already familiar to us all, nor by reason of his power and freedom which we should have to subjugate and utilise for ourselves, nor by virtue of the difference of his attributes which we would have to surmount in the process of cognition or in a movement of sympathy merging us with him, as though his existence were an embarrassment. (TI, 89)

Implied in the ontological subordination of alterity is the view that the other must be 'surmounted, enveloped, dominated' (TI, 89), that is to say, made the same. Levinas claims that the other is 'independent of us: behind every relation we could sustain with him, an absolute upsurge' (TI, 89). The proper relation to the other is one of welcome, one which we discover

in 'justice and injustice'. This welcome in its turn is beyond the characteristic oppositions of the philosophy of being such as 'activity/passivity', '*a
priori/a posteriori*'.

It would be hasty to assume that the terms used to describe the other
('independent', 'absolute upsurge') justify an alignment between the other
and freedom. For the welcoming of the other is indeed no less than the
radical qualification of freedom. With the separation of justice and freedom,
Levinas puts in question one of the basic assumptions of modern political
theory. In the first part of Section C – 'Truth and Justice' – entitled 'Freedom
Called into Question', Levinas argues for the priority of justice over
freedom. Prevailing political theory 'derives justice from the undiscussed
value of spontaneity; its problem is to ensure, by way of knowledge of the
world, the most complete exercise of spontaneity by reconciling my freedom
with the freedom of others' (TI, 83). Justice derived in this way consists in
achieving a balance between one's exercise of freedom and the freedom of
the others: if the exercise of one's freedom compromises that of others, then
it is unjust; if the other's exercise of freedom compromises one's own, then it
too is unjust. From this assumption emerges the calculus of freedom familiar
to modern political theory, namely the weighing of distinct exercises of
freedom for the overall optimal maximisation of freedom and thus justice.

Levinas has a number of fundamental objections to this position, some
of which restate problems already besetting modern political theory, others
which arise from his ethics. He first argues that the subordination of
justice to freedom assumes the 'undiscussed value of spontaneity', and then
calls this value into question by pointing to its own internal limits. These
consist in the paradox, classically stated by Rousseau, of being forced to
be free. In Levinas's version this is put in terms of natality, of being born
into freedom and thus not being able freely to choose it. Freedom is not
itself the outcome of an act of free choice, for, in Levinas's words, 'it finds
itself imposed upon itself' (TI, 83). More significantly, Levinas also argues
that the weighing of freedoms characteristic of modern political theory
assumes that the free agents are part of a totality and that their exercise of
freedoms may be quantified according to a common measure. But this is to
reduce freedom to a quantum, a reduction that once again compromises
the spontaneous character of freedom.

Against these problems with the concept of freedom, Levinas proposes
the priority of justice. This raises the issue of the *investment* of freedom by
the other. Freedom is not rejected in favour of justice, but needs to be
invested by the other through the questioning of the freedom of the I. The
investment of freedom consists in its being put into question by the other,
an interrogation in which the I is left ashamed. The shame of the I arises
out of 'the revelation of a resistance to my powers that does not counter
them as a greater force, but calls in question the naïve right of my powers,
my glorious spontaneity as a living being. Morality begins when freedom,

instead of being justified by itself, feels itself to be arbitrary and violent' (TI, 84). The investment in freedom is its justification by the other, 'justification' being defined earlier as 'lifting from it its character of being a fact, accomplished, past, and hence irrevocable, which as such obstructs our spontaneity' (TI, 82), thus putting in question the claim of freedom to be an absolute. In these terms, justice as the 'welcoming of the other' will entail the experience of the injustice of our freedom.

In order fully to question the absolute character of freedom it is necessary for justice to embody a claim to the absolute. The nature of this claim is discussed by Levinas in Section B under the title of 'The Metaphysical and the Human'. The tone of the section is set by the preceding definition of the transcendence of the other in terms both of its 'eminence', 'height' and 'lordship', and of 'its concrete meaning', its 'destitution', 'exile' and 'rights as a stranger'. The transcendence of the other is manifest in 'the gaze of the stranger, the widow, the orphan' which is recognised 'in giving or in refusing' (TI, 77). The justification of what might appear to be a conflation of a transcendent and an empirical other here weaves together a number of diverse themes into a complex and many-layered argument.

The first step in this argument distinguishes the 'absolute' or divinity from any 'violence of the sacred', that is, from any myth or experience of the sacred. The monotheism that emerges from this distinction is identified with a 'metaphysical atheism'. The separation of the absolute from any experience of participation in the sacred motivates Levinas's location of the transcendent in the social relation: 'A relation with the Transcendent free from all captivation by the Transcendent is a social relation. It is here that the Transcendent, infinitely other, solicits us and appeals to us' (TI, 78). Levinas then paradoxically resorts to an Hegelian description of the proximity of the other as an 'ineluctable moment of the revelation of an absolute presence' (TI, 78), but he clearly intends the 'moment' to be an interruption or a break rather than a mediation with the other, a break moreover that disengages itself 'from every relation'.

The claim that the moment of the expression of the other is a break and not an Hegelian moment in the transition towards absolute knowledge is clarified by the stipulation that the other 'does not play the role of a mediator' (TI, 79) between God and humanity. Levinas underlines his refusal of any Christological account of the other by insisting that 'The Other is not the incarnation of God, but precisely his face, in which he is disincarnate, is the manifestation of the height in which God is revealed' (TI, 79). The face of the other human – the stranger, the widow and the orphan – exceeds its corporeal destitution by 'referring' to the divine Other. The divine Other is not *revealed* to knowledge but is *accessible* 'in justice'. Access to the invisible and unimaginable God is only possible through the 'work of justice' which departs from the break between the circumstances of the destitute other and the reference to the divine Other in the face of the other.

Levinas defines the 'work of justice' as the 'uprightness of the face to face' or the welcoming of the other in the other human, and sees it as 'necessary in order that the breach that leads to God be produced' (TI, 78). The description of the work of justice in these terms brings together religious and social theory in a manner that would be developed further in *Otherwise than Being* and Levinas's later writings. At this point he uses the language of metaphysics that he will later abandon in order to frame the claim that 'metaphysics is enacted where the social relation is enacted – in our relationship with men. There can be no "knowledge" of God separated from the relationship with men' (TI, 78). The inverse also holds, there can be no 'knowledge' of men apart from the relationship with God, but this 'knowledge' is only possible through the work of justice. Soon after, Levinas describes the ethical 'locus of metaphysical truth' as a 'field of research hardly glimpsed at', wherein 'relations with humans...give to theological concepts the sole significance they admit of' (TI, 79). Here Levinas refers forward to a project of religious and social theory that will later prove a major preoccupation and through which he will try to link the 'work of justice' and the 'making of Israel', a linkage greatly complicated by Israel's assumption of the form of the State.

In *Totality and Infinity* the translation of the work of justice into a political project is accomplished in a way that makes any identification of it with a state such as the 'State of Israel' extremely difficult. Indeed, the 'work of justice' is directly contrasted with the 'work of the state' but, as with all the disjunctive oppositions in *Totality and Infinity*, this should not be read too hastily. The most extended discussion of this theme is to be found in Section V of Part C, 'The Truth of the Will', which consists in a presentation of the 'work of the state' identified with 'Hegel's great meditation on freedom' (TI, 241) and its critique in the name of the work of justice.

Levinas sympathetically presents Hegel's critique of abstract freedom, rehearsing the arguments from the *Phenomenology of Spirit* against the freedom of the 'beautiful soul'. The beautiful soul's pursuit of an inner freedom in abstraction from the brutal events of the 'slaughterboard of history' not only compromises its freedom but tends to produce cynicism. Against this outcome, Hegel maintains that freedom must be made concrete, or, in the words of Levinas's commentary, 'Freedom is not realised outside of social and political institutions, which open it to the access to fresh air necessary for its expansion, its respiration, and even perhaps, its spontaneous generation' (TI, 241). Freedom cannot be cherished as a subjective, private possession but must be embodied in institutions; that is, it must become objective. Levinas presents Hegel's argument for objective freedom in terms of the writing of the law: 'Freedom is engraved on the stone of the tables on which laws are inscribed – it exists by virtue of this incrustation of an institutional existence' (TI, 241). This institutional existence – objective freedom – is not an act of 'Bergsonian élan' but rather a

124

'political and technical Existence' in which 'freedom is conserved for man, outside of man' (TI, 241). At this point, having accepted Hegel's critique of subjective freedom, Levinas begins to distance himself from Hegel's account of objective freedom. He does so by returning to the notion of subjectivity assumed by Hegel, and replacing the assumption of its autonomy with that of its extreme heteronomy. With this he begins the re-description of subjectivity and its modes that he will subsequently carry through in *Otherwise than Being*.

Levinas describes Hegel's objective freedom – the translation of freedom into political institutions – as a particular and limited mode of exteriority that he contrasts with those of animality and the Other. Such freedom 'exists reflected by the public order, in the equality which the universality of laws ensures it' (TI, 242). This submission of subjective freedom to the universality of law condemns it to 'exist as though it were dead', subjecting it to 'alienation' or the exteriority of that 'tyranny of the universal and of the impersonal, an order that is inhuman though distinct from the brutish' (TI, 242). This political order subjects the freedom of the individual to a totality, in which its freedom becomes the gift of its totality.

Levinas's account of the 'work of the state' does not of course do justice to the Hegelian concept of ethical life or *Sittlichkeit*, for it describes Hegel's critical account of abstract freedom as though it were the terminus of his system. This forgets the Hegelian analysis of the necessary resort of modern abstract freedom to terror. Levinas chooses not to pursue Hegel's analysis of the ethical state – a theory that exercised some influence on certain currents of Zionism – but returns instead to considering the 'work of justice' in terms of an ethical understanding of subjectivity.

In order to describe the ethical subject, Levinas returns to the interiority of subjective freedom, but now qualifies it as dependence. Subjective freedom is accused by the 'face of the Other – whose very epiphany is brought about by this offence suffered, by this status of being stranger, widow and orphan' (TI, 244). The self that overcomes its separate enjoyment in order to assume responsibility for the other, to orient its actions with respect to the other 'in the incessant overflowing of duty accomplished by ever broader responsibilities' (TI, 246), has been 'elected'. It is a singular election that cannot be equalised or subsumed under a universal. The adventure of the ethical self begins 'in the justice that indicts my arbitrary and partial freedom' but which does not permit 'my pure and simple entry into the universal order' (TI, 245). The indictment is more radical than Hegel's critique of subjective freedom, and accordingly is not satisfied by the move to objective freedom or the totality of the law. In Levinas's words, after the indictment of subjective freedom, 'justice summons me to go beyond the straight line of justice, and henceforth nothing can mark the end of this march; behind the straight line of the law the land of goodness extends infinite and unexplored, necessitating all the resources of a singular presence' (TI, 245). The ethical subject is never under law, but always in pursuit of the promised land of goodness that – an infinite territory – is ever beyond it. The promised land consists in the pursuit rather than the attainment, for the nomadic ethical subject can never arrive at infinity; accomplishment of the duty to the other provokes more responsibility. The self in this way is 'deepened' by the experience of an infinite responsibility and becomes a singularity that cannot be subsumed under the law of a totality: the 'work of justice' exceeds the 'work of the state'.

At this point in his work, Levinas does not fully explore the implications of the 'elected' ethical subject – or the 'new orientation of inner life' (TI, 246) – for what would in Hegel be the passage to objective freedom or the 'work of the state'. This will be attempted in the analyses of *Otherwise than Being*. At this stage, however, it is already clear that the implications of the re-orientation of the subject from autonomy to responsibility are considerable. The ethical self, oriented with respect to an absolute alterity, is enriched and not alienated: the 'work of justice' is thus intended to exceed the institutional and legal totality of objective freedom of the 'work of the state'.

Levinas's reference to the responsibility for the other is intended to free his subject from the Hegelian accusation of providing yet another version of the 'beautiful soul'. The ethical self is inserted in a concrete context of service to widows, orphans and strangers, rather than the institutions of Hegelian objective freedom. What is more, Levinas sees the ethical subject as eminently capable of forming a society, a polity emerging from the 'work of justice' rather than the 'work of the state'. He had already given some intimations of this society in a sketch of a non-totalising polity at the end of Section I.

The depiction of a non-totalising polity begins with the invasion of a totality by infinity, an invasion that produces a 'contraction' that opens a space for singularity. The face of the other here opens the space for the exercise of responsibility for the other. This infinity 'leaves a space for the separated being', and 'Over and beyond the totality it inaugurates a society' (TI, 104). The contraction of infinity into the face of the other is then redeemed by the expansion of responsible acts in the work of justice. This re-creation or recreation is excessive, not driven by needs in pursuit of satisfaction, and inaugurates for Levinas 'the possibility of a sabbatical existence, where existence suspends the necessities for existence' (TI, 104) and where, in its absolute dependence on God, the ethical subject is free 'outside of any system, which implies dependence' (TI, 104). Levinas describes this experience of a society with God as 'religion', a predicament in which 'Creation leaves to the creature a trace of dependence, but it is an unparalleled dependence: the dependent being draws from this exceptional dependence, from this relationship, its very independence, its exteriority to the system' (TI, 104–5).

With the 'work of justice', *Totality and Infinity* returns to its opening question concerning morality and war. The work of justice is the acknowledgement of the infinite, the messianic eschatology of peace beyond the political ontology of war. But it also emerges from it and, Levinas wagers, is inseparable from it. But the mode of co-existence of ethical peace and ontological war remains difficult to imagine. Is Levinas's *Sittlichkeit* achieved through the suspension of security – an act of risk – and can the extent of this risk extend as far as risking the work of the state for the sake of the work of justice and *vice versa*? It is no accident that Levinas repeatedly and consistently described the foundation of the State of Israel in terms of risk, but without specifying where the balance of risk lay. Would the 'work of justice' be risked and perhaps lost in the name of the state, or the 'work of the state' risked and undone in the name of justice? From the non-dialectical disjunctions of *Totality and Infinity*, Levinas moved to intensify the links between ethics, the work of justice and messianic eschatology. This would assume the shape, in *Otherwise than Being*, of a prophetic politics.

4

PROPHETIC POLITICS, OR 'OTHERWISE THAN FREEDOM'

Difficult Freedom

But even if you are free, you are not the absolute beginning.
You come after many things and many people. You are not
just free; you are also bound to others beyond your freedom.
You are responsible for all. Your liberty is also fraternity.

'As Old as the World?' (DF)

Otherwise than Being extends the re-orientation of philosophy from
ontology to ethics, the same to the other, that was begun in *Totality and
Infinity*. Consistent with the earlier text's critique of Hegel and in particular his account of the transition from subjective to objective freedom,
Otherwise than Being explores modes of subjectivity and freedom in a way
that does not add up to the Hegelian universal history of the realisation of
freedom in reason and the rational institutions of the state. Terms such as
'hostage', 'proximity', 'substitution' and 'trace' signify those modes of
subjectivity that, in the words of *Totality and Infinity*, are informed not so
much by the insufficiency of the I but the infinity of the other. The attention to the modes of subjectivity overturns the main premise of traditional
political theory – that the sovereign I and its property are always endangered and in need of the supplement of a social contract and/or a state in
order to protect them. The discovery of the asymmetry and inequality of
the relation of I to other also puts under intense scrutiny the third member
of the 'revolutionary trinity' after freedom and fraternity, namely equality.[1]
   The thought of a 'difficult freedom' distinct from the freedom thought by
Hegel and incarnate in universal history was developed in two complementary contexts by Levinas. The first was the continued reflection on Jewish
identity carried forward in the later essays of *Difficult Freedom* and the
Talmudic commentaries. In these, Levinas developed the hints of a 'messianic
eschatology', disclosed in *Totality and Infinity*, into a 'prophetic politics'.
This complemented and was complemented by the second context, namely
the deepening of the philosophical disengagement from ontology and the

elaboration of an ethics of alterity begun in *Totality and Infinity* and extended into *Otherwise than Being*. This, too, issued in a notion of prophetic politics, but one that was at first glance abstracted from the question of Jewish identity. In this Levinas devotes the difficult freedom expressed in prophetic politics to a re-thinking of the modern political founded on the Declaration of the Rights of Man and Citizen, thus continuing the project begun in the 1930s but now intensified by a new concern with global politics.

The infinity of the other continued to inform the reflections that Levinas pursued during the 1960s and 1970s on subjectivity and politics. From the premise that the 'I' is invested with responsibility for the other, Levinas explored the modes of responsible subjectivity in terms of the modal categories of 'substitution', the 'hostage', 'trace' and 'proximity'. The modality in question is ethical, and is used not only to intensify the critique of ontology but also to derive an ethical theory of society and the state. On the basis of this extension of ethical modality and its modal categories into social and political theory, Levinas is able to sketch an account of 'prophetic politics' and to give an instance of such politics in a reading of the theory of human rights. Another instance of prophetic politics, that of 'Israel', will be looked at more closely in the next chapter.

Levinas's derivation of a prophetic politics is naturally indebted to the precedents described in the historical books of the Bible, which are largely devoted to the tension between the prophetic voice and an emergent monarchic and then imperial politics. The prophetic voice intervenes in politics to judge and correct its course by appeal to the divine. Levinas maintains this vocation for his modern version of prophetic politics, but founds it upon the basis of a sophisticated account of modal subjectivity and the social and political forms that may be derived from it. Prophetic or 'inspired' politics receives its force from the excess of the other over the self, the feature repeatedly analysed by Levinas in terms of the infinity of the other in excess and uncontainable by the self.

It is in the terms of a prophetic politics inseparable from ethics that Levinas conducts his critique of the ontological foundations of political theory and practice. The differences are succinctly stated in the 1976 lecture 'The Ethical Relationship as a Departure from Ontology', part of the series on 'God and Onto-Theo-Logy'. There Levinas asks whether a theory of social institutions and the state can be developed from the ethical categories of 'proximity', 'hostage' and 'substitution'. His answer is framed in terms of a contrast between such a theory and that of the Hobbesian tradition that departs from the premise of insecurity, of 'man being a wolf for man'. He asks, 'What difference is there between institutions arising from a limitation of violence and those arising from a limitation of responsibility?' and answers that there is 'at least one', namely that with the latter, his political theory, 'one can revolt against institutions in the very name of that which gave birth to them' (GDT, 183).

Prophetic politics is both a politics of giving birth to institutions and of rebelling against them 'in the name' of their origin. The 'name' in question is neither freedom nor security, but ethical responsibility. Levinas carefully prepared the way for this political conclusion in a thoroughgoing ethical revision of what he believed were the ontological investments of Western philosophy and its political consequences. In the terms of the 1960 essay 'Forces and Faces', the ethical revision of Western philosophy and the critique of its political consequences in the name of prophetic politics permitted a delay between the philosophical premises of Western political thought and the realisation of their political consequences.

Otherwise than Being I: the ontological supplement

As with *Totality and Infinity*, Levinas's 1974 text *Otherwise than Being or Beyond Essence* emerged from a decade of work in progress. While acknowledging the genesis of the book in a series of articles beginning with 'Substitution' from 1968, Levinas's preface insists that the 'first version preceded the published texts'.[2] The project of the text consists in confronting subjectivity with the 'trauma of transcendence' and so exploring the 'human possibility' of hearing 'a God not contaminated by Being' (OB, xliii). The 'human possibility' in question is inseparable from 'practice and knowledge in this world' – and Levinas insists at the outset that this ethical and political practice be of this world and not of 'the Heavenly City gravitating in the skies over the terrestrial city' (OB, 4). This taking of distance from the Christian distinction between the City of God and the City of Man had considerable implications for ethical and political action, as well as for the understanding of the relationship between holy and universal history.

The insistence on an experience of transcendence with implications for ethical and political practice is further emphasised in the reprise, at the outset of *Otherwise than Being*, of the main theme of *Totality and Infinity* – the derivation of war and commerce from ontology. The section of Chapter One, 'Being and Interest', describes two modalities of being; the first is the war of competing beings driven by *conatus*, the second is a rational peace or 'calculation, mediation and politics' in which 'The struggle of each against all becomes exchange and commerce' (OB, 4). As argued throughout *Totality and Infinity*, war, politics and commerce are modes of being that are characterised by instability: politics and commerce are ever on the point of deteriorating into war. Levinas in his earlier text was unconvinced by Hegel's claim that subjective freedom – *conatus* or the freedom to be – could be rationally governed in the objective freedom of politics and commerce (in Hegelian terms, State and Civil Society). For him, the potential for war that accompanies subjective freedom is carried over into objective freedom, and while 'Commerce is better than war, for in peace the Good has already

130

reigned', such peace is always 'unstable' (OB, 5). He then attempts to under-mine the premise of subjective freedom by a notion of responsible subjectivity invested in a subjectivity 'traumatised' by transcendence.

Otherwise than Being could equally be titled 'otherwise than freedom', since it explores the 'human possibility' of a subjectivity marked by responsibility rather than by the experience of freedom. Levinas argues that responsibility for the other, and all that this will be seen to entail, is antecedent to freedom. Just as the freedom of the subject was shown to be a particular mode of being, so too the responsibility of the subject will evince a modality issuing from beyond being. Given the importance for Levinas of the critique of ontology and its mode of freedom, his path towards the responsible subject describes a modality that is otherwise than ontology and freedom. Yet the significance of the specific discussion of the 'saying and the said' with the term 'saying' used to describe this non-onto-logical modality should not be exaggerated. The modal disjunction between the 'saying and the said' is not the key to Levinas's thought in *Otherwise than Being* but rather one of the many paths out of ontology. This is indicated by the complicity that Levinas reveals between the onto-logical 'said' and the non-ontological 'saying'.

Although Levinas unambiguously contests the primacy of being and ontology over ethics, he does not do so in order to reject ontology. Rather, he sees in ethics that 'basis of proximity' in which 'being takes on its just meaning' (OB, 16). It is through this concession that Levinas is able to elaborate an equivalent movement to Hegel's passage from subjective to objective freedom. The traumatic persistence of the other in the self – 'the anarchical provocation which ordains me to the other' (OB, 16) – opens a way to justice, for alongside the other appears 'the presence of a third party' (OB, 16). Levinas carefully distinguishes between the 'other' and the 'third' by arguing against the view that the third stands to oneself as an other. The 'third' is approached not as an other, but, in so far as it is in relation with my other, 'the relationship between the neighbour and the third party cannot be indifferent to me when I approach' (OB, 16). For there to be justice, this relationship must be thought in terms of compara-bility, a thought which is not available to ethics since, for ethics, the other is always singular. This leaves comparability to ontology: 'There must be a justice among incomparable ones. There must then be a comparison between incomparables and a synopsis, a togetherness and contemporane-ousness; there must be thematisation, thought, history and inscription. But being must be understood on the basis of *being's other*' (OB, 16) – which is to say that, in order for there to be justice, ethics must be supplemented by ontology and ontology by ethics.[3]

The *political* consequences of the supplementation of ontology by ethics and ethics by ontology are considerable. The burden of the argument of *Totality and Infinity* was weighed towards showing that ontology without ethics leads ineluctably to war, and that under the reign of ontology war is omnipresent. Peace could be achieved through the supplementing of ontology by the ethical and its thought of infinity. In *Otherwise than Being*, Levinas's argument moves according to the same logic of the supplement, but in the opposite direction. As has been widely noted, this movement between the ethical and the ontological permits the emergence of justice, but less noted is the further entailment that the resort to ontology also permits the emergence of war at the heart of the ethical. Supplementing the ethical with the ontological permits the emergence of a militant ethics: while in *Totality and Infinity* the ethical supplement sanctioned the ethical qualification of war, in *Otherwise than Being* the ontological supplement sanctions the violent qualification of ethics. This movement is evident in the otherwise enigmatic passage that follows the claim that being is to be understood in terms of being's other: this ethical supplement of ontology transforms the ethical 'approach' into a system of alliances: 'To be on the ground of the signification of an approach is to be *with another* for or against a third party, with the other and the third party against oneself, in justice' (OB, 16). The appearance of the third brings with it a series of complex but tightly structured alliances: the 'I' is ethically 'with' the 'other', but has to decide whether it is for or against the third – at war or in peace with the 'third'. The 'I' can even join with the other in an alliance with the 'third' against the self, but what is hardly entertained is the possibility that the 'I' can be with the 'third' against the other.

The abstract positions outlined here in terms of the triad of 'I', 'other' and 'third' gain historical force if we name the 'other' and the 'third' the 'State of Israel' and the 'Palestinians'. This will be explored further in the next chapter; it is sufficient here to note that such substitution is permitted by the terms of the ontological supplement to ethics necessary to bring abstract ethical relations into history. Levinas, at this point in *Otherwise than Being*, is prepared to bring together the theses of *Totality and Infinity* and *Otherwise than Being*, first by showing that the peace of being secured by reason 'presupposes disinterestedness, passivity and patience', namely the supplement of ethical responsibility, and then by arguing that this responsibility in turn requires an ontological supplement: 'In this disinterestedness, when, as a responsibility for the other, it is also a responsibility for the third party, the justice that compares, assembles and conceives, the synchrony of being and peace, take form' (OB, 16). What must remain in question given Levinas's argument is the status of the 'also' in this sentence. Does the 'I' have a direct responsibility for the 'third', equivalent to its responsibility for the other, or is its responsibility for the third delegated through the other's direct responsibility to the third as its other? Levinas appears to sanction only the second position, insisting that the I must relate to the other's relation to its other and not directly to the third in its quality of being an other. This restriction determines the set of possible alliances between 'I', 'other'

132

and 'third', and, as already seen, rules out the possibility of an alliance between the I and the third against the other.

There is a justified sense in which it may be objected that even to expect a direct relation between 'I' and the 'third' is wholly to misunderstand Levinas's notion of alterity. Nevertheless it is heuristically useful to keep in mind the question of why the third is not the other when following the detail of Levinas's analysis, for what is at stake is the possibility of a passage from subjective to objective freedom, from the ethical freedom of the beautiful soul to the political freedom institutionalised in the modern state. Levinas's insistent discourse of the third and the centrality of the themes of the ethical supplement of ontology and the ontological supplement of ethics in his two major works shows that some form of movement between subjective and objective freedom is essential to his thought, but it is to be distinguished from that of Hegel, which, ultimately for Levinas, dissolves ethics into ontology. It is also important if Levinas is to claim any entitlement to make judgements on the subject of modern politics, and in particular on the State of Israel.

Otherwise than Being II: proximity and substitution

Levinas qualifies the Hegelian passage from subjective to objective freedom by redefining its premise of the freedom of the subject. He states programmatically that this is achieved in a double movement of 'disengagement' and 'presentation': his exposition aims 'to *disengage* the subjectivity of the subject from reflections on truth, time and being in the amphibology of being and entities which is borne by the said', and then to *present* it 'in saying, as a sensibility from the first animated by responsibilities' (OB, 19; my italics). The exposition thus disengages the subject from the categories of quality ('the said') characteristic of ontology – truth, time and being – in order to present it in terms of the modal categories ('the saying') of ethics – proximity, responsibility and substitution. Since to a great extent the work of disengagement had already been accomplished in *Totality and Infinity*, *Otherwise than Being* focuses on the ethical presentation of the subject. It does so through an 'itinerary' or series of stages that begins, in Levinas's own programmatic description, by showing that the subject is a 'sensibility from the first animated by responsibilities' and then claiming 'proximity to be the sense of the sensibility' (OB, 19). He then proceeds classically to show 'substitution as the *otherwise than being* at the basis of proximity' and, in its turn, also 'a relationship between a subject and infinity, in which *infinity comes to pass*' (OB, 19). We can review this itinerary, paying particular attention to its political resonances and the treatment of the question of the 'third' as other.

In the first stage of the itinerary of *Otherwise than Being* Levinas rehearses the disengagement of the subject and sensibility from the structures of intentionality already begun in the writings of the immediate post-war period. However, the terms of Levinas's disengagement from intentional analysis are now somewhat different, since he does not wish to move immediately to the argument for the infinite as an impossible intentional object, as in *Totality and Infinity* and its parerga. According to the itinerary followed in *Otherwise than Being*, infinity is to be the point of arrival, not departure. Instead of lingering with the perplexing modality of the infinite, Levinas returns to develop more fully another of his lines of criticism of phenomenological analysis, namely the disjointedness of the moment, the gap in the moment of what is now named 'diachrony'.

Accordingly, the focus of the analysis of the subject's sensibility falls on time, or, more specifically, on the analysis of time consciousness. Levinas disengages his analysis of sensibility from what he sees as Husserl's emphasis on the continuity of time consciousness and its corollary that 'the time structure of sensibility is a time of what can be recuperated' (OB, 34). Through a series of subtle expositions of the relationship between time and the manifestation of sensation, Levinas relates the Husserlian continuity of time consciousness to the openness of being, describing this as an ontological operation destined to 'exclude from time the irreducible diachrony whose meaning the present study aims to bring to light, behind the *exhibiting* of being' (OB, 34). His move from the disengagement of subjectivity from ontology and on to its ethical presentation thus moves through the diachrony of time consciousness.

Levinas had already explored the theme of the diachrony of time consciousness in his early work, where diachrony is understood in Bergsonian terms as creativity or the production of the new in the moment. In *Otherwise than Being*, he insists that diachrony is not to be thought in terms of the creative freedom and spontaneity of the subject, but rather in terms of its passivity. Such passivity is exemplified by the experience of the 'diachronic temporality of ageing' that ineluctably falls upon the subject and in which 'there is produced despite myself the response to an appeal, direct and like a traumatising blow' (OB, 53). What interests Levinas is not so much the contrast between the phenomenology of the living and the dying present, but rather the mode of production of a response, 'an absolutely heteronomous call' (OB, 53). He will pursue this mode of production not only through the experience of ageing but into the subject itself.

Following the work of disengaging subjectivity from intentional analysis, Levinas permits himself a number of provisional conclusions. The first holds that 'The subject then cannot be described on the basis of intentionality, representational activity, objectification, freedom and will'. Instead it 'has to be described on the basis of the passivity of time' (OB, 53). After thus describing the passage from the disengagement of an ontological to the presentation of an ethical understanding of subjectivity, he insists that 'temporalisation of time, the lapse irrecuperable and outside of all will, is quite the contrary of intentionality' (OB, 53) in the sense of the 'passivity of its patience' (OB, 53). Levinas describes the experience of patience as 'sensibility' or the vulnerability of subjectivity that does not constitute an experience and is not available for intentional analysis. The subject is understood in the accusative rather than the nominative case, as undergoing passively rather than acting. At this point of disengagement Levinas reflects on the task facing his ethical presentation: 'An exposure to the other, it is signification, is signification itself, the one-for-the-other to the point of substitution, but a substitution in separation, that is, responsibility. Our analysis will have to show that. It will examine the proximity which vulnerability signifies' (OB, 54).

Before following him in this analysis it might be helpful to review the change in conceptual vocabulary that Levinas is effecting in the transition from disengagement to presentation. From a language of 'intentionality', representation, objectification, freedom and volition, Levinas is moving towards one of exposure, substitution, responsibility and proximity. It is part of an adventure described at the close of this chapter as leading to 'extreme and irreducible conceptual possibilities' that exceed even the dialectical descriptions of 'order and being' (OB, 58). He emphatically names these possibilities that are 'beyond the possible' as *substitution of one for another, the immemorial past that has not crossed the present, the positing of the self as a deposing of the ego, less than nothing as uniqueness, difference with respect to the other as non-indifference*' (OB, 58). The presentation of these extreme possibilities will lead beyond freedom to a subjectivity elected to responsibility, a responsibility so extreme that the I becomes a hostage of the other. However, although occasionally anticipating this outcome, Levinas remains close to his itinerary, moving from the disengagement of subjectivity from ontology to an analysis of the relationship between the received philosophical concept of sensibility to one of the new 'extreme conceptual possibilities' – namely proximity.

Levinas's task in Chapter Three, 'Sensibility and Proximity', is to show that sensibility emerges not from an intentional relationship between an intention and that which it intends, but from proximity. What will amount to a radical reassignment of sensibility to passivity instead of activity will bring with it a notion of passive subjectivity, or a subjectivity that emerges from its relation with the other. As noted, the reassignment of the qualities of the subject will put in question the links between the freedom and spontaneity of the subject and the transition to objective freedom described in Hegel's universal history.

The first step of the argument locates the proximity of the other in sensibility. Accordingly, Levinas defines sensibility as 'exposedness to the other' and likens this exposure to 'an inversion of the *conatus* of *esse*, a having been offered without any holding back, a not finding any protection in any consistency or identity of a state' (OB, 75). Yet the implications of locating sensibility in the proximity of the other are more radical than the inversion would suggest. First of all it is rigorously distinguished from any agency, even that of giving itself to the other. Sensibility is called to exposure; it does not give itself since the act of giving would entail that some trace of being persist in order to make the gift. Furthermore, the exposure is anachronous, passive and without foundation: 'In the having been offered without any holding back the past infinitive form underlines the non-present, the non-commencement, the non-initiative of the sensibility. This non-initiative is older than any present, and is not a passivity contemporaneous with and counterpart of an act. It is the hither side of the free and the non-free, the anarchy of the Good' (OB, 75). The hither side is described in terms of vulnerability and insecurity; sensibility is 'put in question by the alterity of the other, before the intervention of a cause, before the appearing of the other. It is pre-original not resting on oneself, the restlessness of someone persecuted' (OB, 75). The move from an exposed and vulnerable sensibility to a persecuted subject marks the transition of Levinas's argument from sensibility to the notion of the subject as persecuted by the proximity of the other.

Levinas's use of the charged term 'persecution' is not accidental or merely rhetorical.[4] He will consistently use it, along with the terms 'obsession' and 'trauma', to contrast his view of subjectivity with that in which the subject is free and spontaneous. The subject for him is under accusation, the latter term understood grammatically as signifying the accusative case: in this sense it is exposed and vulnerable to the other. Thus Levinas can bleakly describe proximity as 'not a state, a repose, but a restlessness, null site, outside of the place of rest' (OB, 82). Yet proximity is also defined as 'this being caught up in fraternity' and is referred to as 'humanity' (OB, 83). Levinas illustrates these aspects of proximity by means of the neighbour, who for him is both the other and a brother: 'He is precisely *other*. The community with him begins in my obligation to him. The neighbour is a brother. A fraternity that cannot be abrogated, an unimpeachable assignation, proximity is an impossibility to move away without the torsion of a complex, without "alienation" or fault' (OB, 87). The modality of proximity is thus not that of knowing or recognising the other in his or her freedom, such as in the Hegelian case, or of loving them as much as I love myself; it is rather 'a modality not of a knowing, but of an obsession, a shuddering of the human quite different from cognition...I am first a servant of a neighbour, already late and guilty for being late. I am as it were ordered from the outside, traumatically commanded, without interiorising by representation and concepts the authority that commands me' (OB, 87). Such a traumatic 'relation' to the other is prior to any notion of recognition or indeed of the self; for Levinas this proximity undercuts subjectivity and qualifies any sense of the spontaneity or freedom of the subject.

Having evoked the trauma of proximity and its role in sensibility and the formation of the subject, Levinas proceeds to elaborate the phenomenon analytically and synthetically. The first analytic elaboration consists in tracing the trauma of proximity back to the 'otherwise than being at the basis of proximity' that Levinas calls 'substitution'. This elaboration contributes to Levinas's attempt to locate the divine in the face of the other, linking the trauma of proximity with what he calls at the outset 'a merciless exposure to the trauma of transcendence'. It consists in showing that what appears to the 'substantiality of the subject' or 'hard core of the "unique" in me' 'my unparalleled identity' (OB, xli) is in fact the issue of a modal operation – 'substitution'. The analytic itinerary that leads to modal origins of the subject is accompanied, implicitly and explicitly, by a synthetic movement that passes from substitution and proximity to the question of justice, and on to philosophy in the broad and to ontology in the narrow sense. The first movement comprises the presentation of ethical categories beyond ontology, the second the supplementation of these categories by those of ontology; in short, the transition from the other to the third.

The discovery of the modal category of 'substitution' at the 'basis of proximity' is reported in Chapter Four, 'Substitution', described by Levinas in his introductory note as the 'centrepiece' or, in a footnote, as the 'germ' of the book (OB, xli and 193). The motivation of the discussion is once again the critique of Hegel's alignment of the objective freedom of the state with the subjective freedom of the subject. In Hegel's political speculative proposition this alignment is accomplished by means of recognition, with the subject recognising itself in substance and then substance recognising itself in the subject. In the opening section of the chapter, 'Principle and Anarchy', Levinas strives to interrupt the *principled* speculative movement – one which works through the principle of identity – the rule or *arche* of the One – with an-archy. Levinas's proximity – the traumatising of the subject – disturbs any possible mediation between subject and substance, between subjective and objective freedom. Stated most forcefully, 'Proximity is thus *anarchically* a relationship with a singularity without the mediation of any principle, any ideality' (OB, 100). The disturbed traumatised subject of proximity does not create a 'result', as in the Hegelian movement from subjective to objective freedom, but leaves marks of its disturbance – the 'trace' – in the present.

Levinas's appeal to an-archy and interruption against Hegelian principle and mediation describes the 'praxis and knowledge in the world' of the troubled subject. Anarchy is thus identified by him with 'persecution', but in the sense that it issues from a troubled subject, one perpetually under accusation, rather than a free subject discovering that its subjective freedom is in fact objective and substantial. The political contrast is explicitly laid out in a footnote to this section which begins by professing a debt to

Bergson's *Creative Evolution* in the development of his critique of Hegel's philosophy of the state. What is particularly interesting in this footnote is Levinas's specification of his understanding of political anarchy. Distinguishing his view of anarchy from both Hegel's phenomenology of spirit and his philosophy of the state, Levinas nevertheless hastens to distance his understanding of anarchy from that of the anarchist political movement. His anarchism signifies a politics of the trace, a politics of disturbance rather than of constitution: 'The notion of anarchy we are introducing here has a meaning prior to the political (or antipolitical) meaning currently attributed to it. It would be self-contradictory to set it up as a principle (in the sense that anarchists understand it). Anarchy cannot be sovereign, like an *arche*. It can only disturb the State – but in a radical way, making possible moments of negation *without any* affirmation. The state cannot then set itself up as a whole'.[5] Looking back to the language of *Totality and Infinity*, anarchy is an exteriority that disturbs totality, a retrospective link that Levinas himself underlines when he insists on emphasising the 'exteriority' of anarchy (OB, 102). This description of anarchy also looks forward to his 'prophetic politics' and his understanding of the role of the State of Israel in the global order as the disruption of the system of global government. It will also be seen, but less emphatically, to inform Levinas's own position on the internal relations of the State of Israel.

Returning to the movement from proximity to substitution, Levinas moves forward by criticising the equation of the in- and for-itself of the subject that he attributes to Hegel and now also to Sartre. The movement between the in- and for-itself is a rephrasing of the speculative proposition of subject and substance. Levinas places the subject beyond such speculative movements, insisting in the opening paragraph of the section on substitution that 'The oneself has to be conceived outside of all substantial coinciding of self with self. Contrary to Western thought which unites subjectivity and substantiality, here coinciding is not the norm that already commands all non-coinciding...' (OB, 114). Yet Levinas cannot leave the subject in proximity, traumatised and obsessed, a 'beautiful soul' incapable of the coincidence of subject and substance, subjective and objective freedom. It is necessary for him to show that proximity is indeed responsible, a step which is only possible if he can show that proximity itself is substitution.

The complex discussion of responsibility that opens the section on substitution is in some respects premature, since it introduces responsibility on the basis of proximity. This, however, runs the risk of making 'responsibility' into an asserted and sentimental ethical salve to the tormented subject of proximity, an undesirable outcome for Levinas. Any discussion of responsibility is thus properly prefaced by the theme of substitution, an extended description of which is to be found in the succeeding section on 'Finite Freedom'. The movement of substitution can be formally described in terms of the 'by the other' of proximity being

138

now Responsible for the other as is AE

changed into the 'for the other' of responsibility. Levinas first rehearses the argument of proximity – linking it with his discussion of infinity in *Totality and Infinity* – 'the suffering and vulnerability of the sensible as *the other in me*. The other is in me and in the midst of my very identification', is infinite, or 'beyond its capacity to endure' (OB, 124–5). Yet this does not lead to the collapse or slavery of the self 'because' – and here Levinas signals an important development of his thought –

> because, since an 'immemorial time', anarchically, in subjectivity the by-the-other is also the for-the-other. In suffering by the fault of the other dawns suffering for the fault of others, supporting. The for-the-other keeps all the patience of undergoing imposed by the other. There is substitution for another, expiation for another. (OB, 125)

With this move, from being accused by the other in proximity to being responsible for the other through substitution, Levinas considers himself to have revealed an otherwise than being or condition of hostage at the core of subjectivity.

The 'substitution' or 'expiation' for another is coterminous with responsibility, but the latter is understood modally. In expiation the trauma of proximity is intensified by the self substituting itself for all the others – not only does the self suffer the proximity, but also the proximities suffered by all the others. In substitution the subject expiates for the proximity suffered by others; it is 'a hostage expiating for the violence of the persecution itself' (OB, 127). Furthermore, this act of expiation is infinite, for it involves the substitution for all the others, even for all of creation: 'The self, the subjection or subjectivity of the subject, is the very overemphasis of a responsibility for creation. Responsibility for the other, for what has not begun in me is responsibility in the innocence of being a hostage' (OB, 125). The gravity of this responsibility is emphasised by the use of the term 'hostage', since the responsibility at once radically individuates the subject at the same time as investing it with a universal vocation: in Levinas's words, 'No one can substitute himself for me, who substitutes myself for all' (OB, 126). It is in this way that the subject assumes an infinite responsibility that is beyond its capacity, an assumption that is inspiring and elevating, since it involves the ethical assumption of the infinite by the finite. The contraction of the infinite is experienced as an expansion by the subject, for whom the act of substitution can never fully be discharged.

On the basis of this discussion of substitution, the earlier characterisation of responsibility becomes more transparent. The line of argument that runs from proximity to substitution and arrives at the substitution in proximity is traced in the following passages. The first moves from responsibility through proximity to substitution:

> Responsibility for another is not an accident that happens to a subject, but precedes essence in it, has not awaited freedom, in which a commitment to another would have been made. I have not done anything and I have always been under accusation – persecuted. The ipseity, in the passivity without arche characteristic of identity, is a hostage. The word I means *here I am*, answering for everything and for everyone. (OB, 114)

The passage from proximity as the subject under accusation and *responsible to the other* to substitution and the subject's *responsibility for the other* is then rephrased as a movement from substitution to proximity:

> This passivity undergone in proximity by the force of an alterity in me is the passivity of a recurrence to oneself which is not the alienation of an identity betrayed. What can it be but the substitution of me for the others? It is, however not an alienation, because the other in the same is my substitution for the other through responsibility, for which I am summoned as someone irreplaceable. I exist through the other and for the other, but without this being alienation: I am inspired. (OB, 114)

With inspiration, Levinas returns to the infinity contained in the finite already intimated in *Totality and Infinity*, but now framed in terms otherwise than being.

Levinas properly asks if this description of what he has already termed 'fraternity' is also freedom. He argues that it is, thus aligning two of the three terms of the revolutionary trinity of liberty, equality and fraternity. This alignment involves bringing together inspiration and generosity in an 'anarchic liberation' in which 'the self liberates itself ethically from every other and from itself. Its responsibility for other, the proximity of the neighbour, does not signify a submission to the non-ego; it means an openness in which beings' essence is surpassed in inspiration' (OB, 115). This freedom or, as it is later described, 'gratuity', breaks with any notion of totality such as that informing Hegelian objective freedom.

Hegel also returns at this point in Levinas's exposition, but this time in the context of his critique of the third member of the revolutionary trinity – equality. He refers to the 'venerable tradition' represented by Hegel that maintains 'the ego is an equality with itself, and consequently the return of being to itself is a concrete universality', but argues that, 'viewed out of the obsession of passivity, of itself anarchical, there is brought out, behind the equality of consciousness, an inequality' (OB, 115). Such inequality or dissymmetry is essential to maintain the openness and gratuity of substitution as well as the restlessness that accompanies it. The finite subject can, for Levinas, never be equal to infinity, with the consequence that the

Hegelian concrete universality that produces a speculative unity of infinite and finite – for example, freedom and the state – is excluded as an option. Without a constitutive inequality the subject could return into itself and renege on its infinite obligation. Yet the latter is precisely the risk that Levinas accepts when he concedes that there is a possible passage from substitution and proximity to justice and ontology.

In the chapters of *Otherwise than Being* discussed so far, the statements of the irreducibility of proximity and substitution to ontology seem unambiguous. In the discussion of proximity, Levinas insists that 'In proximity a subject is implicated in a way not reducible to the spatial sense which proximity takes on when the third party troubles it by demanding justice' (OB, 81–2). The effects of the proximity of the other are thus irreducible to the demands of the third for justice. Similarly, in the discussion of substitution, Levinas insists that the sphere of justice is restricted to the other: 'Whatever be the ways that lead to the superstructure of society, in justice the dissymmetry that holds me at odds with regard to the other will find again law, autonomy, equality' (OB, 127). Nevertheless, in the final sections of *Otherwise than Being*, Levinas searches for arguments that will link the ethical categories of proximity, substitution and responsibility with the order of ontology.

At a fairly advanced point in the chapter 'Subjectivity and Infinity', Levinas begins the return passage to ontology, not, it seems, that he ever really left it. He asks: 'Why would proximity, the pure signification of saying, the anarchic one-for-the-other of beyond being, revert to being or fall into being, into a conjunction of entities, into essence showing itself in the said?' (OB, 157). The reversion to ontology is necessary in order to face the question of justice that is provoked by the entry of the third, the other of my other. Levinas moves between the other and the third, finding in the subject's proximity with the other an obsession with the third – the dyad of proximity is supplemented or 'corrected' by the advent of the third and their appeal for justice: 'Justice is necessary, that is, comparison, coexistence, contemporaneousness, assembling, order, thematisation, the visibility of faces, and thus intentionality and the intellect, and in intentionality the intelligibility of a system and the intellect and thence also a copresence on an equal footing as before a court of justice' (OB, 157). Yet in spite of immediate appearances Levinas is far from content to usher back an unreformed ontology, but argues instead that ontology itself has been transformed by the persistence of proximity.

Levinas points to the persistence of proximity in the work of justice by arguing that justice to the third is accomplished by one who is sensitive to remaining within proximity with the other. At this pivotal point both for his text and for his concept of the political he maintains that 'justice is not a legality regulating human masses, from which a technique of social equilibrium is drawn, harmonising antagonistic forces. That would be a

141

justification of the State delivered over to its own necessities. Justice is impossible without the one who renders it finding himself in proximity' (OB, 159). Levinas's concept of political thus emerges in *Otherwise than Being* as the ethical qualification of ontology, of recalling proximity to the work of justice. Proximity acts as a control on the exercise of power or application of judgement. The ambition of this ethico–political project should not be underestimated; indeed, Levinas goes on to claim that:

> Justice, society, the State and its institutions, exchanges and work are comprehensible out of proximity. This means that nothing is outside of the control of the responsibility of the one for the other. It is important to recover all these forms beginning with proximity, in which being, totality, the State, politics, techniques, work are at every moment on the point of having their centre of gravitation in themselves, and weighing on their own account. (OB, 159)

Proximity is called to serve as a control on the equalising operations of the state and its institutions and upon the realm of work and commerce. It is almost as if Levinas, after a sustained critique of Hegel, arrives at an endorsement of a form of ethical life or *Sittlichkeit*.

When Levinas begins to describe how proximity might correct the workings of state and civil society, his thought takes a peculiar turn. He ventures on the impossible task of describing the institutionalisation of proximity, and while his resort to the personalist argument that changing individual ethics will have an impact on the actions of institutions is disappointing, it is not too surprising. What is unexpected is his insistence on the priority of the relation to the other over the third – the third cannot become an other without suffering, in Levinas's word, a 'degeneration' (OB, 159). He insists unambiguously that 'the contemporaneousness of the multiple is tied about the diachrony of two: justice remains justice only, in a society where there is no distinction between those close and those far off, but in which there also remains the impossibility of passing by the closest. The equality of all is borne by my inequality, the surplus of my duties over my rights' (OB, 159). The proposal of a distinction between the near and the far that is not a distinction is severely qualified by the impossibility of passing by the closest. Similarly, the claim that a subject troubled by the proximity of its other will 'forget self', be disinterested and thus capable of justice, does not cover the case of forgetting both self and other in order to do justice to the third. One might expect from Levinas's earlier analysis of proximity that forgetting of self must also entail the forgetting of the other, but here it seems the other must always be remembered *before* the third.

The problem with Levinas's resort to the correction of ontology by means of proximity is that it potentially leaves intact the worst forms of state in the name of the other. It seems as permissible on Levinas's account to wage war by forgetting the self in the proximity of the other as it is to pursue the work of justice. Thus as long as responsibility for the other is given precedence over responsibility for the third, it is hard to see that there is the importance that Levinas claims in the distinction between the state that proceeds from 'a war of all against all, or from the irreducible responsibility of the one for all' (OB, 159). If the responsibility for all is channelled through the other, then the potential of a war against all *except* one's other remains a possibility. Indeed, the reference to 'others' in the remainder of this paragraph is always qualified by the distinction between other and third.[6]

The theoretical reason for maintaining the distinction between the other and the third is the fear that the other will be absorbed by totality. Levinas notes that 'the State issued from the proximity of the neighbour is always on the verge of integrating him into a we, which congeals both me and my neighbour' (OB, 161). Yet this position assumes the fragility of proximity and the superior power of the state; it assumes that the other is always in danger of being reduced to a third. The contrary position in which all thirds become others is relegated to an 'angelic order of justice' and not considered to be an option for this world. With this move Levinas makes himself vulnerable to the same criticism that he himself made on a number of occasions of the corruption that can ensue from the other-worldly orientation of the Christian political theology, namely that the displacement of the 'angelic order of justice' to the city of God is effectively to surrender the possibility of justice in the human city.

The suspicion that perhaps Levinas has conceded too much to ontology and left its structures intact, while opening up just enough space to permit an ethical role for philosophy as the questioning of the state, is confirmed by the end of *Otherwise than Being*. The work ends as it and *Totality and Infinity* began – with war. But this is war – with all the ontological entailments that Levinas has taught us to see – now waged with a bad conscience. The otherwise than being is not otherwise than the war that Levinas has shown accompanies ontology: he ends with the muted hope that 'For the little humanity that adorns the earth, a relaxation of essence to the second degree is needed, in the just war waged against war to tremble or shudder at every instant because of this very justice' (OB, 185). It would be disappointing if, after the journey to otherwise than being, we should be content to arrive at a war waged against war, a just war at whose justice we shudder and for whose violence we repent, but a war nevertheless. This outcome of his inquiry is not exclusive since, alongside it, Levinas also traces another route that passes by means of prophetic politics and the discussion of witness. It opens a strand in his political philosophy that might indeed pass from otherwise than being to otherwise than war.

Illeity and prophetic politics

One of the 'extreme conceptual possibilities' of ethics in *Otherwise than Being* points in the direction of a 'prophetic politics'. This notion of politics emerged simultaneously in Levinas's reflections on Jewish identity, and underlined his insistence upon the universal significance of the particular experience of the Jewish people. The notion of prophetic politics in its turn developed in two directions. One is concerned with its universal implications for a revision of the Declaration of the Rights of Man and Citizen in respect of the understanding of human rights and their global application. This was described by Levinas in terms of the prophetic mission of freedom assumed by the French nation with their revolution. The other direction led to the problems posed by the foundation of the State of Israel for prophetic politics and the sufferings of the Palestinians. The problems posed for prophetic politics by the latter will be discussed in the next chapter. Here, discussion will focus first on the formal characteristics of prophetic politics presented in *Otherwise than Being* and the texts on philosophy and Jewish thought that preceded and succeeded it. This will be followed by an assessment of Levinas's application of prophetic politics to human rights and global politics in an enhanced notion of fraternity. The following chapter will assess Levinas's view of the prophetic mission of Israel and the vicissitudes of the State of Israel.

The section 'Witness and Prophesy' in Chapter Five of *Otherwise than Being* offers one of the most excessive moments of the entire text and perhaps even of Levinas's entire thought. It represents an important meeting of the philosophical, the political and the religious, a meeting that informs all of the text, but is here raised to a particular pitch of intensity. In it Levinas explores prophesy in terms of bearing witness to the infinite and describes it in terms of errancy. Between the lines of this discussion is a philosophical, political and religious preoccupation that was manifest more concretely in the essays of *Difficult Freedom*. There, prophesy was related above all to the separation from history characteristic of monotheism and the associated struggle against idolatry. The latter is not made up of the 'statues of wood and stone' but, in its modern form, includes political ideologies, the idea of progress and, consummately, the ultimate idol of the state. Prophesy is linked to the book and its interpretation, and finally to justice or the designation of 'good and evil without worrying about the meaning of history'.[7] It will also emerge as ethics itself and a mode of thinking within and beyond philosophy, one in which philosophy is troubled and traumatised by what Levinas calls 'Talmudic positions'.

One of Levinas's most elegant and programmatic discussions of the troubling of philosophy by religion is to be found in the 1969 lecture 'The Name of God According to a few Talmudic Texts'. The lecture provides a justification for the style of what became *Otherwise than Being*, couched in terms of a distinction between the troubling of philosophy by the Talmudic mode of thought and the Hegelian claim for the supercession of religion through philosophy. Against Hegel's claim that the allegedly 'partial' representations of religious thought are raised to universal comprehension by philosophical consciousness, Levinas insists that the religious remains a 'presupposition' that philosophy is 'incapable of assimilating' and which, like a traumatic trace, returns ever to trouble it (BV, 211).

Yet Levinas insists that the troubling of philosophy by religion is not to be understood as its subordination, according to an inverted Hegelian logic in which religion comprehends the truth after which philosophy strives but is incapable of attaining. In the extraordinary essay 'God and Philosophy' (1975) from Of God who Comes to Mind, Levinas insists on the ineluctability of philosophy, claiming that 'In sketching the contours of prophetic witnessing behind philosophy where transcendence is always to be reduced, we have not entered into the moving sands of religious experience' (OG, 76). Instead Levinas seeks a mode of thought and a style that is capable of rendering the mutual troubling of the philosophical and the religious. More than this, however, is the further claim that this mode of thought and style – the neither philosophy nor theology characteristic of Otherwise than Being – is also the object of that thought. This is most evident in the intensification of the troubling of philosophy by religion in the section of Otherwise than Being on 'Witness and Prophesy', and especially in the saturation of the concept of illeity.

The extremely concentrated concept of illeity is central to Levinas's notion of a prophetic witness both beyond and within philosophy. It is called at once to name the third mode of thought between philosophy and religion, to epitomise Levinas's critique of phenomenology, and to provoke the most unrestrained version of his ethics, and in extremity even to serve as one of the names of God. Any formal account of Levinas's notion of prophesy will depend on the exposition of this concept, whose extraordinary emergence may be followed, from the 1963 essay 'The Trace of the Other', through Otherwise than Being, to 'The Name of God According to a Few Talmudic Texts'.[8]

'The Trace of the Other' marks an important stage in the development of Levinas's thinking, not only from Totality and Infinity to Otherwise than Being but also beyond the latter. It intensifies the critique of Western philosophy developed in Totality and Infinity, ascribing to it 'since its infancy a horror of the other which remains an insurmountable allergy' ('La trace de l'autre', 188) which, given Levinas's discussion of horror, is a weighty charge. This charge is also directed against Hegel, who is called to 'represent the logical terminus of this fundamental allergy of philosophy' (189). The charge against Western philosophy's investment in structures of identity and return is famously expressed in the comparison of Ulysses and Abraham: 'To the myth of Ulysses returning to Ithaca we would like to oppose the story of Abraham who left for ever his country for a land still unknown and who forbade his servant to lead his son to the point of departure' (191). To the economy of departure and return, giving and receiving, that structures the narrative of loss and recovery of the homeland, Levinas opposes the aneconomy of wandering and homelessness. The former is linked with identity and its ruses of loss and recovery, the latter with excessive desire for the infinite that arises in the encounter with the other.

So far the argument conforms broadly to that of *Totality and Infinity*, with the alignment of desire, infinity and alterity. However, in Section 5 of 'The Trace of the Other', Levinas introduces the themes of the immemorial past and a 'beyond essence', the importance of the latter underlined by its appearance as the subtitle to *Otherwise than Being*. Yet the notion of a beyond essence that is adumbrated in the later sections of 'The Trace of the Other' in many ways exceeds much of the argument of *Otherwise than Being*, reappearing on those occasions of philosophical compression exemplified by the section 'Witness and Prophesy'. Through the concept of the trace Levinas seeks to mark an understanding of the beyond that exceeds the distinction of immanence and transcendence. The attempt at a self-criticism of the position represented in *Totality and Infinity* is evident, since now Levinas no longer conceives of the beyond in terms of a transcendence or 'infinity' opposed to immanence or 'totality'. The attempt to think beyond the disjunctive opposition that structures *Totality and Infinity* will have implications not only for the thinking of alterity, but also for the relation between ethics and politics. It may even be argued that these implications for prophetic politics were never fully worked through by Levinas, but continued to trouble his own troubling of philosophy.

The implications are most evident in Levinas's exploration of the 'beyond' in terms of the third person. He suggests that the '*Beyond of Being is a third person*' who is not defined in terms of self or ipseity. [The third person] represents the possibility of the third direction of a radical unconformity, which escapes the bipolar play of immanence and transcendence characteristic of being, in which immanence is always victorious over transcendence. The profile of the irreversible past assumes by way of the trace, the profile of a 'him' (199). The beyond being is here presented in terms of the 'third' – precisely the 'third' that earlier in *Totality and Infinity*, and also later in *Otherwise than Being*, represented the order of justice and the state, namely the reduction of alterity. From the critique of the 'third' on the grounds of its Hegelian mediation of that which should not be mediated – the I and its other in proximity – Levinas here proposes a thought of the 'third' that is beyond, not below, the opposition of ipseity and alterity, and gives it the name '*illeity*'.

Clearly such a notion of the third cannot be equated with the third of Hegelian mediation, and indeed *illeity* for Levinas does not offer itself as a

146

site for synthesis of self and other. It is described as 'all the enormity, all the excess, all the infinity of the absolutely other that escapes ontology' (199), implying that it escapes even the radical reformulation of ontology carried through in *Totality and Infinity*. Alongside the introduction of *illeity* Levinas also unfolds the 'trace' in terms of temporal irreversibility, but, crucially, of an event that did not take place in time. The theme of irreversibility, which in the 'Reflections on Hitlerism' Levinas criticised in the name of the monotheistic freedom from fate, now returns in the service of a radical conception of responsibility. The irreversibility of the immemorial past weighs on the 'relation' of self and other. Yet it is crucial that the burden of the other – later to be analysed in terms of proximity and substitution – here issues from the third; or, in Levinas's words, the relation of *illeity* and the trace 'is personal and ethical, obliges but does not reveal' (199). The responsibility for the other takes place as *illeity* or the emergence of the sense of irreversibility linked to the immemorial past but producing effects – responsibility – in the present. The arrival of the sense of an irreversible but immemorial past is defined by Levinas as a 'visitation' in order to distinguish it from immanence and transcendence. *Illeity* is thus modal, opening the relation of self and other, but always exceeding the terms of any relation.

Levinas describes the passage of *illeity* in terms of the face, showing that it supplements what is manifest in the face – and thus is unavailable for phenomenological analysis – with a gravity that is not visible. He writes, 'The face is for itself visitation and transcendence. But the face completely open can at the same time be in itself because it is in the trace of *illeity*' (202). Even at the limit case when the face of the other is totally exposed and apparently open for appropriation it nevertheless remains withdrawn by virtue of an immemorial past which cannot be thematised and which is experienced as responsibility. Levinas thus continues, undercutting the claims of ontology, '*Illeity* is the origin of the alterity of being in which the in itself of objectivity participates in betraying' (202). After this derivation of alterity itself from *illeity*, Levinas concludes with a compressed paragraph on God and the immemorial past. God is manifest only by means of his trace; and to go towards him is not to follow his trace as if it were a sign pointing towards him, but to 'go towards the others that hold themselves in the trace' (202). The ending intimates that the third in question in *illeity* is divinity, and that God – beyond immanence and transcendence – is announced in the ethical relation of *illeity* and the trace.

The compressed cluster of themes announced in 'The Trace of the Other' returns in the section on 'Witness and Prophesy' in *Otherwise than Being*. The definition of prophesy follows a discussion of the inspiration of the subject through *illeity* that disrupts the many philosophical distinctions that follow from the founding distinction of immanence from transcendence.

Through the discussion of prophetic inspiration, Levinas is able to bring together the themes of *Otherwise than Being* under the sign of *illeity*. He writes that 'The subject is inspired by the infinite, which, as *illeity*, does not appear, is not present, has always already passed, is neither theme, telos, nor interlocutor' (OB, 148). This subject is no longer subject to 'the originary unity of transcendental apperception', it is not in command of its own identity, nor is it positioned, as with Kant, between heteronomy and autonomy. Just because it is not autonomous – in its inspiration by the other – does not mean that it is subject to heteronomy. Inspiration as *illeity* is 'an inscription of the law in consciousness' that in 'a remarkable way' is able to 'reconcile' autonomy and heteronomy. Yet this is not the Hegelian reconciliation of freedom and law achieved through autonomy or self-legislation; rather, it is the ambivalence of 'being the author of what had been breathed in unbeknownst to me, of having received, one knows not from where, that of which I am the author' (OB, 148–9). Being inspired by the infinite through responsibility for the other provides the context for Levinas's definition of prophesy as the perception of 'the other in the same' or the movement between being the author and the authored.

The distance that Levinas wishes to establish between his view of the encounter between autonomy and heteronomy – between giving and being subject to law – and that of Hegel is restated in terms of *illeity*. Through it, the role played by mediation in Hegel's system is replaced by that of prophesy – namely, bearing witness to a third beyond the opposition of finite and infinite. The distance is taken in Levinas's refusal of the mediatory movement of Hegelian dialectic: 'It is in prophesy that the infinite escapes the objectification of thematisation and dialogue, and signifies as *illeity*, in the third person' (OB, 150). Yet this third does not reconcile, but divides the self and the other, making possible the inauguration of justice: 'This "thirdness" is different from that of the third man, it is the third party that interrupts the face to face of a welcome of the other man, interrupts the proximity or approach of the neighbour, it is the third man with which justice begins' (OB, 150). At the end of this passage Levinas refers parenthetically to his later discussion of justice already examined above, but there is a cleft between them. For while, here, the third of *illeity* is beyond the movement of self and other, making it possible, there the third of justice is the falling from the relation with the other into representation – 'Justice requires contemporaneousness of representation' (OB, 159). The justice of prophetic politics might be read as exceeding representation as well as the relation with the other.

While Hegel would view justice in terms of the reconciliation of opposed claims in a third mediatory instance, Levinas has introduced a notion of justice not as reconciliation, but as its interruption. It would seem at this point that the justice of prophetic politics would even interrupt the proximity of the other, itself an invasion of the identity of the

ipseity
alterity
illeity

subject, but one which might, it seems, become unjust. And indeed, the interruption of *illeity* has a number of peculiar characteristics. In terms of its source it is described as an 'order to come from I know not where', a 'coming that is not a recalling', ' It is the coming of the order to which I am subjected before hearing it' (OB, 150); that is, one that, in terms of its unassignable origin, remains outside of the series of causes and effects. Its consequences are equally unassignable: *illeity* 'does not constrain or domi-nate and leaves me outside of any correlation with its source. No *structure* is set up with a correlate' (OB, 150). The justice that emerges with the interruption of *illeity* is not one which establishes a structure – itself a form of reconciliation – but is anarchic. According to this concept of justice, 'Authority is not somewhere, where a look could seek it, like an idol, or assume it like a logos' (OB, 150); it is not, in short, vested in a state or in a law of nature but is anarchic, 'the pure trace of a "wandering cause", inscribed in me' (OB, 150). This trace – itself beyond immanence and transcendence – has no place, even though it is 'inscribed in me'. Thus the law that orients the interruptions that constitute justice is the inscrip-tion of a trace – anarchic in having no assignable origin or giving rise to any authoritative structure – an inscription that provides the relation of trace and *illeity* that for Levinas describes the Law.

The notion of the inscription of the trace that must be beyond imma-nence or transcendence is clarified by returning to the notion of inspiration and its relation to inscription. This relation is largely taken for granted in *Otherwise than Being*, but is explicitly analysed in the 1979 text 'On the Jewish Reading of Scriptures'. There the book is hesitantly described as 'the modality by which what is said lays itself open to exegesis, calls for it; and where meaning, immobilised in the characters, already tears the textures in which it is held' (BV, 110). The inscriptions making up the book generate meanings; the inscription is an invitation to inspiration, or the interruption of 'another meaning which breaks through from beneath the immediate meaning of what is meant to be said, another meaning which beckons to a way of hearing that listens beyond what is heard, beckons to extreme consciousness, a consciousness that has been awoken' (BV, 111). The inscription of the trace 'awakens' or interrupts by virtue of its call to interpretation or the discovery of the 'other voice resonating in the first'. The trace that is inscribed evokes proximity – the other in the same – and may be described in the same terms as Levinas describes the inspired text, namely as 'the modality, the actual "how" of the ethical code that disturbs the established order of being' (BV, 111). In the section under discussion in *Otherwise than Being*, this disturbance is presented in terms of ethical anachrony – 'this obedience prior to all representation, this alle-giance before any oath, this responsibility prior to commitment, is precisely the other in the same, inspiration and prophesy, the *passing itself* of the infinite' (OB, 150). Meaning and justice consist in the interruption of reconciliation, an interruption and awakening that is never completed but which remains conscious to the other voice which 'drowns out or tears' not only the first voice, but every subsequent voice that would resonate within it. This is the 'other voice' that may be the voice of the other but may also be the voice of the third or *illeity* that will interrupt even the voice of the other in the name of justice.

Prophetic politics opens the possibility for a notion of justice as perpetual interruption, of the self by the other and of the other by the third. The third in question here, and the justice to which it gives rise, is not the third of the state and its justice thought of in terms of equivalence and measure, but the third thought of in terms of divinity and in the divine approbation of human fraternity. It is with fraternity that the section 'Witness and Prophesy' ends, namely with the impossibility of denying fraternity, of prophetically interrupting every fixing of fraternity between self and other in the name of the third. The serious consequences of such politics for the concept of freedom are explored in a preliminary way in 'The Name of God According to a Few Talmudic Texts'.

In the final section of this text on 'Philosophy', Levinas returns to *illeity*, according it the most extraordinary dignity. *Illeity* forms the transition between responsibility and divinity:

> This anteriority of responsibility must be understood in relation to freedom as the very authority of the Absolute which is 'too great' for the measure or finitude of presence, revelation, order and being, and which consequently, as neither being nor non-being, is the 'excluded third party' of the beyond of being and non-being, a third person that we have called 'illeity' and that is perhaps also expressed by the word God. (BV, 128)

The third, God or *illeity*, is 'excluded from being, but orders it in relation to a responsibility' or, in other words, it is *illeity* that, beyond being, provides the authority 'that orders my neighbour for me as a face'. The face of the other is given to me by the third; the responsibility for the other precedes my freedom and will interrupt its exercise. *Illeity* informs the inspiration of prophesy that will be described in 'Revelation in the Jewish Tradition' as 'the anxiety of man caused by the infinite of God which he could never contain, but which inspires him...obedience to the Most-High as an ethical relation with the other' (BV, 147–8). Fraternity emerges as the relation to the other through the divine third, and is here given precedence over freedom.

The notion of prophetic politics is not an exercise in abstract political theology, but is applied by Levinas to hard political cases. Its implications for fraternity mean that it can be used to enrich the understanding of the 'rights of man and citizen' summarised in the revolutionary trinity of 'liberty, equality and fraternity', and, in addition, its reference to the absolute in *illeity* gives it a global reach that makes it significant in the evaluation of globalisation. It provokes extreme difficulty, however, when discussing the significance of the State of Israel, since it seems *prima facie* to call for an interruption of the state in the name of justice. Levinas's tormented reckoning with the question of Israel and the State of Israel will be examined in the following chapter. The remainder of this chapter will examine the implications of prophetic politics for the understanding of human rights and the issues of globalisation and hunger.

The rights of man and citizen

Can democracy and the 'rights of man' divorce themselves without danger from their prophetic and ethical depths? (BV)

Levinas's reflections on human rights published during the 1980s may be approached both as a development of the notion of prophetic politics and as a return to the attempt – begun in the 1930s – to develop a notion of fraternity that would complement liberty and equality without risk of class, national, racial or religious exclusion. The later writings on human rights amount to a reflection on the danger, inherent in the trinity of modern republicanism, that a parochial definition of fraternity as the class, nation, race or church, will compromise the universal aspirations of liberty and equality. Levinas understood the particular figures of fraternity as secularised idolatry, and posed against this idolatry the 'prophetic and ethical depths' that would trouble any particular figuration of fraternity. It will be seen in the next chapter that this troubling of the figures of fraternal identity will also be applied to the problem of the universal or particular character of the fraternity figured in Israel, not to speak of the State of Israel.

Levinas's thoughts on the issue of human rights are most fully expressed in three essays published during the 1980s that mark the final phase of his work. The series opens in 1981 with the 'Prohibition against Representation and the "The Rights of Man"', and continues in 1985 with 'The Rights of Man and the Rights of the Other' and in 1989 with 'The Rights of the Other Man'. The essays derive the *a priori* normative character of human rights from alterity and elaborate a catalogue of distinct particular rights. In them Levinas explores further the 'relations' between rights and institutions such as the state and technology, as well as broader issues of justice and politics. He shows considerable sensitivity to the perversion of rights and begins to show how, if they are rooted in a prophetic politics, they may serve as a corrective to the actions of political institutions. Read together, the essays amount to an attempt to separate rights discourse from its roots in individualism, without, however, lapsing into the fraternal politics of communitarianism. They amount to the vindication of the universal mission of prophetic politics, beyond any particular state including the State of Israel.

In the essays, Levinas insists on the *a priori* character of human rights, *a priori* in the sense of being prior to institutions and acts of association and in possessing an autonomous source of normativity. He derives the *a priori* character of human rights from his ethics of alterity, now developed in the direction of an account of responsibility and love that aspires to universal fraternity. He speaks of the responsibility for the other as an 'Event of sociality prior to all association in the name of an abstract common "humanity". *The right of man, absolutely and originally,* takes on meaning only in the other, as the right of the other man' (AT, 127). The origin of right does not lie in an act of possession but in the event of dispossessing the self before the other, the details and implications of which have already been examined. The *a priori* character of what Levinas calls, in 'The Rights of Man and the Rights of the Other', 'original right' consists in the unique responsibility for the other that was explicated in *Otherwise than Being* in terms of substitution and which contains a relation to the divine. This responsibility is prior to the act of sociality, to institutions, above all those of the state, to 'any authority or tradition' (AT, 145), to any entitlement, to 'all jurisprudence, all granting of privileges, awards or titles' (OS, 117) and even to reason itself, or more precisely to 'all consecration by a will abusively claiming the name of reason' (OS, 117).

Levinas underlines the extent to which this locating of human rights in the right of the other, although intrinsic to rights discourse, also marks a break with its ontological entailments.[9] In 'The Prohibition against Representation and "The Rights of Man"' this break is represented as involving the fundamental tendency of Western culture – which we have seen Levinas identify with ontology – while in 'The Rights of the Other Man' and 'The Rights of Man and the Rights of the Other' he is more specific, in the former locating the break in the Renaissance, and in the latter, during the eighteenth century and thus the Enlightenment. In each case, Levinas recognises the existence of a broad, powerful and liberatory rights discourse established on ontological premises, but argues that it must be reformed on the basis of 'prophetic and ethical depth'.

The most detailed argument raised against the ontological structure of existing rights discourse is to be found in 'The Rights of Man and the Rights of the Other'. Tellingly, Levinas does not put in question the importance of rights discourse in qualifying the actions of institutions and the application of law, but rather its ability to do so on the basis of ontological criteria of possession or entitlement. The 'original right' cannot be conceived in terms of possession or entitlement without the danger of it being applied against itself; instead it must be conceived in terms of the 'right of the other'. Levinas endorses the view that 'the right to respect for the human dignity of the individual, the rights to life, liberty and equality before the law for all men – are based on an original sense of the right, or the sense of an original right' (OS, 116), but cannot accept the prevailing understanding of such original right in terms of 'any power that would be the original share of each human being in the blind distribution of nature's energy and society's influence, but also independent of the merits the human individual may have acquired by his or her efforts and even virtues' (OS, 116–17). Original right must trouble these entitlements – 'tearing loose' from any notion of the proper and of property and finding itself in the traumatic proximity of the other.

By locating 'original right' in proximity and substitution – in what he also called the 'humanism of the other man' – Levinas rigorously distinguished human from natural rights. While the early modern rights tradition used the adjective 'natural' to validate the *a priori* character of human rights, Levinas insists that they transcend nature, thus linking fundamental rights with the 'requirement of transcendence, in a sense, of the inhuman that may be contained in pure nature, and of blind necessity in the social body' (OS, 121). Rights issuing from the 'original right' of the other respect the 'uniqueness and irreducibility of human persons' by 'the diminishing of the violence to which they are exposed in the order, or disorder, of the determinism of the real' (OS, 121). Here Levinas starts to describe the substance of his understanding of rights discourse, while at the same time respecting his earlier critique of the ontological entailments of the biologism of the Nazi–Fascist era and the 'cosmo-politics' of the Cold War.

The extent of the protection of the person that Levinas was prepared to concede to rights discourse is impressive. He includes not only 'original right' and its immediate derivates (such as the right to life that is the correlate of the responsibility for the other expressed in 'thou shalt not kill'), but also the legal rules that condition the exercise of rights. Thus Levinas claims that:

> Behind the rights to life and security, to the free disposal of one's goods and the equality of all men before the law, to freedom of thought and its expression, to education and participation in political power – there are all the other rights that extend these, or make them concretely possible: the right to health, happiness, work, rest, a place to live, freedom of movement, and so on. But also, beyond all that, the right to oppose exploitation by capital (the right to unionise) and even the right to social advancement; the right (utopian or Messianic) to the refinement of the human condition, the right to ideology as well as the right to fight for the full rights of man, and the right to ensure the necessary political conditions for that struggle. (OS, 120)

153

The 'original right' of the other thus extends into a system of diverse 'objective' rights, one which is hierarchically structured in terms of 'urgency, order and hierarchy' but which does not 'recognise any limitation to the defence of these rights' (OS, 120). The potentially radical politics which this concept of right permits can be illustrated by Levinas's discussion of the right to life couched in terms of the inadmissibility of hunger.

The theme of hunger explored in 'Secularisation and Hunger' (1976) and developed in the lectures *God, Death and Time* is revealed to involve rather more than the elementary right to nourishment. It serves as the means by which the right of the other is embodied. Levinas locates the discussion of hunger within what might appear at the outset as an unexpected context – that of secularisation and the assessment of technology. The theme of hunger is introduced after an extended and thinly disguised critique of Heidegger that forcefully restates the link between ontology and paganism that Levinas insisted upon on many other occasions. He describes the move from idolatry to ontology – 'the extraordinary rupture of transcendence that is idolatry, the repose of the earth under the vault of the sky prefigures the reign of the same'[10] – in terms of the secularisation of idolatry. Ontology or, as it has now been revealed, secularised idolatry is then linked through the experience of hunger to the notions of economy and technology. In a fascinating passage, Levinas discloses some of the links between divinity, ontology, economy and technology that are evident throughout his work but rarely thematised so explicitly:

> There is consequently an affinity between the secularisation of the idolatry that becomes ontology (i.e., the intelligibility of the cosmos, representation and presence measuring and equalling each other) and the good practical sense of men gnawed by hunger, inhabiting their houses, residing and building. Every practical relationship with the world is representation, and the world represented is economic. There is a universality of economic life that opens it to the life of being. Greece is the site of this intersection... (GDT, 166)

Thus Levinas describes a link between hunger, the use of technology to satisfy hunger and the ontology that permits the equivalence of representations that underpin technological relations.

Levinas's positive evaluation of global technology will be evaluated below, but already it is possible to gain some sense of his distance from the Heideggerian critique of technology. He sees technology as an agent of secularisation, 'destructive of pagan gods' of nature, the cosmos, place and the elements: 'Technology teaches us that these gods are of the world, and therefore are things, and being things they are nothing much' (GDT, 166). To these are added in 'Secularisation and Hunger' the gods of fate and blood, thus linking these late essays with the early critique of National Socialist ideology in 'The Philosophy of Hitlerism'. Secularisation through technology is joined with secularisation through hunger – a movement that 'begins in human corporeality' and tends 'in the direction of the beyond where a God that is other than the visible gods would abide' (GDT, 169). The privation of hunger excludes consolation 'in the image of a spiritually ordered world' but would be fed: it turns away from the pagan gods and puts the question of its nourishment to God. The question *a dieu* is none other, as seen, than the question to the other. Thus Levinas's discourse on hunger concludes with the 'appearance of transcendence' through the hunger of the other. In place of the cosmological wonder lying at the origin of Greek philosophy that had been discussed earlier in the lectures and in 'Secularisation and Hunger', Levinas ends with the wonder provoked by the ethical response to hunger:

> We cannot wonder enough over the transference, which goes from the memory of my own hunger to suffering and compassion for the hunger of the other man. This is a transference in which an untransferable responsibility is expressed, and with it the impossible evasion that individuates even him who, sated, does not understand the hungry one and does not cease escaping his own responsibility without also escaping himself. (GDT, 171)

The ethical sense for the hunger of the other is a source for the claim of the other on me, of the other's 'original right' over me.

The two trajectories of secularisation – technology and hunger – coincide in 'Secularisation and Hunger' at a point where responsibility for the hunger of the other can be discharged by the development of technology. Against anti-technological rhetorics Levinas insists that the ever-increasing numbers of human beings 'in the path of development...will not be nourished without the development of technology'.[11] Technology is thus essential to discharge the right to nourishment and to life, but the question of the right itself is more fundamental than that of technology. In the Talmudic reading 'The Youth of Israel' (1970), Levinas remembers the European hunger of the war years and the hunger of the camps at the same time as protesting the hunger of the Third World. Here the right of the other to nourishment is described as paramount: 'the problem of a hungry world can be resolved only if the food of the owners and those who are provided for ceases to appear to them as their inalienable property, but is recognised as a gift they have received for which thanks must be given and to which others have a right. Scarcity is a social and moral problem and not exclusively an economic one' (TR, 133). The right of the other to nourishment is also important for recognition of the self, for, as we saw, the one who evades the hunger of the other also evades themselves, or, in terms of the Talmudic reading,

feeding the Third World is essential 'so that the West, despite its abundance, does not revert to the level of an undeveloped mankind' (TR, 133),
one which remains on a war footing for the defence and expansion of its
possession at the cost of its victims. Nevertheless, even if the question of
the hunger of the other is primarily an ethical one, the answer cannot
ignore the issue of how these rights may be institutionalised, and what
dangers attend this process.

In 'The Rights of Man and the Rights of the Other' Levinas warns of
the danger that the rights of man may turn against themselves when they
are institutionalised. They must be institutionalised for the world to be fed,
but this bears with it considerable risk. For as he warns 'the development
of science and technology which is supposed to make possible the actual
respect for the enlarged rights of man may, in turn, bring with it inhuman
requirements that make up a new determinism, threatening the free movements that it was to make possible. For example, in a totally industrialised
society or in a totalitarian society – which are precisely the results of
supposedly perfected social techniques – the rights of man are compromised by the very practices for which they supplied the motivation' (OS,
121). The inversion that Levinas at other points described as 'Stalinisation'
is not an avoidable risk, since the extension of the rights of man in the
West and the Third World depends on the improvement and extension of
technical and political institutions. The development of technology is
necessary to satisfy the right to nourishment and health of the other, while
political institutions are necessary to safeguard the further rights.

It is with respect to the risks attending the embodiment of human rights
in political institutions that Levinas returns to the concept of prophetic
politics. If protected only by law and justice, the 'fundamental principle of
the rights of man remains repressed', the right of the Other is lost in the
equations and measures of conflicting individual rights in state and society.
Levinas describes the political necessities – recourse to a state and its laws
– as 'constituting a determinism as rigorous as that of nature indifferent to
man' (OS, 123). The respect for the rights of the other are 'soon unrecog-
nised in the deviations imposed by the practicalities of the state, soon lost
in the deployment of means brought to bear. And in the eventuality of a
totalitarian state, man is repressed and a mockery made of the rights of
man, and the promise of an ultimate return to the rights of man is postponed indefinitely' (OS, 123). Yet this is a risk that cannot be ignored, but
instead must be taken account of in ethical and political action.

The taking into account of the risks involved in the political and technical pursuit of the rights of man as the rights of the other – keeping open
the promise to the other – is the inspiration of prophetic politics. The latter
is now revealed to involve an 'extra-territorial' vigilance. Taking up again
the Dreyfusard claim for the defence of the rights of man, Levinas writes
that

the defence of the rights of man corresponds to a vocation *outside* the state, disposing, in a political society, of a kind of extra-territoriality, like that of prophesy in the face of the political powers of the Old Testament, a vigilance totally different from political intelligence, a lucidity not limited to yielding itself before the formalism of universality, but upholding justice itself in its limitations. (OS, 123)

The defence of the rights of man in the form of the rights of the other that makes up prophetic politics has two significant features that Levinas now locates in the liberal state, but which will also be of importance when we come to examine the place of Israel in prophetic politics. The first is the *place* of such politics and the other its *inspiration* or concept of justice.

The extra-territorial place of prophetic politics is extremely problematic, and will be discussed further in the following chapter. On one reading its place is outside and above the state, carrying the risk of the separation of the two worlds, but on another it is at the heart of the state. The paradoxical location of prophetic politics is illuminated by Levinas's critique of Buber is 'Utopia and Socialism', where he speaks of a recollection of a promise that should be maintained within the state:

perhaps this recollection, the ever-renewed quest for a society in which the *being-together* of men should be realised, a resistance to the forgetting of this utopian *should-be* at the very heart of State structures setting themselves up as ends in themselves, and the resurgence of conscience against the State's deterioration of social relations – are themselves objective events. Events that mark, in the society State dialectic, the moment of morality limiting politics – an indispensable and unforgettable moment. (AT, 116)

Whether within or without the state, prophetic politics can maintain its extra-territoriality by means of the promise to which it remains faithful; that is, the promise of justice for the other – the respect for the original right of the other which is also the respect for an entire catalogue of human rights.

With the return to a political programme reminiscent of the Dreyfusard defence of the rights of man, the central issue of that defence also returns to the agenda, namely, the relation between liberty, equality and fraternity. In Levinas's prophetic politics, the inspiration of justice requires 'a different "authority" than that of the harmonious relation between wills' – that is to say, one not authorised primarily or exclusively by freedom. Yet, in the closing paragraphs of 'The Rights of Man and the Rights of the Other', Levinas moves towards the thought of a 'freedom in fraternity' through the proximity of the other and the substitution of the rights of the other for one's right of self-assertion. The qualification of the claims of the subject

i.e. FRATERNITY.   understood heterologically vs
understood periodically. autologically.
LEVINAS AND THE POLITICAL

through proximity opens the possibility for 'a goodness in peace, which is
also the exercise of a freedom, and in which the I frees itself from its
"return to self", from its auto-affirmation, from its egotism of a being
persevering in its being, *to answer for the other*, precisely to defend the
rights of the other man' (OS, 124–5). Answering for the Other, defending
their rights, is an exercise of freedom from totality that governs and is
governed by self-assertion.

Levinas ends by emphasising that this goodness in peace is none other
than 'the fraternity that is the motto of the republic' (OS, 125), but now
understood in terms of the proximity of the other. The ethical basis of
fraternity is thus freed from membership of a particular community and
offers an 'original right', orienting justice prior to the institutions of the
state. It permits the re-ordering of the trinity of 'liberty, equality and
fraternity' that inspires the republican defence of human rights. The ethical
basis of fraternity permits 'A freedom in fraternity, in which the responsibility of the one-for-the-other is affirmed, and through which the rights of
man manifest themselves *concretely* to consciousness as the rights of the
other, for which I am answerable' (OS, 125). It is not only the character of
freedom that is changed through proximity from self-assertion to the
responsibility for the other; equality too is transformed by substitution.
Equality is no longer founded in community – the equality of the brothers
– but in difference, in extreme individuation: in responsibility 'I am insti-
tuted as non-interchangeable: I am chosen as unique and incomparable'
(OS, 125). The doctrine of substitution developed in *Otherwise than Being*
now reappears alongside that of proximity in the context of the revision of
the philosophical basis for thinking the nature of liberty, equality and
fraternity, as well as the relations between the three terms.

With this closing argument Levinas seals his restructuring of the philosophical bases of modern republicanism. In place of the premise that the
free expression of my rights are necessarily in opposition to those of the
other – that we are at war – he begins with a freedom invested in responsibility for the other, an equality in terms of a singularity produced in
substitution for the other and a peaceful fraternity that answers for the
rights of the other. In many ways he may be judged to have succeeded in
elaborating the philosophical revision of modern republicanism which he
set out to achieve in the 1930s. It now remains to be seen what became of
this ethical politics when confronted by the Cold War and the wars of the
State of Israel.

cf. AE, 243. where Levinas proposes that
everything must be thought or rethought
on the basis of proximity.

5

ISRAEL IN UNIVERSAL AND
HOLY HISTORY

> The State of Israel, whatever the ephemeral political philosophy of its greatest workers, is not for us a state like any other. It has a density and depth that greatly surpass its scope and its political possibilities; it is like a protest against the world.
>
> (DF, 'How is Judaism Possible?')

Levinas's right to silence?

When asked in the 1986 interviews with François Poirié about the State of Israel, Levinas gave an answer and then insisted he could not answer. Admitting the question affected him deeply – 'You are touching there on too many strong feelings' – Levinas responded: 'I would only say that now, under the given circumstances, as a state is the only form in which Israel – the people and the culture – can survive' (RB, 81). When Poirié persisted with the question, Levinas closed the discussion by saying: 'I will say to you that there are many things about which I cannot speak because I am not in Israel. I forbid myself to speak about Israel, not being in Israel, not living its noble adventure and not running this great daily risk' (RB, 82). What is the meaning of this silence that is professed but not maintained? Why the injunction on himself not to speak of Israel, especially when having just spoken of Israel? The echoes of another philosophico–political silence – that of Heidegger – are deafening and raise the question of Levinas's right to silence on the subject of the State of Israel.

The explicit justification that Levinas cites for his silence is hardly convincing. The claim that it is only possible to speak of a State if one is in the State is little short of an abdication of political and ethical responsibility. It certainly does not square with Levinas's universal prophetic politics of human rights. Thankfully Levinas does not rigorously respect his own injunction, speaking in public on many occasions about the State of Israel. However, while speaking of the State of Israel he partially respects his vow of silence by refraining from saying everything or instead speaking indirectly through proxies. In this way he preserves a silence

159

within his saying, one that paradoxically is loudest around the question of the *State* of Israel. When Poirié asks explicitly about 'the existence of the State of Israel', Levinas does not reply that 'the State of Israel' is the only form under which Israel – people and culture – can survive; instead he resorts to the circumlocution, 'under the given circumstances, as a State' is the only form of survival. The avoidance of the name 'State of Israel' paradoxically echoes other avoidances motivated by very different political denials of the *de jure* right to existence of the State of that name.

In a political situation in which official silences and avoidance of names – whether of the 'State of Israel' or 'the Palestinians' or 'the Palestine Liberation Organisation' – were a mode of conducting war by other means, Levinas's silence is in danger of becoming too eloquent. Yet it is saved by a complexity that expresses more than a particular conflict, even if on occasion it does not seem equal to the terms of that conflict. Levinas's consistency in seeing Israel as more than the State of Israel, while recognising the crucial significance of the latter for Jewish identity in the Diaspora, has been noted and will be discussed further. The basis of his position may be sought in his distinction between two histories of Israel – the universal and the holy. In the first, the Hegelian universal history of nation-states, Israel figures as a nation-state alongside other nation-states, participating in their history. In the second, Israel is more than any nation-state, and its revealed ethical mission exceeds the limits of their violent histories. The distinction also maps onto the diverse readings of ethics and politics anticipated in Levinas's early post-war writings and informing *Totality and Infinity* and *Otherwise than Being*. Universal history is the history of political ontology, while holy history is that of an ethical mission that began in an act of revelation.

The immediate post-war writings, marked by a certain resignation regarding the pagan world, did not entirely surrender the claims of the ethical. For Levinas it was important to keep separate the sacred and the profane, and not to surrender revelation to idolatry. Yet, as observed on diverse occasions, the greatest form of modern idolatry – summed up in totalitarianism – is idolatry of the state, hence raising the expectation that the revealed ethical mission of Israel be directed against the state as the greatest and most powerful of the modern idols. Levinas's interpretation of the Rights of Man is guided by this strategy, showing that the exercise of power by the modern state is contained and even subverted by revealed ethical principles translated into the language of rights. Yet the place of the ethical in the political is fragile, continually beset by the risk of succumbing to the idolatry of power and the state.

In 'The State of Israel and the Religion of Israel' (1951), Levinas acknowledged the modern idolatry of the state while attempting to distance the State in general and the State of Israel in particular from the charge of idolatry in so far as 'it precisely permits full self-consciousness'

(DF, 216). This movement was possible because of the ambiguous place of Israel in universal and sacred history. In terms of universal history – 'national histories' – it would not be enough 'to restore the State of Israel in order to have a political life' (DF, 217), since its 'sovereignty...like the light of satellites, is merely borrowed' (DF, 217). Yet, in comparison, 'a religious history extends the size of its modest territory', and in the case of Israel (but not the State of Israel) this history 'marks the true sovereignty of Israel' that is universal. It is this holy history whose prophetic call for justice 'is placed above the State, but has already achieved the very notion of the spirit announced by the modern state' (DF, 217). What prevents the state from becoming an idol are the principles of liberty, equality and fraternity that for Levinas express the religious sovereignty of Israel and that stand above and check the modern state's potential for becoming an idol of power. The State of Israel uniquely inherits the legacy of Israel through both universal and religious history: as a modern state it acknowledges the declaration of rights inherited by the modern state from the Jewish tradition, while through it 'the Jewish people therefore achieves a State whose prestige none the less stems from the religion which modern political life supplants' (DF, 217). In Levinas's view the dual heritage of the State of Israel, expressed in its Declaration of Independence, gives it a peculiar status and responsibility among the modern nation-states.[1]

In the case of the State of Israel, the risk of surrendering revelation to the idolatry of the state grounded in the necessities of political ontology is critical. The founding Declaration of Independence of the State of Israel of 14 May 1948 combined modern principles of liberty and equality with those of justice and peace bequeathed by the prophetic tradition of Israel. It was this relation between the political and the prophetic that became the central concern of Levinas's work, but it proved the source of as many philosophical political difficulties as the history of the State of Israel. It became necessary to seek points of crossing between the political and the prophetic, between ontology and ethics and, ultimately, between universal and holy history.

Levinas's judgements of the State of Israel embody this difficult adjustment between the demands of a nation-state governed by the logic of political ontology and an unconditional ethics. At one extreme, the prophetic might be surrendered to the political; at the other, the political surrendered to the ethical. This is not simply a case of the state putting considerations of power and security above those of justice and peace. If so, the adverse judgement on many of the actions of the State of Israel would not provoke much difficulty. The difficulty arises when political logic would tend towards greater peace and justice, while considerations of holy history would encourage attitudes and behaviour that provoke war.[2] The relationship between the political and the prophetic thus has always to respond to concrete cases – it cannot stand by itself as a criterion of judgement outside of history.

In the latter case, and in the name of his thought, Levinas does not have the right to silence concerning the State of Israel. While he may not live in the State of Israel, the State of Israel lives in his thought, and it is in the name of that thought and the founding aspirations of the state that Levinas must speak. The tension between political and prophetic aspiration or the place of Israel in universal and holy history can be traced through his words on Israel, and those who may be silenced by the political history of the state but who cannot be silenced by the prophetic demand of justice for the other that is Israel.

The passion of Israel

In 'Beyond Dialogue' (1967) Levinas described the 'Dreyfus Affair and Hitlerism' as 'the two crises that struck European Jewry' (AT, 82). The impact of these crises on the development of his thinking has already been examined; now it remains to consider his views on the Zionist solution to them. While Levinas was aware of the contribution of the Dreyfus Affair to Herzl's formulation of political Zionism and thus to the character of early immigration to Palestine, his understanding of the State of Israel was couched almost exclusively in terms of the crisis of Hitlerism. This gave rise to a particular religious interpretation of the State of Israel which was not shared by the many early generations of immigrants and indeed the founders of the state. Their view was closer to that of Herzl regarding the State of Israel as an event above all in universal history – the creation of a territorial state for a nation that had been condemned by history to live without one. While Levinas partially maintains this perspective, he joins it to a view of the State of Israel as an event in holy history, an event framed in terms of the Passion and Resurrection of Israel.

Levinas describes the 'passion' of Israel on a number of occasions, linking it through the words 'resurrection' and 'adventure' to the foundation of the State of Israel. What is peculiar in this version of holy drama is its source in the Christian tradition of the Passion and Resurrection of Christ. This is underlined in the essay 'From the Rise of Nihilism to the Carnal Jew' (1968), in which Levinas links Auschwitz as the passion of Israel to its 'new beginning' or resurrection in the State of Israel: 'The Nazi persecution and, following the exterminations, the extraordinary fulfilment of the Zionist dreams of a State in which to live in peace is to live dangerously, gradually became history. This passion in which it was finished and this bold new beginning, in spite of the conflicting signs affecting them, were felt, even yesterday, to be signs of the same notion of being chosen or damned – that is to say, of the same exceptional fate' (DF, 221). The passion and the resurrection – Shoah and State of Israel – are thus seen as part of the same holy history or, as Levinas describes it on some occasions, the 'Divine Comedy' of Israel.

The experience of the passion of Israel had earlier been described in 'A Religion for Adults' (1957) in terms of 'total dereliction': 'Among the millions of human beings who encountered misery and death, the Jews alone experienced a total dereliction. They experienced a condition inferior to that of things, an experience of total passivity, an experience of Passion' (DF, 11–12). In drawing what seems a deliberate parallel between the dereliction of Christ on the cross and the Jews in National Socialist Europe as events in holy as well as universal history, Levinas can distinguish the suffering of the victims of the Shoah from that of other victims of the war: 'Their suffering, common to them as to all the victims of the war, received its unique meaning from racial persecution which is absolute, since it paralyses, by virtue of its very intention, any flight, from the outset refuses any conversion, forbids any self-abandonment, any apostasy in the etymological sense of the term; and consequently touches the very innocence of the being recalled to its ultimate identity' (DF, 12). The condition of being without exit forms 'the Passion of Israel' to which the Declaration of the State of Israel is both the resurrection *and* the continuation of the passion – 'the Jewish State beleaguered since its resurrection' (BV, 8).

Levinas regarded the resurrection of Israel in the State of Israel from a number of distinct viewpoints. It could be understood as the literal resurrection of the ancient Hebrew kingdom of Israel, or as the return to a less historically defined aspiration for Zion. In both cases the State of Israel realises the 'Zionist dream, which evolved from the most faithful, durable and implausible of nostalgias, returned to the very sources of the Revelation and echoed the highest expectations' (DF, 221). The resurrection of Israel, its passage from dream to reality, consists in the return to the land of Israel after the disastrous experience of the Diaspora. Yet this is by no means a complacent realisation of messianic aspirations, since, as Levinas insisted, for Israel to live in peace is 'to live dangerously'. It is in this sense that Levinas is prepared to describe the State of Israel as an 'adventure' – self-consciously echoing the tone of Kant's famous footnote on the French Revolution in the *Critique of Judgement*. The dangerous resurrection of Israel in the State of Israel marks the entry of Israel into universal secular history, an entry that represents a considerable risk both for the State and for Israel.

It is important to emphasise Levinas's nuanced understanding of the danger to Israel posed by the State of Israel in order to distinguish his position from that of conservative Zionists such as Menachim Begin and Yitzak Shamir. The latter also linked the Shoah with the founding of the State of Israel, and were repeatedly to compare the enemies of the State of Israel to Nazis and to act as if the State itself was the continuation of the Warsaw ghetto. And there is indeed a sense in which Levinas shared this view of the State of Israel, even generalising it to the twentieth-century human condition. Speaking of the violence, the 'odour of the camps' in the 1975 talmudic commentary 'Damages due to Fire', Levinas describes the State of

163

Israel as 'a category' for twentieth-century humanity, explaining that 'the no-exit of Israel is probably the human no-exit. All men are of Israel. I would say "We are all Israeli Jews" ' (TR, 191). For Levinas, the Israeli Jew has no exit but the sea – their state attacked by enemies motivated by the same anti-Semitism since its foundation – a view apparently not far removed from those of revisionist Zionists such as Begin and Shamir.

Yet physical destruction at the hands of its enemies is not the only nor the main danger that Levinas saw threatening the State of Israel. And it is on these other threats that Levinas is most reticent. Some idea of these threats may be gathered from his sympathetic comments on the position of Vladimir Jankelevitch.[3] After noting that 'the passion of Israel under Adolf Hitler certainly affected [Jankelevitch] in a religious way', Levinas described how Jankelevitch's religious 'faithful affection' for the State of Israel was not incompatible with 'the reservations he has allowed himself to express about the political actions of the Hebrew state that did not appear to him in keeping with prophetic inspiration' (OS, 88). Levinas shared Jankelevitch's view of the importance of prophetic inspiration of the State of Israel, going so far as to see the State as the heir to the vocation of protecting 'Israel's ethics' that was previously undertaken by the reading of the Torah (BV, 9). This meant that the state was in danger, as a modern state among states, of betraying its religious vocation to Israel. The risk that now emerges is less the physical destruction of the state by its enemies, than the destruction of Israel by the actions of the State of Israel: by adopting the form of the state, Israel has entered into the wager that its prophetic inspiration is sufficiently strong to overcome the idolatry of the modern state.

This danger facing the prophetic vocation of Israel in adopting the form of the modern state is most explicitly faced in 'From the Rise of Nihilism to the Carnal Jew'. In a form of indirect communication consistent with his reticence, Levinas does not fully own the criticism, putting it in a paragraph that seems to follow on from the previous paragraph which reads: 'Our enemies began. They cast doubt on the facts and figures' (DF, 222), and thus leaving some ambiguity about who is speaking: he or 'our enemies': 'As for Israel, by dint of insisting on its significance as a State, it has been entirely reduced to political categories. But its builders found themselves abruptly on the side of the colonialists. Israel's independence was called imperialism, the oppression of native peoples, racism' (DF, 222). Even if this is a report of the voice of 'our enemies', it is not reported unsympathetically. It claims that Israel, by becoming a state, has surrendered its prophetic inspiration for the idolatry of power; that its ethical mission has been reduced to 'political categories' and the imperialist logic of power.

Levinas suggests that the reduction of the prophetic mission of Israel to the logic of power can be seen to represent a new form of assimilation.[4] It is no longer the individual Jew who is assimilated within the modern nation-state, but Israel itself, by adopting the form of the nation-state. This assimilation does not involve only the idolatry of the power of the state revealed in its acts of colonial violence, but also other forms of idolatry. Levinas continues to voice the criticism of the State of Israel with the reproach that 'The eschatological dream was substituted by the seductions of tourism, and eighteen years after the creation of the State of Israel, glossy brochures still feed their readers an implausible and invariable visual diet of athletic young girls striding joyfully towards the rising sun. In this world there are no more problems than in the publicity-image world of a modern electrical appliance' (DF, 222–3). The danger that faces Israel is once again that of assimilation – this time not as an individual citizen in a modern state or as a people in a system of modern states – but as a nation-state aiming to maximise its wealth and power through competition, in this case in the global tourist market. Under this general scenario, the State of Israel faces the danger of becoming assimilated betraying its prophetic inspiration and behaving like any other nation-state.

Levinas suggests that a way to avoid this danger is to interpret the State of Israel as no less than 'the return of the possibility of an abnegation' (DF, 224). Here the foundation of the state signifies a preparedness for sacrifice that will prove exemplary for other Jews in the Diaspora as well as for the gentiles. As a state that 'appears worthy of an ultimate sacrifice', the 'State of Israel, in this sense, constitutes the greatest event in modern Judaism' (DF, 225). It is hard to be sure whether Levinas is fully aware of the gravity, the danger and the arguably blasphemous character of his claim. He regards the 'greatest event in modern Judaism' as the return of the possibility of sacrifice – but not in the Temple, but in and for the state. This seems dangerously close to sacrificing to an idol – the most powerful, fascinating and irresistible of the modern idols – the nation-state.

Even if Levinas's view of the state being worthy of sacrifice can be saved from accusations of idolatry, there remain dangers surrounding his use of sacrificial discourse. Writing in the mid-1960s, Levinas seems to hope that Israel will remain the pioneer society of the early twentieth century, precisely the period when it was not a nation-state. The modern mass consumer society of the 1960s fully inserted in the world economy indeed seems remote from Levinas's vision of an Israel prepared for exemplary self-sacrifice. It also seems far from the State that, like all nation-states, was prepared to defend itself with ruthless force and recourse to violent injustice.

The danger of Levinas's position lies in not fully recognising that the State of Israel is a modern state among states. While he does not lapse into the messianic paranoia of the Israeli right, he is nevertheless in danger of promoting idolatry, or the archaic myth of Israel as a settler society, even twenty years after it had become a nation-state. The danger of assimilation that Levinas saw facing the State of Israel, the threat that it would behave like any other state, was not a danger but a fact. And while Levinas's calls for sacrifice may seem at best a quaint nostalgia for the early pioneer phase of Zionism, they may also contain the danger of endorsing the worst forms of sacrifice, not only of self, but also of the other and most significantly of the third. The return of the theme of sacrifice for the State of Israel in the context of Levinas's (1968) essay on the Six Days War, 'Space is not One-Dimensional', is not too surprising given the threat to the State posed by the war. The danger lies in the theme being applied to 'sacrifices' such as those of the settlers in the West Bank after this war, whose religiously motivated return to the self-sacrificial pioneer ethos of early Zionism was compatible with the cruellest injustice. While Levinas did not publicly endorse these colonial adventures, there is a dangerous proximity between them and his view of the exemplary sacrificial mission of the State of Israel. The danger here is one of supporting injustice and forgetting the third for the sake of the Other – and thus indeed sacrificing Israel to the idol of the State of Israel.

The dangers facing the Zionist adventure made it all the more incumbent upon Levinas to specify in what ways the State of Israel must differ from the other states of the world; what it is, in other words, about Israel's place in holy history that makes its contribution to universal history unique. To understand this it is necessary to look more closely at Levinas's view of the messianic significance of Israel.

Israel and messianic politics

Levinas returned repeatedly to the question of messianic politics in his *Talmudic Readings*.[5] The earliest published readings – the 'Messianic Texts' from 1960 and 1961 – appeared in *Difficult Freedom* under the title 'Commentaries', and address precisely the theme of messianic politics. The theme persists throughout the *Talmudic Readings*, returning in the article 'The State of Caesar and the State of David' of 1971 and in 'Who Plays Last' of 1979. At issue in all of these commentaries is the question of whether the state – acknowledged as the highest form of idolatry – is compatible with the messianic mission of Israel. On the response to this question rests the judgement of the State of Israel.

The question of the difficult relationship between the messianic and the state was central not only to these discussions but also to *Totality and Infinity*. As shown in Chapter 3, this text addresses the problem of whether messianism is compatible with political ontology. The argument of *Totality and Infinity* is motivated by the thought of a time 'when the eschatology of messianic peace will have come to superpose itself upon the ontology of war' (TI, 22). Indirectly, through the voice of 'our enemies', Levinas seemed to be suggesting in the 1960s that the contrary had taken place, that the ontology of war (and commerce) has superposed itself upon the eschatology of messianic peace. In this view the State of Israel represented the surrender of Israel to the 'political categories' of the state, all of which, as Levinas had patiently demonstrated in *Totality and Infinity*, are complicit with assimilation to an ontology of war.

Further examination of the link between the argument of *Totality and Infinity* and the *Talmudic Readings* suggests that other possible judgements of the State of Israel were available to Levinas. The ethically unqualified 'ideal type' of the state described in *Totality and Infinity* is in a perpetual state of war, and politics is the art of foreseeing war. A number of possibilities emerge when this characterisation of the state is brought into relation with 'eschatological peace' – discussed at length in Chapter 3. One is that the state will alternatively use and unmask claims for peace and justice as subjective hypocrisy. Another is that the state will mobilise its capacity for war towards the realisation of the 'messianic dream of eschatological peace', while a third is that the 'messianic dream' will transform the state, instituting a new form of state. All of these possibilities may be discerned in the history of the State of Israel, but Levinas attempts to develop the last possibility and to try to regard the State of Israel as bearing witness to the promise of a new kind of state.

This exploration is carried out in the Talmudic commentaries. The 'Messianic Texts' of *Difficult Freedom* explore a number of theses on violence, the state and the messianic epoch that culminate in a sustained and dense reflection upon the messianic implications of the emancipation and the foundation of the State of Israel. The central discussion of the text concerns the very theme of the 'Passion of Israel', but now placing it, and the foundation of the State of Israel, in a new perspective. The discussion concerns pages 97b and 98a of the Talmudic tractate Sanhedrin:

> Rab said: All the predestined dates [for redemption] have passed, and the matter [now] depends only on repentance and good deeds. But Samuel maintained: It is sufficient for a mourner to keep his [period of mourning]. (DF, 69)

Levinas comments on the positions represented by the two discussants. For Rab, the conditions for the appearance of the Messiah – of peace – are already in place, and what is required are individual repentance and good deeds. In this view, 'Moral action, *the individual's work*, is not alienated by a history that denaturalises it and, consequently, does not have to attempt to impose itself by taking the detour of politics and having recourse to reasons of state' (DF, 69). There is no need to form a state, or, in other words 'to become politically allied to assassins' (DF, 69), since good actions and repentance are directly efficacious. Samuel is opposed to this messianic anarchism – 'He attached importance to political realities...*messianic deliverance cannot ensue from individual effort*' (DF, 69). Yet Samuel is by no means an advocate of the formation of a state – making an alliance with the assassins. For the achievement of messianic peace also depends on the identity of the mourner who is to keep the period of mourning.

Levinas retells three options for the identity of the mourner, and then offers a fourth. The first mourner is God – God will ensure deliverance through history at the end of the period of mourning or historical injustice. The second mourner is Israel. Here it is Israel that is suffering, and, Levinas adds, 'This suffering, in the absence of repentance, is the condition for its salvation. (DF, 70)' Suffering 'is the condition for deliverance' (DF, 70). Redemption will follow a suffering that cannot be repented because Israel was the victim of evil. This position, which seems close to that of the 'Passion of Israel' is here qualified on the grounds that it 'reeks of Christianity'. (DF, 70) According to the third position it is indeed Israel that is in mourning, but the end of the mourning will not come by suffering alone: 'it is through suffering that *a freedom may be aroused. Man receives suffering, but in this suffering he emerges as a moral freedom*' (DF, 71). In the fourth position the Messiah is the mourner, suffering for humanity who suffer for him, both of them poised to recognise that time is indeed complete.

In his provisional summary of the discussion Levinas identifies a 'basic alternative' that steers it towards the opening question of *Totality and Infinity*: that of whether we are duped by morality. The alternative, sharpened by the discussion of Rab and Samuel, is whether 'morality – that is to say, the efforts made by men who are masters of their intentions and acts – will save the world, or else what is needed is an objective event that surpasses morality and the individual's good intentions' (DF, 72). Levinas begins to identify the objective event with the third position. The event that causes suffering provokes the need for deliverance: 'The phenomenon of Haman (or Hitler) is placed in the perspective of messianism. Only repentance can cause salvation, but objective events of a political character produce this repentance which is both a manifestation of human freedom and a product of an external cause' (DF, 72). The suffering of the 'Passion of Israel' under National Socialism thus creates the conditions for repentance or the arousal of a freedom. The State of Israel, it is implied, forms part of this repentance – it is not just the result of suffering, but of the repentance or emergence of freedom occasioned by suffering.

Before moving to consider what it is that is being repented, a final element of argument is reintroduced. Rab's objection to alliances with assassins – his being duped by morality – is shown to rely on such an alliance in the phrase 'Has the person who rejects the state not been formed for this rejection by the very state he rejects?' (DF, 76). This rehearses the argument of *Totality and Infinity*: that the political ontology of war underlies morality and cannot responsibly be avoided. From suffering, we are delivered to politics.

In the closing pages of the commentary Levinas returns to the issue of repentance and links this to the State of Israel. Following Hitler and National Socialism, the Emancipation and the compromising of messianism that it entailed (DF, 96) are to be repented and rethought. It is not that Levinas rejects Emancipation, but he wishes to distance it from the dangerous form of citizenship in the nation-state that it adopted during the nineteenth century. He defines Emancipation as 'an opening – not on to humanity, for which [Judaism] always felt responsible, but on to the political forms of that humanity' (DF, 95–6). The political form adopted by nineteenth-century Emancipation was that of citizenship in existing nation-states – a choice replete with dangers and one that for Levinas led to the disaster of the Shoah. Yet the repentance that Levinas sees emerging from the passion or suffering is not the rejection of Emancipation, but of the political form that it adopted, namely citizenship. The new beginning of Emancipation consists in choosing a new political form – not citizenship in an existing nation-state but in adopting the form of the nation-state itself.

Levinas closes his 'Messianic Texts' with a discussion of the adoption by Israel of the political form of the state in the State of Israel. He claims that the messianic sensibility of Judaism would be lost 'if the solution of the State of Israel did not represent an attempt to reunite the irreversible acceptance of universal history with the necessarily particularist messianism' (DF, 96). The 'universalist particularism' that Levinas hastens to distinguish from 'Hegel's concrete universal' is both a withdrawal from and entry into history: withdrawal from the political form of Emancipation as an individual Jewish citizen of an existing nation-state but entry as a state among states that is free to choose the terms of its participation and non-participation. This, in Levinas's eyes, permits the preservation of a 'universalist particularism' in which 'I see the importance of the Israeli solution for the history of Israel. The hypocrisy of those who consider themselves to be outside of history while benefiting from it is annulled by the dangers and risks that the Israeli solution entails' (DF, 96). With the latter, Levinas returns to question of the 'dangers and risks' posed by the State of Israel.

Yet the closing paragraph of the 'Messianic Texts' does not go much further in identifying these risks. Levinas emphasises that 'Israeli Judaism has accepted this danger in its life in the form of the State of Israel and what the State of Israel is to its whole Judaic contents, its vanguard groupings are to the state itself' (DF, 96). The sentence is notable for identifying an 'Israeli Judaism' that is not the whole of Judaism – bracketing, so to speak, the Diaspora – and then regarding the state in terms of a series of risks that range from the risk the state poses to 'its Judaic contents' and what its vanguard groupings pose to the state. The latter implicitly described as diaspora or 'scattering' *within* the state that takes the form of between the 'small grains' of the state 'scattered in the desert, all the remote kibbutzim' that work and take risks indifferent to the 'seething world whose human values they none the less serve' (DF, 96). What it is they risk, however, beyond their lives and perhaps the physical existence of the state is not clear. The central problem of the relationship between the messianic and the political form of the state has not been fully addressed. Nevertheless the transition to a new form of emancipation has been clarified, as has the nature of the passion of Israel, but the nature of the 'adventure' and the risks it entails remain to be clarified.

The necessary clarification is ventured in various ways throughout the series of *Talmudic Readings* that Levinas pursued after the 'Messianic Texts'. It consists in the defence of 'the historical work of the state' and the argument that 'it is not possible to do without [it] in the extremely politicised world of our time', but that its 'work of courage and labour' (another Hegelian echo) can be shaped by 'Israel's unrepentant eschatology' derived from 'Biblical culture' (BV, xv). The philosophical project is the same as that pursued in *Totality and Infinity* – to find an accommodation or 'superposition' of messianic eschatology and political ontology, but the focus is now on the State of Israel as the 'particular universal' that risks the political project of transforming the 'work of the state' by the 'work of justice'.

Levinas synthetically presents the results of his reflections during the 1960s in the 1971 lecture 'The State of Caesar and the State of David'. The examination of the 'idea of kingship which expresses the principle of state control in biblical texts' (BV, 177) is from the outset transparently dedicated as much to the problems facing the 'resurrected' State of Israel as to biblical philology. Levinas presents the biblical and talmudic discussion of the dangers and benefits of importing the political form of kingship (the state) into Israel. He cites the prophetic warnings against adopting kinship the state, and asks two questions as much of the contemporary State of Israel as of the biblical kingdom. The first question is: 'Would the excesses of power be justified when it is a question of assuming the task of the survival of a people among the nations, or of a person among his fellow men? It would seem so' (BV, 178). This concession to the assassins would seem to justify the full use of 'reason of state' by the State of Israel against an enemy that is seen to be dedicated to its destruction. The second question qualifies the first: 'Would a decision for the State be equivalent to choosing life over the Law, while this Law aspires to be the Law of life?' (BV, 178). This is precisely the question of the relationship between the work of the state and the work of justice, of political ontology and messanic eschatology. The answer – couched in terms of 'it would be, unless', sketches a 'provisional abdication' of the law to political power, premised on the fragility of the law. The law, it seems, would require the protection of the state, for 'the Law entering the world requires an education, protection, and consequently a history and a state'; yet it would be betrayed by the state 'unless politics is the path of this long patience and these great precautions' (BV, 179).

Levinas regards his catena of conditions for the adoption of the State by Israel as an attempt 'to go back, very carefully, to the philosophical presuppositions of the "concession" granted by religion to political necessities, and of the "provisional abdication" pronounced by the "spirit of the absolute" before the spirit heedful of the diversity of circumstances and the necessities of place and time to which politics belongs' (BV, 179). But his defence assumes the necessity of the state and underplays the prophetic resistance to the institution of kingship. The argument continues with a reflection on King David, who incarnated both works – that of the state and that of justice. Although the title of the lecture opposes first the 'State of Caesar' to the 'State of David', the actual discussion begins with the superposition of the work of justice and state in the State of David and then examines the State of Caesar. If the case against the 'State of Caesars' had been made first, as is promised in the title, then that for the conditional 'State of David' would have seemed less persuasive.

For the case against the State of Caesar is very heavy. Levinas identifies it as one of the 'four powers' among the States of Babylon, the Parthians and the Seleucid because of its fierce attachment to the rule of law, noting 'The Rabbis cannot forget the organising principle of Rome and its law! They therefore anticipate, with remarkable independence of spirit, modern political philosophy. Whatever its order, the City already ensures the rights of human beings against their fellow men, taken to be still in a state of nature, men as wolves for other men, as Hobbes would have it' (BV, 183). Yet the state, in spite of the work of establishing the rule of law, is also 'the place of corruption' and 'perhaps, the ultimate refuge of idolatry' (BV, 183). This state is 'jealous of its sovereignty, the State in search of hegemony, the conquering, imperialist, totalitarian, oppressive state, attached to realist egoism. Incapable of being without self-adoration, it is idolatry itself' (BV, 184). How would it be possible for the work of justice – frail as it is – to confront this political form and not be submerged by it? Levinas's answer is framed in terms of 'provisional abdication' – that in spite of its imperialist and oppressive work of power, the state keeps open the space for a future work of justice.

In the closing paragraphs of 'Towards a Monotheistic Politics' Levinas situates himself with respect to a body of opinion that saw the mission of Zionism and the State of Israel to be more than ensuring 'a refuge for those who are persecuted' (BV, 187).[6] He cites favourably Dan Avni-Segre's emphasis 'not on the accomplishments of the young State but on the possibilities of political invention that it opens up. At the heart of daily conflicts, the living experience of the government – and even the painful necessities of the occupation – allow lessons as yet untaught to be detected in the ancient Revelation' (BV, 187). The State of Israel, then, is said to keep open the space for political invention, a position justified rhetorically by asking if there is an alternative to 'recourse to the methods of Caesar' –

that is, imperial expansion and oppression (the 'painful necessities of the occupation'?) or the 'facile eloquence of a careless moralism' that would not, in Levinas's words, doom 'the dispersed gathered back together to rapid destruction and a new dispersion?' (BV, 187). But should the work of justice be described as 'a careless moralism', and is it not dangerous to have recourse to the 'methods of Caesar' which are, of course, those of the assassin – namely, murder and oppression of the weak? Levinas continues by evoking a two-thousand-year history of detachment that left Israel 'Innocent of political crime, as pure as the purity of the victim' (BV, 187), contrasting this with the commitment of 1948, but without mentioning the political crimes committed during and after the same War of Independence.

At this point Levinas lapses into a silence masked by the rhetorical flourish that the adoption of the form of the state by Israel marks 'one of the greatest events of internal history and, indeed, of all history' (BV, 187). But this is precisely the 'facile eloquence and careless moralism' with which he reproaches others, except this time in support of the adoption of the work of the state rather than the work of justice. Levinas, in the final analysis and in spite of his insight into the idolatrous nature of the state, remains silent about the dangers posed by the form of the state to the work of justice. For him to speak would entail going beyond rhetorical praise of the commitment of 1948 to a reflection upon the threat that the adoption of the form of the state posed to Israel. For, with the adoption of the state, Israel would not only enter universal secular history but would also break with a millenial tradition and become guilty of political crime. The stark implications of this becomes evident in Levinas's analyses of Jewish identity and the State of Israel and the relationship of the state to its other/third.

Israel and Jewish identity

The introduction to *Four Talmudic Readings* published in 1968, a year after the Six Days War, extends the arguments of 'Space is not One-Dimensional', the reflection on the significance of the war for the State of Israel and Jewish identity that Levinas published the same year in *Esprit*. It offers a precise statement of Levinas's political thought as well as tracing some of its unresolved difficulties. As such it also continues and deepens the reflection on Jewish identity that had been the constant preoccupation of Levinas's thought.

Perhaps the major unresolved problem of the Introduction involves the siting of Jewish universalism. Levinas considered the universal 'Declaration of the Rights of Man and Citizen' to embody the prophetic principle of justice, and saw the modern state as founding itself upon these claims. The 'Rights of Man and Citizen' limited the idolatry of power implied in the modern state in the same way as the Biblical prophets limited the power of their kings by prophetic admonishment. There is a sense in which Levinas believed that the declaration of the Rights of Man marked a partial and fragile realisation of the universal vocation of Israel, one that needed to be deepened, especially with respect to the notion of fraternity. He alludes to this view in the Introduction to his *Four Talmudic Readings*: 'we assume the unity of the consciousness of mankind claiming to be fraternal and one throughout time and space. It is Israel's history which has suggested this idea, even if mankind, now conscious of its oneness, allows itself to challenge Israel's vocation, its concrete universality' (TR, 6). Here Levinas contrasts the realisation of the universal aspirations of Israel in the unity of mankind – expressed in the notion of universal human rights – with the hostility of the nations to the 'concrete universal' of Israel, in the form of anti-semitism, and the State of Israel in the form of anti-Zionism.

Levinas's views on universal human rights and the State of Israel have considerable implications for his understanding of modern Jewish identity. Not mentioned here, but deeply informing his discussions elsewhere, is the problem posed by the prophetic roots of universal human rights. The view that such rights mark a realisation of prophetic politics runs the risk of assimilation, namely the dissolution of a particular Jewish identity in the realisation of universal human fraternity through the declaration of universal human rights. This, of course, can be interpreted in two ways: one in which Judaism is dissolved into the universal; the other in which it is raised to the universal. In the one, Jews are assimilated by means of citizenship; in the other, citizenship is assimilated into Judaism. In both cases there is assimilation, but in the first Jews become modern citizens, forsaking their particular identity for the universality of modern citizenship, while in the second, modern citizens become Jewish, with the significance of Jewish identity here extending far beyond what Levinas described as 'flesh and blood Jews'.

Levinas certainly explored both these possibilities, fearing both equally, but perhaps for different reasons. However, the existence of the 'concrete universal' of the State of Israel complicated the otherwise formal dialectical movement between universal and particular. Returning to the Introduction of *Four Talmudic Readings* we can see that Levinas has described an almost Hegelian irony of history: the realisation of the Jewish prophetic inspiration in the universal fraternity of human rights is used against the alleged particularism of Israel and the 'concrete universal' of the State of Israel. It is on this basis that Levinas continues with the claim that 'Immortal anti-Semitism continues in the form of anti-Zionism, at the moment in which Jewish history wishes also to be a land upon the earth that its concrete universalism contributed to unite and upon which the rigidity of the alternative national-universal is weakening' (TR, 6). This is a complex passage that demands reflection. In the first place, the notion of 'immortal anti-Semitism' is adopted directly from Herzl and was one of the legitimating principles of political Zionism; for Herzl, and also it would seem here for Levinas, Jews would never be secure outside of their own state.[7] The danger in making an absolute out of anti-Semitism consists in creating a Manichean world of constant struggle between absolute good and evil, a division which can provoke the most terrible and violent actions in the name of the good. It also blunts the concept of anti-Semitism, allowing such rhetorical gestures as the equation of anti-Zionism with anti-Semitism. There are many circumstances in which anti-Zionism is indeed masked anti-Semitism, but the equation does not hold for all cases of anti-Semitism, nor for all cases of anti-Zionism. There have been and are anti-Semitisms that are pro-Zionist and there have been and are anti-Zionisms that are not anti-Semitic.

The equation of anti-Semitism and anti-Zionism also bears the risk of equating Jewish with Israeli identity. This of course would deny the experience of non-Jewish Israelis – who historically have constituted between 12 and 20 per cent of the population of the State of Israel – as well as that of Jews who are not citizens of Israel, over two-thirds of the world's Jewish population. This, it will quickly become apparent, is far from being Levinas's own position. The second part of the sentence on 'eternal anti-Semitism' provokes further difficulties, not only because it links the translation of 'eternal' anti-Semitism into historical 'anti-Zionism' by means of the foundation of the State of Israel. It also stages the irony of the universal claims of human rights being turned against the actions of the State of Israel while seeing the latter as 'loosening the rigidity' of the 'national-universal' or nation-state. At this point the two historic vehicles of prophetic politics – universal human rights and the State of Israel – collide. The adoption of the form of the state by Israel does not for Levinas necessarily denote a new form of assimilation, this time to the idol of the state rather than to citizenship of states (although Levinas was not absolutely certain of this), since by virtue of *its* adoption of this form Israel promises to transform it. Yet from Levinas's perspective there emerges an unspoken problem: if the universality of rights is a realisation of prophetic politics, why then must the immense risk be run of adopting the idolatrous form of the state. If the idolatry of power that Levinas has shown to be the essence of the state prevails over the prophetic mission of Israel, if the State of Israel ignores human rights, then this means that through a brutal irony of history the prophetic mission of Israel becomes endangered by its own adoption of the form of the state.

In the language of the state, what matters is that the state ensures the security of its citizens, and consequently the actions of the State of Israel, if it was like any other state, could be understood in these terms. But for Levinas, the State of Israel cannot be a state like all the others but has the prophetic mission of transforming the meaning of the state, divesting it of its idolatry of power. At this point Levinas is silent on the evidence of the extent of the *Realpolitik* conducted by the State of Israel during and since 1948 and develops a new line of argument. In this, the Diaspora is given an important role in reminding the State of Israel of its prophetic mission. The state is in the position of the Biblical king who is admonished in the name of justice by the prophet, in this case the Jews of the Diaspora. But who they are remains open to question. What Levinas begins to sketch is a link between the Judaism of the Diaspora and the reading of the Talmud. The latter 'suggests a reading in search of problems and truths and that, no less than a return to an independent political life in Israel, is necessary for an Israel wishing to preserve its self-consciousness in the modern world but may yet hesitate in the face of a return that would see itself in purely political terms' (TR, 9). The adoption of the form of the state along with the study of the Talmud in the diaspora and in the State of Israel thus provides a means of avoiding the dialectical movement of universal and particular described above – it proposes an exteriority to the State of Israel, but one that is complementary.

Levinas underlines this middle position by referring to the role of the Hebrew University in developing the reading of the Talmud, the university being an institution both universal and located in a particular place. It is called here to 'translate' the wisdom of the Talmud into the Greek tradition, making possible 'a Western Jew, Jewish and Greek, *everywhere*' (TR, 10). Does not the 'University of the Jewish State' thus offer, asks Levinas, 'the solution of a contradiction dividing both the Jews integrated within the free nations and the Jews who feel dispersed?' (TR, 9). Levinas elaborates a vision of the 'autonomous political and cultural existence' made possible by Zionism and embodied in the Hebrew University. This is neither the 'Loyalty to a Jewish culture closed to dialogue and polemic with the West [that] condemns the Jews to the ghetto and to physical extermination', nor the 'Admission into the city that makes them disappear into the civilisation of their hosts' (TR, 9). In this scenario, the State of Israel can represent either the worst or the best of both scenarios: it can become a ghetto and vulnerable to its enemies at the same time as it is assimilated to the idolatry and *Realpolitik* of the state or, as in the Hebrew University it can aspire to 'concrete universality'. Levinas is silent on the probable outcome, but evokes instead Kant's footnote in the *Critique of Judgement* on the astonished spectators of the French Revolution: 'The Judaism of the Diaspora and a whole mankind astonished by the political renewal of Israel await the Torah of Jerusalem. The Diaspora, struck in its living forces by Hitlerism, no longer has either the knowledge or the courage needed for the realisation of such a project' (TR, 10). The State of Israel and the Diaspora here unite in the work of prophetic politics, of bringing the Torah to the nations.

Levinas regards the unity/non-unity of Israel in the State of Israel and the Diaspora as a new form of the political that marks the transformation of the territorial nation-state. This is not an Hegelian sublation, in which the Diaspora is gathered into the territorial nation-state – a totalitarian project horribly familiar from the pan-German and pan-Serbian adventures – but a new political form in which Diaspora and state coexist. In it the involvement of the Diaspora in the struggles for human rights and the study of the Jewish tradition serves as a form of prophetic control upon the potential idolatry of power inherent in the form of the nation-state. Yet the latter also serves to focus consciousness of Jewish identity in the Diaspora and to act as a 'city of refuge' from the potential violence of the nation-states that host the Diaspora. Levinas regards this new form of the political as challenging the rigidity of the territorial nation-state, and becoming appropriate to a global condition in which the coexistence of nation-states and Diasporas is becoming increasingly the norm.

Levinas's invitation to regard Israel as promising a new form of the political that combines Diaspora and territorial nation-state, while theoretically provocative, carries with it a high degree of practical risk. As the repository of prophetic consciousness the Diaspora needs to have channels of communication that allow it to influence the actions of the nation-state. Levinas sees these as founded on Jewish identity, the shared tradition of the Diaspora and the State of Israel. Yet in this equation it is important to recall that both state and Diaspora face different dangers of assimilation – in the first case assimilation to the political form of the state; in the second to the political form of citizenship in a state. Each thus serves to emphasise Jewish identity to the other: the State of Israel reminds the Jewish citizens of the Diaspora of their identity as Jews, and the Diaspora reminds the State of Israel that it is a state inspired by the prophetic principles of justice. The model of the Dreyfus resistance is evident, but now the role of the press and public demanding respect for the principle of justice is given a global and a quasi-institutional form in the Diaspora and institutions such as the university.

Given this mutual responsibility, Levinas's claim to a right of silence regarding the actions of the State of Israel reneges on his own political philosophy. As part of the Diaspora he has, according to his own theory, not only the right but the obligation to question those actions of the State of Israel that are idolatrous or that diverge from its prophetic inspiration. Indeed we shall see that, on some occasions, Levinas did act according to his political principles, but also that on others he either remained silent or, it might be argued, privileged the work of the state over the prophetic principles of the work of justice. The possibility of the latter – in the face of Levinas's own thought – is not unconnected with the persistent discourse of sacrifice that attends his reflections on Israel. This cannot but bring him into an uncomfortable proximity with idolatry and the risk of the consequent deflation of his own political and ethical thought.

Two important texts from 1963 and 1968 – either side of the Six Days War – develop the vision of a Jewish identity inseparable from an understanding of Israel as the unity in non-unity of the sovereign and the prophetic moments – State of Israel and Diaspora. These are 'Means of Identification' and the magnificent reflection on the Six Days War, 'Space is not One-Dimensional'. The former is reminiscent, in its defence of Western Judaism and critique of Zionism, of the early Brunschvicg essays and opens with some words on the difficult temporality of Western Jewish identity. Suspended between *already* and *still*, Western Jewish identity is 'already lost' by the fact of Jews having to question it and yet, for the same reason, still persists in being questioned. The source of this already-lost but persisting identity is referred to as an 'immemorial past', 'an adherence that pre-exists any form of allegiance' (DF, 50), a reference that anticipates the philosophical elaboration of this theme in *Otherwise than Being*. For this reason, identity is something to be searched for (or avoided), but in either case where to search or how to avoid cannot be determined in advance.

The complex view of identity to which Levinas refers puts in question any notion of Jewish national identity such as that of Zionism that turns the 'primordial experience...into politics and nationalism' (DF, 50). Observing that 'For many Israelis, their identity card is the full extent of their Jewish identity as it is, perhaps, for all those potential Israelis who are still in the Diaspora' (DF, 51), Levinas goes on to question the risk posed by assimilation with the ideology of nationalism.[8] The confusion of identity with nationalism, the transformation of a Jewish identity into a national one is a form of assimilation to a modern ideology – nationalism – in which the reflective Western Jew, assimilated to the 'Western mentality' 'uncovers something savage' (DF, 51). Once again Levinas refers to the university as the site for this reflection, and ends with a plea for the role of study in the constitution of identity. In quiet opposition to any assimilation to national identities, whether in Israel or the Diaspora, Levinas proposes the study of the inassimilable – 'the source, the forgotten, ancient, difficult books' in which 'Jewish identity is inscribed' (DF, 52–3). This demand for a correction of the tendencies of assimilation by means of the study of the inassimilable, the discovery of the unthought in the tradition, is here opposed to Israeli national identity, again underlining Levinas's ambivalence; however, with the Six Days War, Levinas began to theorise the complementary roles of state and Diaspora.

Nowhere does he take this reflection as far as in 'Space is not One-Dimensional'. The choice of *Esprit* for this article was not accidental; since 'Reflections on the Philosophy of Hitlerism' published in *Esprit* in 1934, Levinas had used the pages of the journal to publish his reflections on politics and the political. The upsurge of solidarity between the Diaspora and the State of Israel during the war inspired Levinas's vision of a new form of the political, but it also provoked the resurgence of old political responses, notably the resurgence of anti-Semitism in France. Levinas addresses this reprise of anti-Semitism by evoking the French Revolution and the unresolved tension between universal citizenship and national fraternity that was its legacy (a tension examined by Hannah Arendt in *The Origins of Totalitarianism*, 1973). As seen, Levinas had been working on this question since the 1920s in connection with the Dreyfus Affair and the prophetic principles of justice inherent in the Declaration of the Rights of Man and Citizen. He now returned to this theme in the context of his response to the anti-Semitic *canard* of the double allegiance of Jewish citizens, this time in terms of an allegedly conflicting allegiance between the States of France and Israel.

The article reaffirms the significance of the French Revolution for Levinas's thought; he goes as far as to claim that 'Adherence to France is a metaphysical act, of course; it had to be France, a country that expresses its political existence with a trinitarian emblem which is moral and philosophical, and is inscribed on the front of its public buildings' (DF, 260–61). The 'moral and philosophical' trinity of liberty, equality and fraternity brings together the ethical and the political in an 'exceptional essence epitomised by France, in which political and moral life came together, and on the basis of the ideals of the 1789 Revolution and the Declaration of the Rights of Man' (DF, 261). Levinas considered the 'metaphysical act' of adherence[9] to these principles for Jewish French citizens to have a 'religious source' that was gradually forgotten – namely, the recognition of the prophetic sense of justice. The security of French Jewish citizens was shaken by the Dreyfus Affair and, while noting that 'to the extent that justice triumphed in the Affair, and politics once more rejoined ethics, a new pride in being French could be added to the ancient one' (DF, 261), Levinas also saw it as creating 'a new vigilance, a new attention paid to the world, a new way of being stirred and tense in one's existence, a reunion with an old religious experience' (DF, 262). Such vigilance for justice and injustice was inseparable, as was shown in *Totality and Infinity*, from a messianic eschatology, and is here joined to the defence and extension of human rights.

The possibility of events of injustice such as the Dreyfus Affair was nested in the revolutionary trinity itself. Liberty, equality and fraternity, like the Father, Son and Holy Spirit, remains an equivocal formula susceptible to a host of interpretations. The revolutionary trinity, like the Christian trinity before it, invites a choice as to which person of the trinity is to be given the most importance. Throughout his writings Marx, for example, showed the contradiction that arose in bourgeois societies between liberty and equality – economic liberty producing inequality that then compromises the liberty of the disadvantaged – and pitted against it the fraternity of the international proletariat. But, as we have seen, other versions of fraternity were also conceivable that were able to 'trump' liberty and equality in the same way as the Son trumps the Father and Holy Spirit in the Arian heresy – the Jacobin fraternal nation of brothers in arms; the Gallo–Catholic fraternal confession and the fraternal race. Jewish citizens, whatever their entitlement to liberty and equality, were always in danger of their claims being compromised by confessional or racial fraternity.

Levinas's response to the resurgence of this threat in 1967 was to argue that political space was no longer, even if it had ever been, one-dimensional. The French nation was beginning to 'open up to new experiences, seek new *raisons d'être*, and shift everyone's sense of nationality' (DF, 261). Attachment to the State of Israel is but one aspect of the extension of the fraternal dimension beyond the nation, 'not the cause, but the effect of this change' (DF, 261). Under a broader notion of fraternity such as Levinas had been working towards all of his life, recognition of being both a French citizen fully adhering to the principles of the French Republic and a member of the Jewish Diaspora was entirely consistent. Thus Levinas criticises the reduction of fraternity to the nation for its one-dimensionality: '*Does being French, short of Euclidean space, mean moving only in one dimension?*' (DF, 259). Levinas then takes his argument beyond even a claim for the enrichment of the dimension of fraternity to the call for the invention of a new, non-Euclidean political space stretching beyond the three dimensions of liberty, equality and fraternity.

The fragility of the existing dimensions of the political was exposed by 'what happened in Europe between 1933 and 1945', namely an event that no longer leaves even the comfort of a three-dimensional political space. Levinas describes the Shoah in terms of a topological analogy, referring to 'human events which tear open their own envelope' – in this case the three-dimensional envelope of the modern political trinity. The transgression of political dimensionality following the Shoah puts in question the three dimensions of liberty, equality and fraternity, let alone attempts to reduce the three to a single dimension. The non-Euclidean politics to which Levinas alludes requires the supplement of an extra, religious dimension of politics deliberately unthematised in the revolutionary trinity and prefigured in the new relation between nation-state and diaspora. It was precisely the deliberate exclusion of the religious that provoked those issues that came to be collected by the Nazis under the chilling title of 'the Jewish Question'.

The rethinking of the relationship of the French Jewish citizen to France and to the State of Israel must take account of the fourth religious dimension of the political. This entails a number of different considerations, ranging from the prophetic inspiration of the original Declaration of the Rights of Man and Citizen to the understanding of the place of Israel in the modern world. By the latter, Levinas intends the broad inquiry into the religious–political of Israel – that is, of the Diaspora and the State of Israel, and not just the politics of the State of Israel. Given that the latter is a part of Israel, it cannot be overlooked, but Israel and the State of Israel cannot be reduced to a simple identity. The issue of Israel and modernity cannot be separated from the tension that informs it between 'holy' and universal history. The tension is ubiquitous in Levinas's analyses of Israel and the State of Israel, and is manifest in 'Space is not One-Dimensional' when he writes: 'The Nazi persecution and, following the exterminations, the extraordinary fulfilment of the Zionist dream, are religious events outside of any revelation, church, clergy, miracle, dogma or belief' (DF, 263). But as religious events they must not be relegated to a separate dimension of holy history as in the Christian City of God, nor absorbed into a contin-uous universal history; rather, they must be seen to inhabit a dimension that is related to the political dimensions of universal history but which can neither be totally separated from nor absorbed into them.

The plurality of dimensions that characterise universal and holy history allows Levinas to distinguish between Israel and the State of Israel while not entirely separating them from each other. Yet the force of Hegelian universal history often prevails over the Rosenzweig-inspired pluralism of holy and universal history. This is evident in Levinas's closing remarks on the State of Israel. According to the pluralist notion of history, the dimen-sions of the State of Israel would always be in tension between universal and holy history, with the state, its civil society and the Diaspora suspended between the political and religious dimensions. In contrast, according to Hegelian universal history, all historical events are located within the progressive actualisation of the idea of freedom in the state. An account of the State of Israel would in these terms locate the foundation of the state as the historical outcome of a sacrifice for the sake of freedom. Levinas, as already noted, seems on occasion to come close to this posi-tion, but in 'Space is not One-Dimensional' he succeeds in aligning universal and holy history through an inversion of universal history. The State of Israel is not, as might be expected from the logic of universal history, *founded* upon sacrifice, but *produces* the sacrifice that is consistent with the prophetic vocation of Israel:

> It is not because the Holy Land takes the form of a State that brings the Reign of the Messiah any closer, but because the men who inhabit it try to resist the temptation of politics; because this State proclaimed in the aftermath of Auschwitz, embraces the teaching of the prophets; because it produces abnegation and self-sacrifice. (DF, 263)

The state does not actualise freedom but provokes sacrifice. The dangers of combining holy and universal history on the basis of sacrifice have already been noted. Another possible reading emerges at this point, one for which the combination of holy and universal history is not a fusion, not the evocation of a messianic *Sittlichkeit*. It is rather an unsettling of the state – and the idolatry of power it commands – by awakening a 'demand for the absolute' that cannot be satisfied by a state, one that lends power to 'the messianic institutions of Israel' (*not* the State of Israel) 'that tear us out of our conformism and material comforts, dispersion and alienation' (DF, 263–4). The messianic institutions of which Levinas speaks are not those real existing institutions of the State of Israel, but nor are they forms of the ideal state in the manner of Plato's *Republic* or Augustine's *City of God* – they are more properly understood as postponements or corrections of existing institutional structures in the name of justice, in particular justice for the other. According to this historical logic there arises the possibility - and this is one that Levinas never publicly addresses - that perhaps even the state must be sacrificed for the sake of justice.

One way to clarify Levinas's position is to situate it in the context of a debate within the history of Zionism that has recurred throughout the (universal) history of the State of Israel. Viewed from the standpoint of universal history, the State of Israel is primarily a political event set within a particular political history: this view would be consistent with the Zionism – shared by Herzl – that saw in the State of Israel the realisation of a civil freedom that could not be guaranteed to Jews in the Diaspora. An opposed view would see the wars and the politics of the State of Israel as secondary and, in extreme formulations perhaps, even obstructive to the messianic mission of Israel in holy history. The combined dimensions of universal and holy history may be seen to have produced a political logic that combines aspects of both and situates the actions of the State of Israel on a scale calibrated between the secular extreme of sacrificing the messianic mission of Israel in order to ensure the security and prosperity of the State of Israel and the holy risk of sacrificing the State of Israel for the sake of the messianic mission of Israel. It is a tension that has been played out in terms of territory: how far must attempts to realise the religious claims to the Holy Land in holy history be qualified by considerations of protecting the existence of the State of Israel within limited borders?

Levinas tries to sustain the tension between the dimensions of holy and universal history by holding that 'holy history' involves a reference to 'This truth and this destiny [that] are not contained within political and national categories' (DF, 264)[10] while referring to a 'destiny confusedly felt' with respect to the events of May–June 1967 that concerned the very existence of the state and fell under the political categories of universal history. He describes this tension between the dimensions in terms of 'an awkward position in being' (DF, 264) that cannot be understood solely in terms of universal history, but challenges the very dimensionality of its concept of the political and points to the need for extra dimensions of political experience that would include the ethical and the religious. The 'awkward position in being' also characterises the State of Israel as a hybrid product of holy and universal history: 'a Holy Land resuscitated by the state' that leads a 'dangerous and pure life' (DF, 264). The state in short is always suspended between the claims of the two histories, with the omnipresent danger of one of its aspects conflicting with the other and leading potentially to mutual ruin.

Although throughout 'Space is not One-Dimensional' Levinas insists on increasing the number of dimensions of the political to accommodate both universal and holy history, his conclusion seems on balance to judge the actions of the State of Israel according to the criteria of universal history.

After a reference to 'you too, my Muslim friend, my unhated enemy of the Six Days War', to whom Levinas also concedes an 'awkward place in being' (along with fully conscious Christians and Communists), the conclusion subtly produces the continuity between the France of the Declaration of the Rights of Man and Citizen and the State of Israel that is urged throughout the essay. Once again echoing Kant's footnote on the French Revolution (and, like Kant, without naming the state in question) Levinas concludes that 'it is from adventures such as these run by its citizens that a great modern State – that is to say, one that serves humanity – deserves its greatness, the attention it pays to the present and its presence in the World' (DF, 264). At this point it becomes necessary to ask about those who were displaced by the 'place in the sun' taken by a 'great modern state' and of those others who are sacrificed to its political adventures.

Threatening others

The closing flourish to 'Space is not One-Dimensional' might seem to mark a lapse in Levinas's ethical and political judgement, the point where the prophetic demand borne by holy history for justice to strangers, widows and orphans – those without protection – has been forgotten. The exhilaration of the political adventure of the State of Israel as an event of universal history seems to occlude holy history at this point. Yet such a judgement would be too hasty, not only simplifying the problem of political judgement that emerges at this point but also containing it. For it is at this point – the point of victory – that Levinas's entire ethics and politics is shaken. For the event of victory and the blatant abdication of responsibility for the vanquished brings to light a dimension of Levinas's thought that was, in retrospect, always there but otherwise contained.

It is not the acceptance of war that is in question, for we have seen that Levinas's work is unsentimentally addressed to the question of war and the horror that it brings; nor is it the readiness to forget, on this occasion, the responsibility of holy history in the face of the events of universal history. What emerges in the victory of the state 'that serves humanity' is an unexpected complicity between universal and holy history. Holy history is not quite what it seemed, an unconditional call for justice, but suffers from the equivocations arising from its unacknowledged partiality towards universal history.[11] Holy history, it seems, is vulnerable and its universal claims open to compromise or distortion, addressing only a part of humanity, or, perhaps even more disastrously, addressing that part of humanity that considers itself to be the whole of humanity.

The partiality of holy history becomes unhappily joined with what can only be described as a fear of Asia. At its most general this appears in the context of discussions of Jewish and Christian solidarity in terms of a shared holy history against a threatening other. In 'Jewish Thought Today'

(1961), Levinas refers to 'the rise of countless masses of Asiatic and under-developed peoples... peoples and civilisations who no longer refer to our holy history, for whom Abraham, Isaac and Jacob no longer mean anything' (DF, 165). He continues: 'under the greedy eyes of these count-less hordes who wish to hope and live, we, the Jews and Christians, are pushed to the margins of history, and soon no one will bother any more to differentiate between a Catholic and a Protestant or a Jew and a Christian...' (DF, 165). Levinas – not without irony – refers to Marxism as a possible vector of holy history in Asia, but what prevails is a narrow notion of Christian and Jewish fraternity. In 'Beyond Dialogue' (1967), Levinas goes even further by citing Jewish/Christian solidarity before the threat of Hitler as a precedent for solidarity in the face of Asia: 'I am not thinking exclusively of our kinship in the face of Nazism. But behold, upon the world's stage, innumerable masses advancing out of Asia. In the eyes of these crowds who do not take holy history as their frame of refer-ence, are we Jews and Christians anything but sects quarrelling over the meaning of a few obscure texts?' (AT, 83). The violent dehumanising of the peoples of Asia is striking – 'the two billion eyes that watch us' – as is the closure of holy history and the devaluation of the non-European other.

What is most striking in this parochial version of holy history is the absence at this point of the third Abrahamic religion – Islam – a religion which shares and even enhances prophetic holy history and for which Abraham, Isaac and Jacob are of the utmost significance. Fortunately, this exclusion is not consistent; indeed, in the 1959 address 'Monotheism and Language', Levinas pays eloquent homage to the significant place occupied by Islam in and with respect to holy history. Yet there remains an ambiva-lence over whether Islam is indeed part of holy history or whether Moslems are to be counted among the dehumanised 'masses' of Asia. This surfaces a year later in 'The Russo–Chinese Debate and the Dialectic' (1960), an essay published in *Esprit* that must rank as Levinas's ugliest and most disturbing published work.

The essay was published in the same year as 'Principles and Faces', the essay in which Levinas reflected upon the possibility of a universality other than that of the state and a freedom other than that defended by Hegel and Marx. Such difficult reflections, he claimed, went beyond Hegel and Marx by putting into question the foundations of Western metaphysics. In the context of the search for a notion of the political beyond the frontiers of Western metaphysics, 'The Russo–Chinese Debate and the Dialectic' is a grave disappointment. Given the title, Levinas might have been expected, when speaking of Asia, to confront Europe and its dangerous metaphysics with new sources of universality and freedom drawn from the East. That he does not even contemplate this step is one of the many mysteries of this tormented text whose political motivation becomes apparent only in its closing lines.

The immediate occasion of the article was Sino–Soviet tension, a geopolitical situation to which Levinas responded with some disquieting reflections on the geopolitics of the Soviet Union and Asia. Or, to be precise – 'Russia' – for Levinas is not concerned with the Euro–Asian empire that was the Soviet Union, but with a Russia that should in his view form an alliance with Europe against Asia. In an appeal to the worst kind of universal history, Levinas writes:

> The exclusive community with the Asiatic world, itself a stranger to European history to which Russia, in spite of all its strategic and tactical denials, has belonged for almost a thousand years, would this not be disturbing even to a society without classes?...In abandoning the West, does not Russia fear to drown itself in an Asiatic civilisation which, it too, is likely to carry on existing behind the concrete appearance of dialectical resolution?' (IH, 171)

The evocation of a national and then a European identity that must be protected against a culture that is a stranger to its history, the figuration of contact with the other in terms of drowning, would seem to invert all of the theses of Levinas's thought.

Levinas's development of the 'argument' is hardly more encouraging, with a passage that begins:

> The yellow peril! It is not racial, it is spiritual. It does not involve inferior values; it involves a radical strangeness, a stranger to the weight of its past, from where there does not filter any familiar voice or inflection, a lunar or Martian past.' (IH, 172)

It is difficult to imagine any circumstances in which the phrase 'the yellow peril' can not be racist, let alone in the context set by Levinas that consigns a phantasm of Asia to the moon or another planet, thus figuratively stripping Asians of their humanity. It is almost as if, at its most charitable construal, Levinas was undertaking the rhetorical experiment of mounting an extreme particularist argument against the universalism of Hegelian–Marxist philosophy of history. This might be supported by his provisional conclusion that 'progress towards a universal society would pass by paths where the diverse human groups do not have to overcome their histories. There would exist dialectically indispensable forms of particularity' (IH, 172). Yet surely this defence of Russian and European particularism is not the new universality and freedom that Levinas intimated in 'Principles and Faces'?

In the light of the phobic references to an alleged spiritual 'yellow peril', the 'spirit' of monotheistic freedom evoked in 'The Philosophy of Hitlerism' against National Socialism begins itself to seem uncomfortably parochial. Indeed, the parallel Levinas suggested elsewhere between the threat to monotheistic 'holy history' posed by National Socialism and 'Asia' seems here to be indirectly confirmed. With its references to the 'Graeco, Judaic, Christian West', the 1960 essay seems to have converted the monotheistic 'Popular Front' against Nazism of the 1930s into a Cold War spiritual and geopolitical bloc, uncannily similar in its simplifications to Heidegger's geopolitical 'analysis' of the place of Germany between the USA and the USSR.

The reason for the exclusion of Islam on this occasion becomes clearer towards the end of the essay, and in particular in the final paragraph which reveals that its object is other than the debate between Soviet and Chinese Marxism. The essay ends with the sentence: 'It thus would have been necessary to be a little Chinese, to again call a cat a cat and to recognise in the anti-capitalist nationalisms the shadow of National Socialism' (IH, 173). Far from exploring the openness to the Asian other, the essay is here revealed as pursuing a particular political agenda. In closing, Levinas describes one of the main points of tension between 'Russia' and China to be the former's support for radical nationalist movements: the Chinese criticised the Soviet Union for its support of nationalist movements regardless of their commitment to socialist or communist principles. Levinas concurred, criticising the Russian faith in the dialectic that allowed it 'to support anti-communists if they represented a stage towards socialism and to show sympathy to those who torture communists in their prisons. It would appear reasonable to take seriously socialist pretensions and anti-imperialist slogans made by aggravated and avid nationalists' (IH, 172). It is hard to avoid the suspicion that this critique is motivated less by hitherto-undisclosed Maoist sympathies on the part of Levinas, nor even by an ethical protest on behalf of communists imprisoned by radical nationalist regimes, but in obedience to a different political agenda.

It is likely that Levinas has a particular radical nationalism in mind at this moment, namely Arab nationalism and above all the Nasserite regime in Egypt and other radical Arab nationalisms supported diplomatically, economically and militarily by the Soviet Union. These nationalisms were united in their implacable 'anti-imperialist' hostility towards the existence of the State of Israel. This reading is confirmed by the claim regarding the 'shadow of National Socialism' falling upon these regimes, one which was consistent with a contemporary discourse that emphasised the alleged historic and political links and similarities between Arab nationalism and German National Socialism. While the claim is controversial, the existence of such a discourse is not, and it is likely that Levinas subscribed to it in this essay. If this is true, then the absence of Islam and the warnings against 'Asia' plausibly refer to Arab nationalism in conflict with the State of Israel. Whatever the final judgement of the meaning of this tormented essay, it does reveal an aspect of Levinas's thought that arguably compromises many of his universalist ethical claims.

Having said as much, it must also be recalled that Levinas's judgement of the non-European world, of Islam and indeed of Arab nationalism and the case for the Palestinians, was ambivalent. His homage to Islam's role in holy history has already been noted, as has his ethical recognition in the Talmudic reading 'the Youth of Israel' of the claim of the non-European other to nourishment.

The ambivalence is most exposed on those occasions when Levinas speaks of Arab nationalism and the Palestinians. It is here that his ethical and political thought and their commitments to holy and universal history are placed under most strain. This can be shown through Levinas's comments on the struggle between the State of Israel with the Palestinians and Arab nationalists from the three-year period 1979–1982: 'Politics After' (1979), the preface to *Beyond the Verse* (1981) and the radio discussion 'Ethics and Politics' (1982).

In the foreword to *Beyond the Verse*, Levinas cites from his own essay on Paul Claudel, 'Poetry and the Impossible', published in 1969. Following a discussion of 'the Passion of the Holocaust' (a Claudelian formulation that Levinas adopted) and Zionism, Levinas begins a meditation upon responsibility for suffering. This begins 'Of course, it is the West, not the Arab world, which bears the responsibility for Auschwitz' (BV, xvi). With this, Levinas faces what was claimed by many as the injustice of requiring the Palestinian Arabs to pay with their suffering for the suffering imposed upon the Jewish people by the colonial nations of the West. Levinas begins tentatively to answer in terms of the universality of responsibility – under which all humans, including the Palestinians, are responsible – but then breaks off with an extraordinary self-citation from *Difficult Freedom*.

The act of self-citation in *Beyond the Verse* is of a complexity that verges on the irresponsible. Levinas writes: 'In *Difficult Freedom* I published the following lines, written more than ten years ago' (BV, xvi), and then makes a long citation. He does not give the source of the citation, nor the fact that the paragraphs from which he cites are in the original essay carefully framed as reports of Claudel's views and not necessarily his own. What must be owned, however, is the act of citation along with the selections and the ellipses, not all acknowledged, by means of which it is constructed. The 1969 essay returns to consider Claudel in the light of the Six Days War, resuming the objections to Claudel's view of sacred history as a passion played and replayed in the 'Old' and 'New' testaments stated in the early 1950s. In 1969, Levinas admires Claudel's grasp of the uniqueness of the Shoah, his placing 'the martyrdom of Auschwitz out on its own' (DF, 129), and even the manner in which he interprets this event in terms of Christian theology as a sacrifice of innocence or 'holocaust'. Then, in the course of an extended reflection on the notion of sacred history and the passage from 'the despair of the camps to the new beginning in Israel' (DF, 129), Levinas arrives at the question of historical responsibility and the fate of the

Palestinians – especially the refugees of the 1948 War of Independence – as discussed by Claudel. The discussion thus reports Claudel's position, but without marking any distance from it, thus giving the impression that Levinas is speaking through a mask, that is, paradoxically retaining his right to silence on the subject of the State of Israel by using the voice of a Catholic, questionably anti-Semitic poet and theologian whose work he had already uneasily denounced twenty years earlier.

It is from this discussion that Levinas makes the following citation, comprising three questions and a response separated by two ellipses, in the foreword to *Beyond the Verse*:

> What is the suppression of national distinctions if not an indivisible humanity, that is to say, responsible in its entirety for the crimes and misfortunes of the few?...Are all human relations reducible to the calculations of damages and interest, all problems to the settling of scores? Can anyone amongst mankind wash his hands of all this flesh gone up in smoke?...The gesture of recognition which would come to Israel from the Arab peoples would no doubt be replied to by a brotherly zeal such that the problem of the refugees will lose its unknown elements. (BV, xvi)

The citation opens by entertaining the thought that all humanity is responsible, adding that perhaps human relations are not reducible to a movement of wrong and reparation and that all are guilty. These general thoughts on responsibility and the calculations of damages are then linked to a call for 'a gesture of recognition' from the Arab peoples that would bring a reply from the State of Israel that would in turn would solve the problem of the refugees. In order fully to appreciate the significance of Levinas's citation of his own call for a 'gesture', four years after such a gesture had been made in the visit of Egyptian President Sadat to Israel, it is necessary to examine more closely the elements of the collage of citation that was assembled for the purposes of *Beyond the Verse*.

The sentences that make up the citation are drawn from two paragraphs, the first of which begins by evoking a holy history that touches the flesh of all humanity, beyond national differences. The fact that all are touched by holy history leads to the question of whether then we are not all responsible. The ellipsis after the first citation deletes a rhetorical flourish that links universal responsibility to the claims of the Arab peoples to have suffered an injustice at the hands of the State of Israel: 'The Arab peoples would not have to answer for German atrocities, or cede their lands to the victims of Hitlerism! What deafness to the call of conscience!' (DF, 131). The argument seems to be that the Arab peoples would have a case only if it were true that all humanity were not responsible for the crimes of the few. To believe this to be true, Claudel/Levinas claims, is indeed to be deaf to the call of conscience. There follows the second sentence of the citation, referring to the impossibility of 'calculations of damages' and 'settling of scores' that, in its context, does more than make a general philosophical point, but also works to corroborate the previous allegation of an Arab 'deafness' to the call of conscience.

The second passage of Levinas's citation then moves to the figure of unabsolvable, universal guilt before 'that flesh turned to smoke'. Yet between the two sentences are two further sentences, this time invisibly deleted. These sentences once again serve to make specific the general claims represented in the cited sentences. Thus, between the 'settling of scores' and the evocation of universal guilt, there are two sentences on the Palestinians, notable in addition for the emergence of a split between the Claudel/Levinas voice. The first sentence reads 'The right to a "birthplace" invoked by Arab refugees can certainly not be treated unjustly, and Paul Claudel is not one to speak lightly of an attachment to one's native sort and the nostalgic value of the church tower (or minaret)' (DF, 131). The justice of the Palestinian's case is reduced, first by referring to it in the conditional double negative – it 'can not be treated unjustly' as opposed to 'must be treated justly' – and then by comparison with Claudel's own sentimental attachment to native soil, finally to be reduced to a 'nostalgic value' itself deflated by the simile of 'church tower (or minaret)'. All this prepares to trivialise the claim of the refugees before the next sentence: 'But can the call of the land silence the cries of Auschwitz which will echo until the end of time?' (DF, 131). Is this anything other than the weighing of suffering that Claudel/Levinas has just condemned? The cry for justice of the refugees has been reduced to a nostalgic 'cry of the land', which is then weighed and found wanting beside the cries of the murdered at Auschwitz. There then follows the powerful figure of the unabsolvable guilt of all for the murdered of the Shoah.

The final sentence of the citation in *Beyond the Verse* moves into the next paragraph, moving over two sentences in which Levinas distinguishes his voice from that of Claudel – the second referring to Claudel's 'frightening apostrophe' and 'excessive phrase', circumlocutions for the fact that perhaps Claudel had not overcome the racism discerned earlier by Levinas, but merely transferred it to another victim. The final cited passage calls for an Arab gesture of 'recognition' that would evoke fraternity and allow a solution to the problem of the refugees. Then, in the remainder of 'Poetry and the Impossible', Claudel/Levinas evoke the new possibilities that will arise 'if, on both of Israel's frontiers, the swords are turned into ploughshares and the tanks become tractors' (DF, 131). The vision, however, is immediately followed by apologetics, namely the argument familiar in Israeli political discourse that the Palestinian problem is in fact an Arab problem, and that the territorial claims of the State of Israel are modest in respect to the vast territory occupied by the Arab nations.

At this point Levinas interrupts the equivocal reportage to ask, 'Is it for a Jew to say?', thus qualifying everything that was said before as not necessarily his own. But after his ethically ambiguous 'saying' of Claudel's 'said', the call to the historical responsibility of the survivors of National Socialism not to remain silent seems if anything to intensify the ambiguity. The survivor of the 'Hitlerian massacres' is *Other in relation to martyrs'* – He is 'consequently responsible and unable to remain silent'; the shared responsibility of Jew and Arab 'ought to help them talk to each other...There is an obligation to speak' (DF, 132). And yet it is as if Levinas has not spoken, but allowed his voice to be confused with that of a Christian with a questionable record with respect to anti-Semitic and anti-Islamic sentiments.

It can now be appreciated how the bewildering avoidance of speech, while claiming the obligation not to remain silent in 'Poetry and the Impossible', complicates the citation in the foreword to *Beyond the Verse*. In short, Levinas uses selective citations from a report on the musings of Claudel as a vehicle to express his thoughts on the future of Israel following the visit of Sadat to Jerusalem in 1977. His comment on the passage cited is: 'Today, I will no longer say refugees, but Palestinians. Zionism is not at an end, for all that' (BV, xvi). Levinas's response to the 'gesture of recognition' made by Sadat substitutes for the juridical status of 'refugees' the political name of the 'Palestinians'. In terms of conservative Israeli politics the admission that the Palestinians are a people might have seemed radical, but in fact Levinas's naming of the Palestinians did not represent his taking an ethical lead over the political, but merely reflected the Camp David Accords in which the Likud government conceded the name of a people to the Palestinians.[12] The ethical is trailing behind the political, conceding speech according to political rather than prophetic criteria. Whatever the judgement of the significance of Levinas's naming of the Palestinians, how far can it be said to meet the earlier promise of Israel's fraternal zeal in response to a 'gesture of recognition'? For even the recognition of the 'Palestinians' by Levinas seems restrictive, since he has no more to say to them: the remainder of the foreword is concerned less with the Palestinians than with the challenge to the meaning of Zionism represented by the acknowledgement of their existence.

The definition of Zionism that Levinas proposes has two dimensions: peace with neighbours, and the necessity 'not to continue being a minority in its political structure' (BV, xvii), the latter ensuring that attacks on Jews do not remain an 'uncontrolled and unpunished phenomenon' (BV, xvii). It is difficult to interpret exactly what political strategy he is recommending – there is a clear, demographic recommendation that Jewish people remain a majority in Israel, but how this is to be achieved politically – by withdrawal from the occupied West Bank or by deportation of Arab Israeli citizens – remains unsaid. Even more disturbing is the final modulation of 'responsibility for others' into '*my* family, *my* people, despite the possessive pronouns, are my "others", like strangers, and demand justice and protection' (BV, xvii). This introduces the notion of a political choice between others, one framed in terms of such others as 'my' family and people and those who are the third or the stranger. Such an understanding of the other puts into crisis the universal and foundational claims of an ethics of alterity, but, as noted in the discussion of *Otherwise than Being*, it is a restriction intrinsic to Levinas's thought on the relationship between other and third rather than a contingent lapse in its application.

The closing comments on Zionism in the foreword to *Beyond the Verse* were more fully worked through in Levinas's 1979 response to Sadat's peace initiative, 'Politics After!'. The references to the Israeli–Arab/Palestinian conflict are governed by the plea for the recognition of the extraordinary and novel character of the adventure of the State of Israel. This state will, for Levinas, 'have to incarnate the prophetic moral code and the idea of its peace' (BV, 194), and, after 'the realism of its political formulations at the beginning' (BV, 191), Zionism is now in the course of doing so. Levinas further claims that Zionism combines 'Politics and a precarious state of being from which the despair beyond which one must go is never absent' (BV, 193). The relationship between politics and the 'precarious state of being' that describes Jewish identity remains static, with the co-existence of different intersecting political temporalities. According to the first, the struggle for the State of Israel 'will always have been the struggle of the Warsaw ghetto up in arms but with no ground to which to withdraw' (BV, 194). This is the 'truth' of the State of Israel that lies behind its posture as 'An armed and dominating State, one of the great military powers of the Mediterranean basin, against the unarmed Palestinian people whose existence Israel does not recognise!' (BV, 193). Yet qualifying the injustices of the state coexisting with this past and present is the promise that 'all injustices [are] capable of being put right' – the 'prophetic promises that are hidden behind the Zionist claim to historical rights and its contortions under the political yoke' (BV, 194) an aspect of Zionism intuited by Sadat. However, it is not necessary to be an Hegelian to expect a more nuanced sense of historical development from Levinas, and a more explicit acknowledgement of the possibility that the past and present of the State of Israel is capable of ruining the promises of its future.

With the invasion of Lebanon in 1982, any remaining historical justification for Levinas's view of the defensive character of the State of Israel was put in question. The objectives of establishing a client state in Lebanon and destroying the political infrastructure of the Palestine Liberation Organisation (PLO) that had been established there were represented by Prime Minister Begin as a defensive operation, claiming at a cabinet meeting that 'the alternative to fighting is Treblinka',[13] and then in a telegram to the President of the United States making comparisons between the invasion of Lebanon and the Allied attack on Berlin during the Second World War, and comparing the PLO with the Nazis. With the assassination of the Israeli client President, the Phalangist Bashir Gemayel on 14 September, Israeli forces entered West Beirut and Defence Minister Sharon gave the fateful order to Israeli Defence Force Commanders to permit Phalangist Militias to enter the Palestinian refugee camps of Sabra and Shatila in search of militant members of the PLO. From Thursday 16 September to Sunday 19 September the Phalangist Militia murdered Palestinian refugees – men, women and children, claiming 700–800 victims according to Israeli estimates, 2000 according to those of the Palestinian Red Crescent.[14] The Israeli soldiers present outside the camps were already aware of the murders on the Thursday but did nothing. Begin apparently first heard of the massacre on Saturday, on the BBC, but the tenor of his response was captured by his comment to the *New York Times*: '*Goyim* kill *goyim*, and they immediately come to hang the Jews.' Yet the revulsion within Israel and the Diaspora at the complicity of the State of Israel in a war crime led to demonstrations and a call for a commission of inquiry, initially resisted by the government but which under Yitzhak Kahan eventually reported in February 1983 that Israel was complicit in the war crime and recommended removal of the Minister of Defence and senior officers.

The war crime perpetrated at Sabra and Shatila can be interpreted in a number of ways – as confirmation of the violence of the Israeli State, or, given the revulsion and protest provoked by the murders in Israeli civil society and the Diaspora, as confirmation of its prophetic vocation. In this context, Levinas's response to the crime is clearly important as a touchstone for his ethical and political principles as well as his views on Israel and the State of Israel. A little more than a week after the murders, Levinas participated in a radio broadcast with Shlomo Malka and Alain Finkielkraut that addressed the theme of Israel and Jewish ethics. Malka introduced the programme, evoking the shock felt by Jewish communities throughout the world at the murders. Levinas replied evasively to his opening question on whether Israel was innocent or responsible for the deaths at Sabra and Shatila, prejudging the question of guilt - 'Despite the lack of guilt here – and probably there, too' (perhaps referring to France/the Diaspora and Israel/Lebanon?) - and then claiming the 'honour of responsibility'. But the latter is not the squalid responsibility of the Israeli soldiers who looked on but did not intervene to stop the bloodshed, but a noble responsibility universalised as the responsibility of the innocent for the other.

Finkielkraut returned the discussion to the events themselves, asking Levinas about the temptation to escape responsibility. Levinas replied by returning to 'the facts', and describing the protests against the murders by the majority of Israel and the State of Israel as an 'ethical reaction', but then instead evoking the Holocaust and the qualifications that this introduces for responsibility 'in myself'. Thus, and still in the context of the discussion of a war crime, Levinas claimed that, 'along with this feeling of unbounded responsibility, there is certainly a place for a defence, for it is not always a question of "me", but of those close to me who are my neighbours. I'd call such a defence a politics, but a politics that is ethically necessary' (LR, 292). After a further intervention by Finkielkraut, Levinas returned to link Zionism with military preparedness and to define the neighbour, consistently with the position adopted at the end of the foreword to *Beyond the Verse*, as 'my people and my kin'.

Levinas at this point distinguishes between two ethical calls, limiting the first to the defence of a specific other, in this case the Jewish people: 'When you defend the Jewish people, you defend your neighbour' (LR, 292); and then claiming that 'there is also an ethical limit to this ethically necessary political existence' (LR, 293). He saw this ethical limit as now at issue in Israel, thus linking the question of the second level of ethics to the promise of political invention that he consistently sought in the State of Israel. Finkielkraut then challenged Levinas by citing Begin's precept, 'Jewish blood [shall] not flow with impunity', bringing the reply that, although invaluable, this phrase is not itself ethical, that it 'does not set the limits within which a political action, or even warlike measures, would be justified' (LR, 293). It is in the context of the justification of such measures that Levinas then brought forward the two phases of the Israeli invasion, 'Peace for Galilee' and the siege of Beirut, claiming that the ethical was interrupted at Sabra and Shatila. However, he again quickly universalised the responsibility, diverting discussion once more from the issue of the specific ethical and political responsibility for the event.

At this point Malka intervened to ask: 'Emmanuel Levinas, you are the philosopher of the "other". Isn't history, isn't politics the very site of the encounter with the "other", and for the Israeli, isn't the "other" above all the Palestinian?' (LR, 294). Faced with this unavoidable question that went to the heart not only of his philosophy but also of his political judgement, Levinas's reply is chilling and, to use his idiom, opens a wound in his whole œuvre:

> My definition of the other is completely different. The other is the neighbour, who is not necessarily kin, but who can be. And in that sense, if you're for the other, you're for the neighbour. But if your neighbour attacks another neighbour or treats him unjustly, what can you do? Then alterity takes on another character, in alterity we can find an enemy, or at least then we are faced with the problem of knowing who is right and who is wrong, who is just and who is unjust. There are people who are wrong. (LR, 294)

An apologetic response to the revelation of the other as enemy would be to distinguish between empirical and transcendental others, and to maintain that here Levinas was speaking of the former. A harder thought is that Levinas's claim is rigorously consistent with his philosophy, which we have argued recognises the inevitability of war. To describe the other as enemy at this point is thus entirely consistent with such a reading of Levinas's ethics.

It is also consistent with the detail of his understanding of the wars of the State of Israel. The 'Moslem friend' of 'Space is not One-Dimensional' is also the unhated enemy, and the neighbour Levinas has already identified in the same interview as the 'Jewish people'. But a characteristic ambiguity also enters into Levinas's response. At its most general, the question may be asked, who are the neighbours who are at war with each other? Or, in this specific case, who is the neighbour that attacks, and who is attacked? Malka has identified the other with the Palestinian, and Levinas has replied that his definition of the other is 'completely different' – suggesting that the Palestinians are not the other, are not neighbours. But who, then, is attacking whom? Is Levinas's neighbour – the State of Israel – attacking another neighbour – the Lebanon? Or is the State of Israel being attacked by the Palestinian 'neighbour'? Or again, is Levinas referring to the attack by the neighbour Israeli civil society upon its neighbour, the government of the State of Israel?

Even without being able to identify the neighbour, Levinas's view of the subsequent problem of 'knowing who is right and who is wrong, who is just and who is unjust' uncharacteristically reduces ethics to the problem of knowledge. If this claim is meant seriously, then Levinas opens not only the political problem of identifying *who* is right and who is wrong, but also of knowing *what* is right and what is wrong. If such knowledge is of more than tactical or strategic utility, that is, if it is ethical, then it will become less easy to identify in the other an enemy. In *Totality and Infinity* the necessary link was the messianic, so unsurprisingly the discussion now turns to the messianic, once again identified by Levinas with sacrifice – 'the daily sacrifice made by people who've left secure positions and often abundance in order to lead a difficult life, to lead an ethical life...' (LR, 295). Yet, perhaps in the case of the war in Lebanon, those of whom Levinas spoke did not make a sacrifice, but were sacrificed by the state to its own pursuit of power. On this possibility, that of the idolatrous, sacrificial state, Levinas remained silent until his last words in the discussion.

In the closing exchanges Levinas referred to 'the shock that the human possibility of the events of Sabra and Shatila – whoever is behind them – signifies for our entire history as Jews and human beings' (LR, 296). The evocation of the shock in this case led Levinas tacitly to suggest a departure from classical Zionism, calling as he always had for the defence and protection of 'our books'. The supreme threat is that levelled at the books, by which Levinas means the interpretation of the prophetic word or 'work of justice'. The protection of the books may be interpreted as the raising of the prophetic principle of justice above the claims of the state or territory, for it is 'The books which carry us through history, and which, even more deeply than the earth, are our support' (LR, 296). In his final words

Levinas is even more explicit, arguing that Zionism must be distinguished from 'some sort of commonplace mystique of the earth as native soil' (LR, 296). It is instead 'a relationship to the world and to a human being', one which, Levinas now seems to claim, is beyond any territory. His last words seem to place the call of justice beyond even the occupation of the Holy Land: 'A person is more holy than a land, even a holy land, since, faced with an affront made to a person, this holy land appears in its nakedness to be but stone and wood' (LR, 297). With this, ethics seems once more to prevail over politics and the state.

When looked at more closely, Levinas's final word is even harder on Zionism. He arrives by way of a Talmudic reference to a text from the book of Numbers in which the explorers sent ahead by Moses to the Holy Land calumniate it. Levinas's explicit line of argument at the end of the broadcast maintains that, if calumny of 'stones and trees' merits death, how much more serious the affront to a person. Yet the message of the Talmudic reading to which Levinas refers, his 1965 'Promised Land or Permitted Land', is far more sombre in its implications even than this. The calumny of the land by the explorers is linked by Levinas to the scruples of intellectuals – the 'beautiful souls' concerning the Zionist adventure – the explorers calumny 'the Zionists of that time...They have decided, in the name of truth, to confound the Zionists' (TR, 56). The explorers argued against the right to the land, against the utopian project of occupying it. Thus they calumny not only the land, but also the Zionists and the Jewish people who dream of the promised land.

So far, it would seem as if Levinas's veiled reference to this Talmudic reading does not support his conclusion that holy land is but stone and wood compared to an offended person. Yet this overlooks the final lesson of the reading – those who are about to conquer a country

> not only commit themselves to justice, but also apply it rigorously to themselves...They assume a responsibility without indulgence and are summoned to pay for their own injustice with their exile. You see, this country is extraordinary. It is like heaven. It is a country that vomits up its inhabitants when they are not just. There no other country like it; the resolution to accept a country under such conditions confers a right to that country. (LR, 69)

In this light, Levinas's last words are a warning that the State of Israel is only justified if it obeys the prophetic call for justice – if it ceases to do so, then its inhabitants will be expelled. The claims of prophetic ethics carried in the books are maintained in their interpretation and will condemn any injustice on the part of a state that claims to act in their name.

Assimilations

The concluding section of *Beyond the Verse* is entitled 'Zionisms', under-lining Levinas's view of the existence of a plurality of philosophical and political perspectives on the political future of Israel. Another perspective on this future may be provided by a reading of his views of assimilation, or rather assimilations, for this too is a plural phenomenon with many possible futures. The problem of assimilation is intrinsic to Levinas's understanding of the vocation of Israel, consistently defined by him as the alignment of the universal and the particular. Levinas repeatedly distin-guished his view of this alignment from the logical subsumption of the particular by the universal, insisting on an 'excessive' or 'awkward' rela-tionship between them. Levinas was aware not only of the danger of such 'assimilation' of the particular by the universal, but of the dangers that attended such assimilation. His memory of National Socialism was insep-arable from that of the failure of a particular cultural programme of political assimilation. Yet there were other assimilations beyond that of the nineteenth- and early twentieth-century experience of assimilation to citizenship. There was also the assimilation to Western 'culture' and to the political and cultural form of the nation-state – Zionist 'normalisation' of the status of the Jewish nation – with different dangers attending them. There is also a radical understanding of assimilation to which Levinas seems to have approached during the 1980s which does not assume the assimilation of Judaism to the West, but of the West to Judaism.

The third essay making up 'Zionisms', following 'The State of Caesar and the State of David' and 'Politics After!', is 'Assimilation and New Culture' (1980). The address in the State Presidential Palace in Jerusalem is an invaluable meditation on assimilation, not only in itself but also as the statement of a position that changed during the 1980s, along with Levinas's views on the State of Israel. In it Levinas declares the task of creating a new 'culture' that is situated within the powerful claims to artic-ulate the universal made by the 'forms of European culture'. Levinas paradoxically both over- and underestimates the phenomenon of assimila-tion. He overestimates it in the view that

> The forms of European life have conquered the Israelites to the extent that these forms reflect the spiritual excellence of univer-sality, the norm of feeling and thinking, and the source of science, art and modern technology, but also the thought of democracy and the foundation of the institutions linked to the ideal of freedom and the rights of man (BV, 196–7).

In this view the threat of assimilation is posed in terms of the universalist technical, cultural and political institutions and aspirations of the West, in the light of which Judaism is in danger of becoming particularistic 'folklore'.

The underestimation of the phenomenon of assimilation lies in the hope that the 'State of Israel will be the end of assimilation' (BV, 201). By seeing resistance to assimilation taking the form of the nation-state, Levinas forgets the extent to which adoption of this nation-state is itself an act of assimilation, replete with danger. The form of the nation-state may undermine what Levinas saw as the 'beyond of universalism', informing a Judaism that had been awoken by assimilation. The 'beyond' of assimilation to universalism is 'what completes or perfects human fraternity', an experience that presents the task of expressing 'in Greek those principles about which Greece knew nothing' (BV, 200). Levinas concludes by claiming that 'The explanation and elaboration of these concepts are decisive for the struggle against assimilation' (BV, 201). Yet this defensive posture with respect to assimilation returns to its overestimation.

The overestimation of assimilation as a total phenomenon of Western culture, one that Levinas suggests is linked in some way with totalitarian politics, may be regarded as a misapprehension. It was indeed Levinas who saw that the 'foundations of the institutions linked to the ideal of freedom and the rights of man, (BV, 197)' cited as part of the universality of the West, were themselves assimilated by the West from Judaism. In his writings of the 1980s Levinas became increasingly sensitive to the complexity of assimilation, no longer seeing it as a unilateral movement from the universal to the particular, but as a mark of an irreconcilable disturbance between them.

The complexity is figured in a late talmudic reading, 'The Nations and the Presence of Israel' (1987), which mediates upon the determination of the nations 'to take part in the Messianic age!' (TN, 97). This reading considers the claims of the nations to bring gifts to the Messiah, that is to say, to be assimilated to Judaism and through it 'the constitution of a new humanity' (TN, 96). The gifts of Egypt – that once offered refuge – and of Cush who made no offence, are acceptable, but the question of the homage of the 'criminal Roman Empire' inspires debate. 'Rome' is a type for Graeco–Roman modernity – 'a monstrous city of countless skyscrapers…The accumulation of useless wealth' (TN, 96), in short 'the distant West, a future America' (TN, 100). The condemnation of Rome prefigures that of 'a certain political and ethical model' made of an inhuman formalism, colonial expansion and the hypocrisy that attends 'a social equilibrium established through warfare' (TN, 106). Intensifying the critique of Rome and the West, Levinas sees it as also prefiguring the idolatry of the modern state; it is a colossus of 'Universal legality, though lacking in nuance and cumbersome, unloving, merciless, unpardoning' (TN, 107). The claim of Rome to be admitted to the messianic age of peace and justice thus demands close legal scrutiny.

Levinas confronts 'Rome' with the 'word of the Lord, consecrating fraternal bonds of love between beings', and asks whether it is possible for Rome to grasp this word. The answer is a qualified no, since Rome is only capable of understanding 'formal brotherhood' (TN, 100) and not the full talmudic concept of fraternity. The full implications of the question are revealed towards the end of the reading, when 'Rome' is identified with totality and ontology. As in *Totality and Infinity*, the 'rays of messianic light'

> break the evil spell of *having* by which being insists on being. They offer a glimpse at a future suspension of the heaping up, the amassing, the accumulation by which, for being – in the advent of its being – is ever and again a question of its own being. A forgetting, a failure to recognise the other! A piling up, amassing, unending totalisation of the objects and money that mark the rhythm and essential structure of the perseverance of being in its being. Its concrete modes: stock piling and banks. But also men at war. A suspect ontology! (TN, 108)

Messianic peace and justice consist in the suspension of totality – here identified both with Heideggerian ontology and with the idols of commercial totality, or capitalist accumulation and the political accumulation of military power by the state. The messianic is manifest as the promise of a sabbath, or suspension of the 'suspect ontology' informing the idols of the accumulation of wealth and power.

In this late reaffirmation of the messianic dimension of the political, the role of the State of Israel is conspicuously reduced, almost to the point of disappearance. The emphasis now falls on the universality of Judaism, a movement paralleled in the writings of the 1980s on universal human rights which develop, among the nations, the prophetic inspiration of a universal human justice. Levinas thus changes emphasis, moving from the dangers posed to Judaism by assimilation to the assimilation by the nations of Jewish universal fraternity in the declarations of human rights. It implies less that the Jewish people enter universal history by becoming a nation among the nations than that the nations become part of holy history, not in being subsumed under it, but by homage to its aspirations of human fraternity, peace and justice. The implications for Jewish identity and assimilation are profound – rather than the Jews becoming a nation, the nations may become Jewish, an intersection of holy and universal history whose implications were already recognised by Franz Rosenzweig and endorsed by Levinas in the words 'And Israel, beyond the Israel of flesh and blood, encompasses all people who refuse to accept the purely authoritarian verdict of History' (OS, 65).

With the resistance to history, discussion might turn back to the 'Philosophy of Hitlerism' and the national and racial communities of fate that were criticised there. It might also return to the origins of Levinas's thought in the Dreyfus Affair and the political options that this event brought to light. One was represented by Herzl's conviction that the

Jewish people, in order to be protected from future injustice, needed to adopt the form of the nation-state. Another, represented by Brunschvicg and Durkheim, maintained the hope that the Declaration of the Rights of Man and Citizen, if deepened and extended, would itself help to ensure justice and the security of the Jewish people. Levinas's thought was informed by this tension, recognising the prophetic inspiration of universal human rights and the universal notion of fraternity that they embodied. His understanding of the political was shaped by the tension between the political strategies of Herzl and Brunschvicg, one that towards the end he tried to reconcile in his notion of Israel as exceeding any particular means of identification.

AFTERWORD: STRANGE FIRE

> The fire on the altar shall be kept burning, not to go out:
> every morning the priest shall feed wood to it, lay out the
> burnt offering on it, and turn into smoke the fat parts of the
> offering of well-being. A perpetual fire shall be kept burning
> on the altar, not to go out.
>
> (Leviticus 6:5–6)

> Now Aaron's sons Nadab and Abihu each took his fire pan,
> put fire in it, and laid incence on it; and they offered before
> the Lord alien fire, which he had not enjoined upon them.
> And fire came forth from the Lord and consumed them; thus
> they died at the instance of the Lord.
>
> (Leviticus 10:1–2)

> After the earthquake – fire; but the Lord was not in the fire.
> And after the fire – a soft murmuring sound.
>
> (I Kings, 19, 12)

> For a multiplicity to be maintained, there must be produced
> in it the subjectivity that could not seek congruence with the
> being in which it is produced. Being must hold sway as
> revealing itself, that is, in its very being revealing itself, that
> is, in its very being flowing toward an I that approaches it,
> but flowing toward it without ever running dry, burning
> without being consumed. (TI, 221)

The equivocal blessing and danger of fire is to be found throughout
Levinas's writing. Fire is both the vehicle for Jewish identity and the agent
of its destruction, but beyond this it is also the means of vengeance. It
requires responsible handling but is always potentially out of control.
Strange or alien fire may have unforeseen destructive consequences, and at
the moment that it seems most benign it may ignite into a terrible and
uncontrollable force, not of nature but of spirit.

In the extended reflection on Jewish identity, 'Means of Identification'

(1963), Levinas moves from Zionism as a site for the transmission of Jewish identity to 'forgotten, ancient, difficult books'. He asks:

> Are the true books just books? Or are they not also the embers still glowing beneath the ashes, as Rabbi Eleazer called the words of the Prophets? In this way the flame traverses History without burning in it. But the truth illuminates whoever breathes on the flame and coaxes it back to life. More or less. It's a question of breath. (DF, 53)

Here, reading the text is substituted for the perpetual burnt offering in the Temple. The ritual of the burnt offering is preserved in the embers of the book and the reader breathing upon it takes the place of the priest attending the fire, with the difference that unlike the priest the reader does not have to be in a state of purity to attend the offering, but is purified by it, inspired and illuminated by the light of the flame. The life of the sacrificial animal which in the Temple stood in for the breath of life – 'the Lord God formed man from the dust of the earth. He blew into his nostrils the breath of life, and man became a living being' (Genesis 2:7) – is now the breath breathed on the embers exciting them into flame, the life spent in study.

The embers of the book provoke fire and light when breathed upon, a light which exceeds the breath sacrificed to raise it. In one of the 'Messianic Texts' of *Difficult Freedom* the 'sparks of enlightenment' provoked by debate between individual readings combine into a messianic blaze brighter than the sun that consumes history: 'The ultimate truth is set ablaze by all those sparks as the end of History embraces all histories' (DF, 94). This blaze of the many readings that make up the Diaspora contrasts with the uniform light of philosophy, politics and the state; it is a flame that not only traverses history without burning but its blaze is now compared to the messianic completion of history.

On the question of the perpetual renewal of the fire, Levinas remains ambiguous. By identifying the holy text as an ember that lives on beneath the ashes, Levinas keeps a fire in reserve – even after the consummation of the sacrifice the ember and the ash remain. Yet elsewhere Levinas insists on a fire that burns without consuming and without leaving ash. In 'Revelation in the Jewish Tradition' (1997) the questioning of the self by the other is likened to 'an inextinguishable flame which burns yet consumes nothing. Is not this prescriptive of Jewish revelation, in its unfulfillable obligation, its very modality? An unfulfillable obligation, a burning that does not even leave any ash, which would still be, in some respect, a substance based on itself' (BV, 150). The putting into question of same by other is similarly likened in 'From Consciousness to Wakefulness' (1974) to 'the burning without consumption of an inextinguishable flame' that does not even leave 'a cinder' (GM, 32). This strange fire that burns without consuming or leaving ash is nevertheless capable, in the words of 'God and Philosophy' (1975), of 'devastating its site like a devouring fire' (GM, 66), of giving a light that consumes sight – 'A dazzling where the eye holds more than it can hold' – and finally of igniting flesh, 'an ignition of the skin that touches and does not touch that which, beyond the graspable, burns' (GM, 67).

The danger of this fire that is beyond history and can yet carry identity through it is emphasised by Levinas's evocation of flesh and the burn. In 'From the Rise of Nihilism to the Carnal Jew', Levinas refers to the survival of Nazi persecution in terms of the scar: 'Contemporaries retained a burn on their sides, as though they had seen too much of the Forbidden' (DF, 221), a mark also described in 'Beyond Dialogue' as the incurable 'stigmata of so many burns' (AT, 81). The livid scar is neither ash nor ember, it continues to burn even though it does not need fuel, it traverses history but as suffering and not as an ember – the burnt body is neither ember nor ash, but continues to burn. It has no substance and leaves no ash. The burns left by the strange fire force a rethinking of the fire that burns without fuel and residue, one that is carried through in Levinas's two magnificent reflections on fire, 'The Light and the Dark' from 1961 and the Talmudic reading 'Damages due to Fire' of 1975.

Levinas's meditation upon the festival of Hanukkah in 'The Light and the Dark' begins with a contrast between the domestic fire of the hearth and the strange fire of the lights of Hanukkah. The candles successively lit over the days of the festival – 'this growing expanding light' – differs from 'the flame that burns in the hearth' (DF, 228). It does not give the heat and light of domesticity and hospitality, but a light that shines out onto the street – a political light. The light of Hanukkah marking the violent re-sistance of the Maccabeans sustained Jews during the centuries of persecution, and 'No doubt even today, it sustains the magnificent combat-ants of the young State of Israel' (DF, 228). Yet it is strange fire, and Levinas is immediately alert to the risks of violent resistance – of the 'polit-ical and warlike paths' – that 'finds itself caught up in a world it wanted to destroy' (DF, 229). He reminds his readers of the Talmudic justification of the festival. During the struggles for the Temple, the Greeks defiled the oils, except for one flask with a day's supply of lighting that lasted eight days. This was the miracle of strange fire commemorated in the candles of Hanukkah, 'the miracle of a light richer than the energies feeding it, the miracle of "more" from "less", the miracle of surpassing' (DF, 229).

For Levinas, this justification of the festival 'restores to a national war, a war defending a culture, the permanent horizon of marvel. It is the daily marvel of the spirit that precedes culture. It is a flame that burns with its own fervour' (DF, 229). The flame, identified with a militant spirit, possesses infinite resources – it can burn forever – and 'as a creator, surpasses the prudence of techniques; without calculation, without past, it joyfully pours forth its feelings in space, freely and prodigiously entering into the cause of the other' (DF, 230). Beyond the calculations of politics, free of fate, this 'revolutionary essence of the spirit' is 'Creation, freedom, permanent renewal' (DF, 230), undertaken in the cause of the other, for the ethical. But it is strange fire, and Levinas cautiously reminds the reader that this light cannot cannot burn gratuitously; before the blaze it is necessary to remember that what made it possible was the remnant of oil that was preserved – 'ignored by everyone, but unchanging' – an oil that figures first of all the 'best part of oneself' that was kept apart from 'war or political struggle'and is likened to the Jewish scholarly tradition. For this oil is 'a liquid lying dormant on the edge of life like a doctrine preserved in some lost yeshiva' (DF, 230). Before kindling the flame that burns without fuel and without ash it is necessary to retain some material from the triumphal blaze – the cinder or the text that needs effort to be coaxed into flame – and it is in the light of this remnant that Levinas looks on the lights of Hanukkah and not the triumphant glory of political and warlike struggle.

In 'The Light and the Dark', Levinas also alludes to another danger of the strange fire of Hanukkah, that of the fire spreading out of control. For the 'revolutionary essence of the spirit...blows where it will' (DF, 230) and not necessarily where *we* will. The fire of militant struggle can destroy itself, absolute principles can betray themselves in the fight to be realised. The call to keep 'the best part in reserve' – to keep 'a transparent oil intact' – is none other than a call to responsibility. The ethical is here the reservation – the holding back – from the revolutionary renewal of spirit, even, perhaps especially, when this is conducted 'in the cause of the Other' (DF, 230). The question of the responsibility for the fire carried by the wind – of violence or the damage done in the name of the other – is the subject of discussion in the sombre talmudic reading 'Damages due to Fire' (1975).

Levinas begins his reading of Baba Kama 60a–b, 'Damages due to Fire', by linking the theme of fire to those of war, the fatality of destruction and Auschwitz, and then moves to the question of responsibility. The text affirms responsibility for disasters originating in human freedom but executed through fire which 'escapes the powers of the guilty party. Fire, an elementary force to which other elementary forces will add themselves, multiplying damages beyond any rational conjecture! The wind adds its whims and violences to it' (TR, 185). Yet freedom is not so far removed from the elementary force of fire – it too is strange fire, and so Levinas begins to move from fire to war and the uncontrollable. The question becomes one of the reason of the war, its irrationality and perhaps even its complete disorder beyond reason, its perversion or inversion. The home itself is no longer refuge from this horror, nor is being just or unjust, since 'to the angel of extermination freedom is given' (DF, 187). In the condition of absolute insecurity that ensues, 'outside it is the sword, inside it is terror'

– this, for Levinas, is the 'odour of the camps', the 'abyss of Auschwitz or the world at war' as well as 'the State of Israel' as a category, 'That inside in which there is fear is still the only refuge. It is the the no-exit. It is the no-place, non-place (TR, 191). The vision of freedom as strange fire engulfing everything and destroying freedom culminates in a vision of the omnipresence of the angel of death in which 'There would be no radical difference between peace and Auschwitz' (TR, 193) in Levinas's words, that approaches the limit of pessimism, a limit that on occasion he too touched.

The reading does not end here in the complete spread of destructive fire, but with the Aggadah of the rabbi-blacksmith who is aware that 'the peaceful handling of fire' calls for the absolute responsibility for damages due to fire. We are responsible for the damage caused by our possessions, and this responsibility is aggravated by fire. Damages due to fire are compared to those caused by an arrow fired with destructive intent. The rabbi-blacksmith knows both the creative and the destructive potential of fire, and by reserving to it absolute responsibility preserves justice from the freedom of the exterminating angel and supports the call for justice directed to those responsible for the 'National Socialist holocaust'.

Yet Levinas ends the reading with the equivocation of strange fire. The destructive power of fire can be turned upon those who lit it in the first place – the most fitting punishment of the Nazi war-criminals is that 'Zion will be rebuilt' (TR, 196). Jerusalem will be reconstructed 'by the very means which were used to destroy it, precisely through fire, become protector' (TR, 196). Yet this is to depart from the lesson of the rabbi-blacksmith on the creative uses of fire; for fire is not only used to build, but has become the fire of protection. Levinas asks: 'But where is the glory of His presence among us, if not in the transfiguration of consuming and avenging fire into a protective wall, into a defensive barrier?' (TR, 196). The protective wall of fire is not all that it seems, since it too is strange fire and what it protects it may equally destroy, for with a change of wind the fire directed without, toward the enemy, may turn within.

Levinas thankfully gave another answer in 'The Light and the Dark', advocating there a withdrawal from the blaze of glory and its cycle of consuming, protecting and avenging fire in order to find the glory of the presence in an ember or 'a little flask of pure oil' that keeps alight 'our failing memory' for the future.

NOTES

Introduction

1 See Alain Finkielkraut's article 'Une philosophie affectée par l'histoire du Xxe siècle' in the collection *Emmanuel Lévinas et l'histoire*, edited by Nathalie Frogneux and Françoise Mies (1998).
2 Jewish prisoners of war in camps in the east of Europe were not similarly protected from deportation and murder by the SS.
3 The biography by Marie-Anne Lescourret (1994) is a beginning, but does not provide a consistent level of insight into Levinas's political positions and commitments. It may be supplemented with Simon Critchley's chronology from *The Levinas Companion* (CUP forthcoming) and the not entirely reliable biographical sketch of Levinas's relationship to Zionism by Françoise Mies and Pierre Sauvage, 'Lévinas et le sionisme' in Frogneux and Mies 1998: 339–48.
4 For a beautiful reading of the question of peace and fraternity that departs from very different premises and arrives at a diametrically opposed conclusion see Catherine Chalier's *de l'intranquillité de l'ame* (1999). Chalier's reading is anti-political, resting on persons rather than institutions: peace consists in 'fullness or perfection' (p. 29) and is located above all in human interiority.
5 Feminist readings of Levinas other than Chalier, and notably those inspired by Irigaray, have begun to transform the theme of fraternity into that of love. See Luce Irigaray and Tina Chanter's contributions to *Re-Reading Levinas* (Bernasconi and Critchley 1991), and more recently Stella Sandford's *The Metaphysics of Love* (2000). For a sustained reading of fraternity in terms of a Christian concept of love as charity see Gianluca De Gennaro, *Emmanuel Levinas: Profeta della Modernita* (2001).
6 The great exception is Derrida who, since 'Violence and Metaphysics' (1964) through 'At this very moment in this work here I am' (1980) to *Adieu to Emmanuel Levinas* (1997), has developed the rethinking of fraternity in his work on friendship and hospitality.

Chapter 1

1 In the 1982 Radio-France dialogues with Philippe Nemo reprinted in *Ethique et infini*, Le Livre de Poche, Paris, 1990, 73
2 'The second dedication to *Otherwise than Being* guards against losing touch with the particularity of a strictly Jewish destiny. Written in Hebrew, it is inaccessible to many of Levinas's readers. It records the names of Levinas's father, mother, brothers, father-in-law, and mother-in-law, in whose memory the book

is offered.' (Robert Bernasconi, 'Only the Persecuted: Language of the Oppressor, Language of the Oppressed', in Peperzak, 1995: 83.)

3 See, for example, Poirié RB, 36.

4 Written for *Le Nouvel Observateur* in 1988 and translated in *Critical Inquiry* 15 (Winter 1989), 485.

5 See also the Nemo interviews, *Ethique et infini*: 'Heidegger will never in my eyes be cleared of his participation in National Socialism' (1990: 32).

6 A striking instance of Levinas's ambivalence with respect to Heidegger and the mourning of the victims of National Socialism is delicately analysed by William J. Richardson, 'The Irresponsible Subject', in Peperzak 1995: 123–31.

7 Charles E. Scott's suggestive essay 'A People's Witness beyond Politics', also in Peperzak 1995: 25–35, may be read in this context, emphasising the radical but still Husserlian notion of intentionality that informs Levinas's ethical and political thought.

8 The intense republican ethos of the university was due to its being re-founded after the return of the region, city and university to French administration following almost half a century of German control. The cultural significance lent to the re-founded university by the French state is described by Jacques Le Goff in his preface to the Strasbourg historian Marc Bloch's history of 'the royal touch': 'After the war, the University of Strasbourg, having returned to the French, received particular attention from the public authorities in order to erase the memory of the German university and to make of the retrieved institution an intellectual and scientific showcase for France before the German world.' (Jacques Le Goff, preface to Marc Bloch, *Le rois thaumaturges*, Paris, 1983.) Along with the work of Levinas, the Annales school of history founded by the Strasbourg historians Marc Bloch and Lucien Febvre remains an enduring monument to the interwar ethos at the University of Strasbourg.

9 For a discussion of Levinas's teachers at Strasbourg see Lescourret 1994: 56–64.

10 In 1968 Levinas described 'the Dreyfus Affair and not the creation of the State of Israel (although the Dreyfus Affair lay at the origins of political Zionism)' as the 'turning point' in French anti-semitism and the Jewish community's perception of its vulnerability. This was in spite of 'the extent that justice triumphed in the Affair and politics once more joined ethics' (*Difficult Freedom*, 261).

11 Although she adds that the Affair was part of the reason 'why France fell an easy prey to Nazi aggression' (Arendt 1973: 93).

12 Arendt 1973: 90. The French army did not officially and publicly accept the innocence of Dreyfus until 1995. Even in 1985 the proposal to erect a statue to Dreyfus in the École Militaire excited opposition and led to it eventually being placed in the Tuileries.

13 The *League* had a precedent in the 1860 *Alliance Isrealite Universelle* founded in response to the 'Mortara case', the kidnapping of a Jewish child, Mortara, by the Papal authorities in Bologna after the child had been secretly baptised by a servant of the family. The *Alliance* dedicated itself more generally to the cause of emancipation, with particular respect to education, opening schools throughout the Mediterranean basin. Levinas worked for the Alliance at its École normale israélite orientale from 1930 until 1963.

14 Arendt 1973: 92

15 Bergson was also a victim of an *Action française* campaign, the post-Dreyfus action to block his election to the Academie Française successfully countered by Peguy.

16 'The Diary of Leon Brunschvicg', *Difficult Freedom*, pp. 38–45. The essay is also noteworthy for its critique of some of the aspects of classical Zionism, see the discussion on pp. 81–3.

17 Tr. S. and J. Lukes, *Political Studies,* xvii, 14–30; see also Lukes 1973.

18 EN, 224. It is indicative of the power of the phenomenological reading of Levinas that the only response that the interviewer can make to this long defence of Bergson is to say 'Let's get back to phenomenology'. Beyond the homage paid in interviews, Levinas refers favourably on several occasions to Bergson's work, as in his late essay 'The Old and the New' (1980) where he again reflects on 'the importance of Bergsonism for the entire problematic of contemporary philosophy' (TO, 132).

19 See EI, 28 where Levinas ranks *Time and Free Will* as one of the most beautiful books in the history of philosophy along with Plato's *Phaedo,* Kant's *Critique of Pure Reason,* Hegel's *Phenomenology of the Spirit,* and *Being and Time.*

20 Pierre Trotignon's 'Autre voie, meme voix: Levinas et Bergson' remains a unique and provocative study of the parallels between the work of the two philosophers. However, while his focus on Bergson's *Les deux sources de la morale et de la religion* (1932) casts light on Levinas's notion of prophesy, the article on the whole underestimates the *philosophical* presence of Bergson in Levinas's work.

21 In a later essay, 'Ethics as First Philosophy', Levinas described Husserl as 'one of the culminating points of Western philosophy', and Heidegger's *Being and Time* in *Ethique et infini* as 'a model of ontology'; as early as 1927–8 he urged his friend Maurice Blanchot to read it.

22 For the protocols of the Davos conference see the translation of Heidegger's *Kant and the Problem of Metaphysics*; for the mountain walks, see Lescourret 1994: 77.

23 Lescourret 1994: 81.

24 The major articles are 'Friborg, Husserl et l'ontologie' (1931), 'Martin Heidegger et la l'ontologie' (1932), 'Phenomenologie' (1934), and 'L'oeuvre d'Edmund Husserl' (1940)'.

25 Catherine Chalier's work of the early 1990s focuses on the question of freedom in Levinas, but almost exclusively from the viewpoint of autonomy. In 'La cité humaine', Chapter Five of *L'utopie de l'humain*, the discussions of Levinas's concepts of freedom and political legitimacy are couched almost entirely in terms of a contrast with Rousseau, overlooking Bergson. For a summary in English of this argument see Chalier's essay 'The Philosophy of Emmanuel Levinas and the Hebraic Tradition' in Peperzak 1995: 3–12.

26 It is inevitable that, in a commentary that advertises its fidelity to the original, the most innovative and perhaps telling philosophical developments must perforce be relegated to the footnotes, since they are outside the full jurisdiction of the commentary.

27 We can already detect in the commentary the cumulative rhythm of Levinas's thought that Derrida has likened to waves breaking on a shore.

28 See his critique of the multiple intentionalities of the medieval doctrine of intentionality on p. 24 of his commentary.

29 'The conceptual essence that Bergson criticises is a geometrical ideal which results not from *ideation* (which grasps the essence of things with all the vagueness proper to them) but from the idealisation which transposes to an ideal limit the given concreteness of things' (THP, 119).

30 Initially proposed in *Formal and Transcendental Logic* of 1928.

31 Levinas notes that the account of historical consciousness that he describes 'occupies a very important place in the thought of someone like Heidegger...' (THP, 156).

32 For analysis of the *Esprit* articles see H. Caygill 'Levinas's Political Judgement: The *Esprit* articles', *Radical Philosophy* 104, Nov/Dec 2000.

33 Mounier, *La pensée de Charles Peguy*, Paris, 1931.

34 Bergson was always reticent, refusing to comment publically on the Dreyfus trial and preferring Peguy to defend him against the anti-Semitic attacks of *Action française*. He held consistently to this position, even refusing Mounier's request for public support of a manifesto against anti-Semitism in 1933, claiming that his opposition to anti-Semitism was obvious and that such a manifesto 'is only of interest if done by a non-Jew'. On the other hand, Bergson in his will refused to convert to Catholicism in spite of his inclination because of the wave of anti-Semitism and his wish 'to remain with those who tomorrow will be the persecuted' (*Magazine litteraire*, 386, April 2000, 22–3). He indeed refused the opportunity to avoid wearing the yellow star or to be declared an 'honourary arian' – privileges which were not lightly turned down by a sick man in his 80s.

35 Levinas still stands out among modern philosophers as one of the few to have read *Mein Kampf*.

36 These often underestimated and little-read essays, discussed on pp. 40–8, should thus be interpreted as aspects of a broader anti-Nazi cultural politics.

37 Overall, Levinas's reading of Nietzsche is as subtle and equivocal as his reading of Marx – his interpretation of *Also Sprach Zarathustra* in 1934 may be compared with that in 'Humanism and Anarchy' that alludes to the moments of excess and generosity in Nietzsche (CP, 127).

38 *Paix et Droit* was the journal of the l'Alliance israélite universelle for which Levinas published a number of articles during the 1930s. These have been reprinted as '*Epreuves d'une pensee*' (1935–39), with a valuable introduction by Catherine Chalier in the first (1991) edition of the Cahier de l'herne dedicated to Levinas. Unfortunately they were not reprinted in the more widely available Le Livre de Poche edition.

39 Levinas refers to them as being the product of the 'leisure of a man of spirit', namely Gobineau in his *Essay on the inequality of human races* (1853–55),

40 Victor Klemperer's diaries, kept in Dresden during the period of National Socialism, give examples of Jews who not only accepted Nazi racial definitions of Judaism, but also approved of Nazi anti-Semitic policy.

Chapter 2

1 The protection of the *Wehrmacht* was precarious – further east, in German-occupied Poland and Russia, the Geneva Conventions proved little protection for Jewish POWs.

2 RB, 41, where Levinas contrasts the attitude of the guards and locals with that of a stray dog.

3 'We organised a facsimile of a university with programs, courses, hours, enrolments, examinations', *Critique and Conviction* (Ricoeur 1998: 18). Speaking of his Jewish colleagues, Ricoeur noted, perhaps too complacently, 'the German army had always succeeded against the SS in retaining control of the prisoner-of-war camps. The SS never commanded these camps, and for this reason it was possible for Ikor and Levinas not to have to worry. I know that a certain number of Jews were sent to separate camps, sometimes with prisoners reputed

to be subversive; but I have not read that these Jewish prisoners who were moved were made to suffer harsh treatment' (Ricoeur 1998: 19–20).

4 In the preface to *Existence and Existents*, Levinas links the work to 'studies begun before the war' and 'continued and written down for the most part in captivity...' (15).

5 Bobby, the dog that greeted the prisoners as they returned to the Stalag from forced labour, 'was the last Kantian in Nazi Germany'; 'The Name of a Dog, or Natural Rights', DF, 153.

6 Foreword to *Difficult Freedom*, xiii.

7 RB, 45. In the preface to *Existence and Existents*, Levinas acidly notes: 'The stalag is evoked here not as a guarantee of profundity nor as a claim to indulgence, but as an explanation for the absence of any consideration of those philosophical works published with so much impact between 1940–1945' (EE, 15).

8 As a forced labourer in the forest, Levinas's *Holzwege* were far removed from the tourist strolls of a commuter village such as Todtnauberg.

9 For further reflection on Levinas and Hegel, see Derrida's 'Violence and Metaphysics' in *Writing and Difference* (1997: 79–153), and Robert Bernasconi, 'Levinas, Hegel. La possibilite du pardon et de la reconciliation', in *Emmanuel Levinas: Cahier de l'herne* (1991: 357–79).

10 Levinas also characterises the 'there is' as an 'inextinguishable "consummation" of being' – an early instance of the 'strange fire' that glimmers throughout his post-war writing.

11 The classic study of this dependence is Derrida's 'White Mythology', in *The Margins of Philosophy*.

12 See TO, 48, where the event of nothingness, 'the *there is* (the way existing is affirmed in its own annihilation...)' is characterised by 'a vigilance without possible recourse to sleep'.

13 The latter point is clarified in the later texts where the retreat from *there is* is described as hypostasis.

14 As will be seen, Levinas's resistance to the logic of sacrifice was not entirely consistent; on some occasions he brought into proximity the murdered of the Shoah and the foundation of the State of Israel.

15 For a different reading of the two texts of 1947 see Jacques Taminiaux, 'La premiere replique a l'ontologie fondamentale' in *Emmanuel Levinas: Cahier de l'herne*, 278–92.

16 EE, 30; he uses the same example of lifting a weight as Bergson in *Time and Free Will*.

17 See Sternhell, *The Founding Myths of Israel*, Princeton University Press, 1999.

18 In *Time and the Other* Levinas apologised for his repeated returns to Shakespeare, reflecting that 'it sometimes seems to me that the whole of philosophy is only a meditation of Shakespeare' (TO, 72).

19 Levinas defines hypostasis in *Time and the Other* as 'the event by which the existent contracts its existing' (TO, 43).

20 See Levinas's article on Delhomme in *Noms Propres*, Livre du Poche, Paris 1987, pp. 57–64

21 Levinas's essay responds to a change in the climate of international relations evident during 1956. In spite of the repression of the Hungarian Revolution, 1956 witnessed important changes in the domestic and international policies of the USSR, with Khrushchev's denunciation of the Stalinist 'cult of the personality' and the announcement of an new international policy of 'peaceful co-existence' between the nuclear superpowers.

22 'Etre juif', *Confluence* 7, 1947, pp. 256–7.

23 The connections between Heidegger's thought and Christianity are most extensively explored in 'Heidegger, Gagarin and Us' (esp. DF, 233).

24 'The catholicity of Christianity integrates the small and touching household gods into the worship of saints, and local cults. Through sublimation, Christianity continues to give piety roots, nurturing itself on landscapes and memories culled from family, tribe and nation. This is why it conquered humanity' (DF, 233–4).

25 'This religion, in which God is freed from the Sacred, this modern religion was already established by the Pharisees through their meditations of the Bible at the end of the Second Temple' (DF, 217).

Chapter 3

1 Victor Klemperer (in *The Language of the Third Reich: LTI – Lingua Tertii Imperii: A Philologists Notebook*, with an epigraph from Rosenzweig: 'Language is more than blood') describes totality *Totalität* as 'one of the foundations on which the LTI is built', referring to how 'every expression and situation in life is caught up in [the National Socialist] network'. Furthermore '*Total* is also a number of maximum value, and in its concrete reality as pregnant with meaning as the Romantic excesses of *zahllos* and *unvorstellbar*. The terrible consequences for Germany itself of the total war that it declared as part of its own programme are still fresh in everyone's mind. But it is not only in relation to the war that one comes across the ubiquitous 'total' in the LTI: an article in the *Reich* extols the 'total learning environment' in a rigidly Nazi girls' school; in a shop window I saw a board game described as the 'total game'.

2 In his most profound meditation upon Levinas, 'A Word of Welcome', Derrida approaches this space with questions addressed to hospitality and to political invention. He begins with the claim '*Totality and Infinity* bequeaths to us an immense treatise *of hospitality*' (Derrida, 1999: 21) and ends with the question of the political invention of peace in Israel. Quite properly, the space between hospitality and political invention is left uncharted, for perhaps this is the space of war and perhaps *Totality and Infinity* is more properly described as an immense treatise *of hospitality and war*.

3 For a comprehensive study of Levinas's debt to Rosenzweig see Robert Gibbs, *Correlations in Rosenzweig and Levinas*, 1992; for the wide range of interpretations see Richard Cohen, 'La non-indifférence dans la penseé d'Emmanuel Levinas et de Franz Rosenzweig', in Catherine Chalier and Michel Abensour, *Cahier de l'herne*, 1991; Handelman 1991; and above all Stéphane Mosès, 'Rosenzweig et Lévinas. Au-delá de la guerre', in Frogneux and Mies 1998.

4 The reference to the work of memory in this passage should be distinguished from those of Hegel, Durkheim, Freud and Heidegger, to mention those cited by Levinas on p. 272 and at other points throughout TI. The past that is recalled is not necessarily an event, but an 'immemorial past' – what is important is the event of remembrance and not the event recalled.

5 '...infinity overflows the thought that thinks it. Its very *infinition* is produced precisely in this overflowing' (TI, 25).

6 The title of Catherine Chalier's anti-political reading of Levinas (Chalier 1993).

7 'Labour can surmount the indigence with which not need, but the uncertainty of the future affects being' (TI, 146).

Chapter 4

1 Levinas's disruption of the theme of equality has been carefully analysed in the work of Fabio Ciaramelli, who, while aligning equality and totality, discerns an ethical pre-original that can serve as a corrective to totality – 'The political institution of equality must aim at this pre-originary dimension of the ethical, which is the only warranty of its difference from totality' ('The Riddle of the Pre-original', in Peperzak 1995: 93).

2 OB, xli; the other articles mentioned by Levinas are 'Beyond Essence' (1970), 'The Saying and the Said' and 'Proximity' (1971), and 'Truth as Unveiling and Truth as Witness' (1972).

3 'Justice is this very presence of the third party and this manifestation, for which every secret, every intimacy is a dissimulation. Justice is at the origin of the claims of ontology to be absolute, of the definition of man as an understanding of being' (OB, 191).

4 For a confrontation with the radicalism of Levinas's understanding of persecution see Robert Bernasconi, 'Only the persecuted...: Language of the Oppressor, Language of the Oppressed', in Peperzak 1995.

5 The description of anarchy and anarchists as pursuing a principle of disorder is probably not defensible, although the main target of this criticism is probably Deleuze's case for 'crowned anarchy' that is a sovereign anarchy made in *Difference and Repetition* and later works. The suspicion of a crypto-debate between Levinas and Deleuze, both working through Bergsonian heritage, is supported by the attack on the notion of the 'face' in *A Thousand Plateaus* and the case for a body without organs.

6 Levinas at this point refers obliquely to the importance of knowing 'that war does not become the instauration of war in good conscience', as if aware of the problem of a disinterested war that his theory is here admitting.

7 'From the Rise of Nihilism to the Carnal Jew' (DF, 223).

8 In both *Otherwise than Being* and 'The Name of God According to a Few Talmudic Texts', Levinas explicitly refers to the reprinted version of the 1963 essay in *Discovering Existence with Heidegger and Husserl*.

9 The recovery of the ethical from within an ontological rights discourse that emphasises property and possession is analogous to Levinas's recovery of infinity and alterity from within the metaphysical tradition.

10 GDT, 164: Levinas's lectures on 'Transcendence, Idolatry and Secularisation' and 'Don Quixote: Bewitchment and Hunger' draw closely on 'Secularisation et faim'.

11 'Secularisation et faim', *Cahier de l'herne*, 25.

Chapter 5

1 The doubling that constitutes the State of Israel may be compared with the doubling of the state as an idol that worships itself, discussed in the 1972 Talmudic commentary 'And God Created Woman': 'Idolatry, that is no doubt the state, the prototype of idolatry, since the state adores being an idol' (TR, 176).

2 Notably the messianism of the Israeli right that succeeded the Six Days War, and from which Levinas maintained an ambiguous distance.

3 The difference between the philosophical and political positions of Levinas and Jankelevitch is nicely described by Taminiaux: 'Je l'entends encore, lors de la soutenance en Sorbonne de son doctorat d'État dont *Totalité et Infini* formait la thèse principale, riposter avec obstination a Jankélévitch qui le couvrait

d'éloges empoisonnés pour avoir enfin exorcisé la pensée francaise de ces sirènes germaniques: "Mais, Monsieur, détrompez-vous: je suis phénoméno-logue!"' 'Levinas et l'histoire de la philosophie' in *Emmanuel Lévinas et l'histoire*, p. 50.

4 This position is consistent with that of orthodox and hassidic critics of Zionism; see the contributions in Selzer 1970.

5 For some useful reflections on the methodology of reading the Talmudic commentaries, see Gilles Bernheim, 'A propos des lectures talmudiques', and Annette Aronowicz, 'Les commentaires talmudiques du Levinas' in *Emmanuel Levinas: Cahier de l'herne*, pp. 397–409 and 413–27.

6 See the Talmudic reading 'Cities of Refuge' for a sustained discussion of the limits of the politics of refuge – 'A civilisation of the law, admittedly, but a political civilisation whose justice is hypocritical and where, with an undeni-able right, the avenger of blood prowls' (BV, 52). In such a 'political civilization' it is important not to be duped by its claims to justice, for they are but the masks of perpetual war.

7 See Arendt's critique of the 'immortal antisemitism' thesis in her 1945 essays 'Organised Guilt and Universal Responisbility' and 'The Seeds of a Fascist International' (Arendt 1994).

8 Levinas's silence with respect to non-Jewish Israeli citizens already noted is perhaps defensible at this point given the focus of discussion, but Moslem, Druze and Christian Israelis become increasingly obtrusive by their absence from his discussion of the State of Israel and Israeli identity.

9 The motion of adherence as a metaphysical act should be read in the context of the description of adherence to Jewish identity in 'Means of Identification' as that which 'pre-exists any form of allegiance' (DF, 50).

10 The echo of Heidegger's notorious reference to the 'inner truth and greatness of the National Socialist movement' from the *Introduction to Metaphysics* is disquieting but surely not intentional.

11 This partiality, or rather provinciality, of the relation between universal and holy history is exposed in Levinas's notorious comment in an interview with Raoul Mortley: 'I often say, although it's a dangerous thing to say publicly, that humanity consists of the Bible and the Greeks. All the rest can be translated: all the rest – all the exotic – is dance' (*French Philosophers in Conversation*, Routledge 1991, 18). This position is not an exceptional lapse in Levinas's thought, but is consistent with his views on Asia and his repeated critiques of anthropological thought; in this connection his implacable hostility towards the work of Levi-Strauss is particularly worthy of note.

12 The English text of the first of the Camp David Accords, 'A Framework for Peace in the Middle East', referred to the 'legitimate rights of the Palestinian people and their just requirements' and to the 'Palestinians', while the Hebrew version referred to 'the Arabs of the Land of Israel'.

13 Cited in Avi Shlaim (2000: 404); see also details of the Reagan telegram comparing the PLO with 'Hitler and his henchmen' (2000: 411), and the objec-tions made by prominent Israelis to this historical delirium – notably Chaika Grossman, a veteran of the Warsaw ghetto who 'implored Begin – "Return to reality! We are not in the Warsaw ghetto, we are in the State of Israel"'.

14 Shlaim: 416ff.

BIBLIOGRAPHY

Works by Emmanuel Levinas

Alterity and Transcendence (1995), tr. Michael B. Smith, London: The Athlone Press, 1999

'As if Consenting to Horror', tr. Paula Wissing, *Critical Inquiry* 15 (Winter), 1989

Basic Philosophical Writings, Adriaan T. Peperzak *et al.* (eds), Bloomington: Indiana University Press, 1996

Beyond the Verse: Talmudic Readings and Lectures, tr. Gary D. Mole, London: The Athlone Press, 1982

Cahier de l'Herne: Emmanuel Levinas, Paris: Editions de l'Herne, 1991

Collected Philosophical Papers, tr. Alphonso Lingis, Dordrecht: Martinus Nijhoff, 1988

De l'évasion, Fata Morgana, 1992

Difficult Freedom: Essays on Judaism (1963–76), tr. Seán Hand, Baltimore: The Johns Hopkins University Press, 1990

Discovering Existence with Husserl, tr. Richard A. Cohen and Michael B. Smith, Evanston: Northwestern University Press, 1998

Entre nous: Essais sur le penser-à-l'autre, Paris, Éditions Grasset, 1991

Existence and Existents, tr. A. Lingis, The Hague: Martinus Nijhoff, 1978

Ethique et infini, Paris: Libraire Arthème Fayard et Radio-France, 1982

Emmanuel Levinas: Essai et Entretiens, Arles: Actes Sud, 1996

God, Death and Time, tr. Bettina Bergo, Stanford: Stanford University Press, 2000

In the Time of the Nations, tr. Michael B. Smith, London: The Athlone Press, 1994

Is it Righteous to Be? Interviews with Emmanuel Levinas, ed. Jill Robbins, Stanford: Stanford University Press, 2001

'La trace de l'autre', *En decouvrant l'existence avec Husserl et Heidegger*, Paris: J. Vrin, 1974

Les imprevus de l'histoire, Fata Morgana, 1994

L'intrigue de L'infini, Paris: Flammarion, 1994

New Talmudic Readings, tr. Richard A. Cohen, Pittsburgh: Duquesne University Press, 1999

Nine Talmudic Readings (1968–1977), tr. Annette Aronowicz, Bloomington: Indiana University Press, 1990

Noms Propres, Paris: Livre du Poche, 1987

Of God Who Comes to Mind, tr. Bettina Bergo, Stanford: Stanford University Press, 1998

On Thinking-of-the-Other (1991), tr. Michael B. Smith and Barbara Harshav, London: The Athlone Press, 1998

Otherwise Than Being or Beyond Essence, tr. Alphonso Lingis, The Hague: Martinus Nijhoff, 1981

Outside the Subject, tr. Michael B. Smith, London: The Athlone Press, 1993

'Reflections on the Philosophy of Hitlerism' (1934), tr. Seán Hand, *Critical Inquiry* 17 (Autumn), 1990

The Levinas Reader, ed. Seán Hand, Oxford: Basil Blackwell, 1989

The Theory of Intuition in Husserl's Phenomenology, tr. Andre Orianne, Evanston: Northwestern University Press, 1973

Time and the Other, tr. Richard A. Cohen, Pittsburgh: Duquesne University Press, 1987

Totality and Infinity: An Essay on Exteriority, tr. Alphonso Lingis, Pittsburgh: Duquesne University Press, 1969

Works cited in the text

Arendt, Hannah, *The Origins of Totalitarianism*, New York and London: Harcourt, Brace, Jovanovich, 1973

——*Essays in Understanding 1930–1954*, Jerome Kohn (ed.), New York: Harcourt Brace and Company, 1994

Bergson, Henri, *Oeuvres*, Paris: Presses Universitaires de France, 1959

Bernasconi, Robert and Critchley, Simon, *Re-Reading Levinas*, Bloomington: Indiana University Press, 1991

Burggraeve, R., *Emmanuel Levinas: une bibliographie primaire et secondaire*, Leuven: Centre for Metaphysics and the Philosophy of God, 1990

Chalier, Catherine, *Lévinas: l'utopie de l'humaine*, Paris: Albin Michel, 1993

——*de l'intranquillité de l'âme*, Paris: Manuels Payot, 1999

Cohen, Richard A., *Elevations: The height of the Good in Rosenzweig and Levinas*, Chicago: The University of Chicago Press, 1994

De Gennaro, Gianluca, *Emmanuel Levinas Profeta della Modernita*, Rome: Edizioni Lavoro, 2001

Derrida, Jacques, *Writing and Difference*, tr. Alan Bass, London: Routledge, 1997

——*Adieu to Emmanuel Levinas*, tr. Pascale-Anne Brault and Michael Naas, Stanford: Stanford University Press, 1999

Durkheim Emile, 'Individualism and the Intellectuals', tr. S. and J. Lukes, *Political Studies*, XVII, 14–30

——*The Elementary Forms of the Religious Life*, tr. Joseph Ward Swain, London: George Allen and Unwin, 1971

Frogneux, Nathalie and Mies, Françoise, *Emmanuel Levinas et l'histoire*, Paris and Namur: Les Editions du Cerf/Presses Universitaires de Namur, 1998

Handelman, Susan A., *Fragments of Redemption: Jewish Thought in the Literary Theory of Benjamin, Scholem and Levinas*, Bloomington: Indiana University Press, 1991

Heidegger, Martin, *Being and Time*, tr. John Macquarrie and Edward Robinson, Oxford: Basil Blackwell, 1978

——*An Introduction to Metaphysics*, tr. Ralph Mannheim, New Haven and London: Yale University Press, 1987

Herzl, Theodor, *The Jewish State*, New York: Dover Books, 1989

Hourani, Albert, *A History of the Arab Peoples*, London: Faber and Faber, 1991

Husserl, Edmund, *Ideas: General Introduction to Pure Phenomenology*, tr. W. R. Boyce Gibson, New York: Collier Books, 1962

——*Cartesian Meditations*, tr. Dorion Cairns, Dordrecht: Martinus Nijhoff, 1988

Lescourret, Marie-Anne, *Emmanuel Levinas*, Paris: Flammarion, 1994

Llewelyn, John, *Emmanuel Levinas: The Genealogy of Ethics*, London: Routledge, 1995

Lukes, Steven, *Emile Durkheim, His Life and Work: A Historical and Critical Study*, Harmondsworth: Penguin, 1973

Mortley, Raoul, *French Philosophers in Conversation*, London: Routledge, 1991

Peperzak, Adriaan T., *To The Other: An Introduction to the Philosophy of Emmanuel Levinas*, West Lafayette: Purdue University Press, 1993

——(ed.), *Ethics as First Philosophy: The Significance of Emmanuel Levinas*, New York and London: Routledge, 1995

Poirié, François, *Emmanuel Levinas, Essai et Entretiens*, Babel 1996, 90

Ricoeur, Paul, *Critique and Conviction: Conversations with François Azouvi and Marc de Launay*, tr. Kathleen Blamey, Cambridge: Polity Press, 1998

Rosenzweig, Franz, *The Star of Redemption*, tr. William W. Hallo, London: Routledge and Kegan Paul, 1971

Sandford, Stella, *The Metaphysics of Love*, London: The Athlone Press, 2000

Sebbah, François-David, *Levinas*, Paris: Les Belles Lettres, 2000

Selzer, Michael (ed.), *Zionism Reconsidered*, London: Macmillan, 1970

Shlaim, Avi, *The Iron Wall: Israel and the Arab World*, Harmondsworth: Penguin, 2000

Sternhell, Zeev, *The Founding Myths of Israel*, tr. David Maisel, New Jersey: Princeton University Press, 1999

INDEX

p 5 -
cf. Blanchot.

p 79 : separation of freedom + autonomy.

p 83 - Malraux quote.

p 92 : political ontology
development of a non-ontological philosophy.

p 96 -

p. 122 -

p. 125 - new modes of defining the
subject.

(p. 129 - "modal" categories.
  cf. 133 modal categories vs categories of
                                    quality.

p. 146, 148 : illeity. (definition)

p.101 · primacy of orientation over the terms in the orientation.

p.158 ·

p.152   separate rights discourse from its
roots in individualism.

p.155 responsibility

chapter on BGE. ?

1) diversion of Heidegger -
ontological difference .

2) deflation of Hegelian dialectic

} pp. 50 -
54

p.74 definition of Tode Ti
the thisness of the thing -
individuality of the thing

illeity - pp. 145 . 147